D

Qualitative Methods in Human Geography

edited by

John Eyles and David M. Smith

Polity Press

Copyright © Polity Press 1988

First published 1988 by Polity Press
in association with Blackwell Publishers
Reprinted 1992

Editorial Office:
Polity Press, 65 Bridge Street
Cambridge CB2 1UR, UK

Blackwell Publishers
108 Cowley Road, Oxford, OX4 1JF, UK

British Library Cataloguing in Publication Data

A CIP catalogue record for this book is available from the British Library.

ISBN 0–7456–0370–X
ISBN 0–7456–0371–8 (pbk)

Typeset in 10 on 12pt Times
by Downdell Ltd., Abingdon, Oxon.
Printed in Great Britain by T. J. Press Ltd, Padstow

Contents

List of Contributors   vii
Preface   xi

1   Interpreting the Geographical World   1
    Qualitative Approaches in Geographical Research
    John Eyles

2   Constructing Local Knowledge   17
    The Analysis of Self in Everyday Life
    Susan J. Smith

3   Racial Conflict and the 'No-Go Areas' of
    London   39
    Michael Keith

4   Definitions of the Situation   49
    Neighbourhood Change and Local Politics in Chicago
    Peter Jackson

5   Topocide: The Annihilation of Place   75
    J. Douglas Porteous

6   Decoding Docklands   94
    Place Advertising and the Decision-making Strategies
    of the Small Firm
    Jacquelin Burgess and Peter Wood

7   Social Interaction and Conflict over
    Residential Growth   118
    A Structuration Perspective
    David Evans

8   The Geography of Popular Memory in
    Post-Colonial South Africa   136
    A Study of Afrikaans Cinema
    Keyan G. Tomaselli

9   The Concept of Reach and the Anglophone
    Minority in Quebec   156
    Courtice Rose

10 'When you're ill, you've gotta carry it'   180
    Health and Illness in the Lives of Black People
    in London
    Jenny Donovan

11 Participant Observation   197
    The Researcher as Research Tool
    Mel Evans

12 A Case-Study Approach to Lay Health Beliefs   219
    Reconsidering the Research Process
    Jocelyn Cornwell

13 From Fact-world to Life-world   233
    The Phenomenological Method and Social Science
    Research
    John Pickles

14 Towards an Interpretative Human Geography   255
    David M. Smith

Index   268

List of Contributors

Jacquelin Burgess is a Lecturer in Geography at University College London. Her interests in urban imagery began with her PhD research at Hull University where she first explored the links between media and the meanings of places. Her recent work has focused on representations of places and landscapes in a variety of popular cultural forms, notably newspapers and television. She is also engaged in qualitative research using in-depth small discussion groups to explore popular values for open space. She is co-editor and contributor to *Valued Environments* (1982) and *Geography, the Media and Popular Culture* (1985).

Jocelyn Cornwell studied History and Social and Political Sciences at King's College, Cambridge before taking a Masters degree in Sociology as Applied to Medicine at Bedford College, London and studying for the PhD at Queen Mary College. In 1984, she published *Hard-Earned Lives: Accounts of Health and Illness from East London*, a case-study of beliefs about health and illness in the working-class community of Bethnal Green. Since then she has concluded an investigation at the Open University into the health beliefs of elderly people, and has contributed to the work of the Primary Health Care Group at the King's Fund Centre on services for disadvantaged groups. She is currently working as a Locality Manager in Islington Health Authority's newly decentralised community health services.

Jenny Donovan was, until December 1987, Arthritis and Rheumatism Council Research Fellow, at Birmingham University, working on an ethnographic study of a rheumatology clinic, looking particularly at the effects of lay perceptions of health on the doctor–patient relationship and issues surrounding the provision of patient information. She has subsequently moved to the London Hospital Medical College. She is the author of, *'We don't buy sickness, it just comes': Health and Illness in the Lives of Black People in London* (1986), based on a PhD thesis prepared at Queen Mary College and lives in Tottenham, London.

David Evans was educated at the University of Leeds, followed by postgraduate work in Toronto. He is currently working as a research consultant in a joint partnership between the Department of Geography, Loughborough University and a private multidisciplinary practice. He also lectures and tutors part-time, specializing in social geography, planning studies and information technology. David Evans' main academic research interest is in the social geography of the suburbs and exurbia. In 1987 he completed a major study examining resistance to residential growth on the urban fringe using case-studies from Britain, the United States and Canada. He has previously published on this theme and is a committee member of the Rural Economy and Society Study Group of the British Sociological Association.

Mel Evans is currently an Action Research Worker in Newham Docklands for Community Economy Ltd, a national organisation researching and promoting community initiatives in local economic enterprise. He is also a Tutor Counsellor in Social Science for the Open University. He is presently completing research on ideology and the local community, begun as a postgraduate student at Queen Mary College.

John Eyles, formerly Reader in Geography at Queen Mary College, London, now teaches at McMaster University, Hamilton, Ontario. He has held visiting positions in Australia, Poland, New Zealand and Israel. His research interests are in the fields of social geography and the geography of health care in which his most recent book is *The Geography of the National Health: An Essay in Welfare Geography* (1987) as well as in the theoretical and methodological issues of human geography, on which he has recently edited *Research in Human Geography* (1988).

Peter Jackson has been a Lecturer in Geography at University College London since 1980, having been educated at Oxford University. Since completing doctoral research on the Puerto Rican migration to New York he has undertaken a variety of ethnographic studies in New York, Chicago and Minneapolis-St Paul with funding from the American Council of Learned Societies, the British Academy and the Fulbright Commission. He is the joint author of *Exploring Social Geography* (1984, with Susan J. Smith) and the editor of *Race and Racism* (1987). His current research focuses on the cultural politics of British racism.

John Pickles is Assistant Professor of Geology and Geography at West Virginia University. His main research areas are the philosophy of the human sciences and social theory, particularly phenomenology, hermeneutics and critical theory; geography, education and democratic empowerment; and regional policy in South Africa. He is currently engaged in a project funded by the National Science Foundation addressing the role of industrial decentralization in the regional policy of South Africa. His publications include two books: *Phenomenology, Science, and Geography: Spatiality and the Human Sciences* (1985) and *Geography and Humanism* (1987) and several articles dealing with geographic theory, education and democratic empowerment, and South Africa.

J. Douglas Porteous was born in York, and migrated via Oxford, Hull, Harvard, and MIT to become Professor of Geography at the University of Victoria, British Columbia. His teaching and research interests are eclectic, including urban planning, environmental aesthetics, literary geography, geoautobiography and the problems of resource frontier settlements and isolated islands. He has published over 100 articles and four books, *The Company Town of Goole, Canal Ports, Environment & Behavior* (1977) and *The Modernization of Easter Island.* Three more books, *Planned to Death, Otherscapes* and *Degrees of Freedom* will appear shortly. For recreation Dr Porteous travels the world, having visited over 100 countries at last count. He also heads the Saturna Island thinktank.

Courtice Rose is Associate Professor of Geography at Bishop's University in Lennoxville, Quebec. He graduated in geography from the University of Western Ontario and then completed at PhD degree at Clark University. Interest in the situation of the Anglophone minority in Quebec was stimulated by research completed for the Secretary of State's office in Ottawa during the year 1981–2. Dr Rose has also contributed articles on philosophical problems in human geography to journals such as *Tijdschrift voor Economishe en Social Geographie* and *Society and Space.*

David M. Smith is Professor of Geography at Queen Mary College, University of London, having held previous posts in the USA, South Africa and Australia as well as in Britain. He is author or editor of a dozen books in economic and social geography, including *Human Geography: A Welfare Approach* (1977) and *Geography, Inequality and Society* (1987). His interest in qualitative approaches, as an extension of long-standing concerns with the place of humankind in geographical research, owes much to the work of post-graduate students in the Health Research Group in Geography at QMC, some of whose work is included in this volume.

Susan J. Smith completed her undergraduate studies and doctoral research at Oxford University. She has held research and teaching positions at the Universities of Oxford and Brunel, and at the University of California, Los Angeles. She is now a research fellow at the ESRC's Centre for Housing Research at Glasgow University. Her work currently centres on race and gender-related inequalities in the housing system, as well as on aspects of crime and neighbourhood change. Her books include *Crime, Space and Society* (1986).

Keyan Tomaselli is Professor and Director of the Contemporary Cultural Studies Unit, University of Natal, Durban. A former professional documentary film-maker, he graduated in urban geography with Honours at the University of the Witwatersrand. He is author of four books on South African cinema, and has also published in geographical journals.

Peter Wood is Senior Lecturer in Geography at University College, London. He graduated at the University of Birmingham, developing research interests in the West Midlands. More recently his studies of industrial location and regional development have extended to the South-East, London and Docklands. He also has a growing interest in the regional significance of service sector employment. He is co-editor and contributor to *London: Problems of Change* (1986) and *Regional Problems, Problem Regions and Public Policy in the United Kingdom* (1987).

Preface

Research in human geography has changed significantly over the past three decades. The 1960s saw the ascendance of quantitative methods and mathematical models, while much of the 1970s was preoccupied with a reaction in the form of approaches which placed primary emphasis on structural features of society. In the 1980s competing '-isms' have proliferated in the search for something less mechanical and more in tune with the complexity of human existence than is provided by positivism and structuralism. The importance of human agency has emerged (or reasserted itself), to broaden and deepen the perspective on individual action characterized by the behavioural school. An important outcome has been methodological innovation, recognizing that human experience, and the process of assigning meaning to it, require something more subtle than the tools and techniques of the 'quantitative revolution' or evocation of the mega-structural forces of crude Marxism.

The purpose of this book is to put forward a range of approaches to the description and interpretation of the geographical world to which the term 'qualitative' is assigned. The aim is to demonstrate by example, and to this end we have assembled case-studies to show something of the variety of qualitative methods in current use. They are almost all place-specific, in the contemporary spirit of the importance of locality as well as of individuality in human affairs, though what they actually tell us about particular people in particular places is secondary to the research process and experience that they reveal.

In the first, introductory, chapter, John Eyles provides a prelude to the case-studies by setting qualitative approaches in a methodological and philosophical context. This is followed by a sequence of chapters which exemplify the analysis of what place means to people, in terms of images, sense and signs, and how they are to be interpreted. In chapter 2,

Susan Smith takes us straight to the heart of Britain's contemporary inner city problems by explaining the social construction of an urban image promoted by the press, in which the association between crime and race provides people with a means of making sense of local expressions and experiences of social disorder. Then Michael Keith looks at a different facet of the same issues: the symbolic significance of so-called 'no-go' areas defined and contested in the practice of social conflict. In a change of continent Peter Jackson considers the experience of neigh-bourhood change in Chicago, as mediated by local politics. At the extreme, change may include the annihilation of place, or 'topocide' as Douglas Porteous terms it in chapter 5, with traumatic consequences for those (including Porteous himself) for whom the place in question had special meaning. In chapter 6, Jacquelin Burgess and Peter Wood return to image-creation in their attempt to 'decode' the version of London Docklands created by advertising designed to attract small businesses. Then, David Evans examines interaction and conflict over residential growth in which certain kinds of suburb take on a symbolic life-style or status. Chapters 8 and 9 concern a broader spatial scale, as Keyan Tomaselli turns to the medium of film to show how it may, through textual analysis, reveal aspects of the 'geographical memory' and experience of a particular people (Afrikaners) in South Africa, while Courtice Rose explores spatial dimensions of the identity of the Anglophone minority in Quebec.

The studies in chapters 2 to 9 are all concerned with the interpretation of different kinds of 'text', whether newspapers, other documentary records, advertisements or films, in which semiotics and interpretation are underlying methods. The emphasis shifts in chapters 10 to 12, to explore the implications of somewhat different methods. Jenny Donovan explains the use of informal surveys in an ethnographical approach to the understanding of black people's perceptions and experiences of health. Mel Evans considers the practice and demands of participant obser-vation, with the researcher as self-aware research tool. Jocelyn Cornwell offers some retrospective observations on a case-study in which extended tape-recorded interviews comprised the material used to place lay health beliefs in the broader context of people's everyday lives.

The final two chapters stand back from the locality-based case-studies which form most of the substance of this volume. John Pickles puts forward phenomenological method as the key to the approaches that we have termed 'qualitative', bringing together questions of philosophy and technique. In the concluding chapter, David Smith identifies and summarizes the main findings and themes of the other chapters and relates them to some aspects of the changing practice and internal structure of human geography.

While we would not claim that our choice of contributors is representative of institutional affiliation with qualitative approaches in British (or English-speaking) human geography, the prominence of Queen Mary College and Oxford reflects more than chance or personal knowledge on the part of the editors. At QMC John Eyles' work on environmental satisfaction and sense of place in the 1970s and early 1980s provided a relevant setting for post-graduate students who brought in or acquired an interest in qualitative-interpretative approaches. At Oxford, Clyde Mitchell in anthropology as well as the supervision of Ceri Peach were especially influential. David Smith's role as external examiner of two Oxford PhD theses provided some cross-fertilization. Seven of the twelve studies in this volume owe their origin to post-graduate research supported by studentships from the Economic and Social Research Council (ESRC), formerly the Social Science Research Council (SSRC). These are the chapters by Smith, Keith and Jackson (all Oxford PhDs), Mel Evans, Donovan and Cornwell (QMC), and David Evans (Loughborough). The assistance of the Council is gratefully acknowledged.

As editors, we have refrained from imposing our own sense of order and coherence on the content of this book, save for our own introductory and concluding contributions. We have preferred to permit and indeed encourage our authors to speak (write) for themselves, subject only to an initial brief, suggestions to improve clarity in places, and an invitation to consider some helpful and incisive comments on their drafts from Derek Gregory and Tony Giddens. We are grateful to them all for what they provided and for their response to queries, sometimes to an unreasonably tight deadline, and hope that they find this volume to be some compensation for their efforts. We also hope that our collective endeavours help to secure qualitative approaches a central place in the emerging redefinition of human geography as part of a critical and interpretative social science.

John Eyles
David M. Smith

1

Interpreting the Geographical World
Qualitative Approaches in Geographical Research

John Eyles

This book is about method. It is not so much a book which tells readers how to carry out qualitative and interpretative research – there exist many such books in anthropology and sociology (e.g. Schwartz and Jacobs, 1979; Burgess, 1982, 1984; Marsh, 1982; Hammersley and Atkinson, 1983; Plummer, 1983; Silverman, 1985) – but rather one which informs on how particular pieces of research were carried out. Its express purpose is, therefore, to demonstrate by example, although many of our contributors also feel that they must locate their empirical work in its philosophical and methodological contexts. But our contributors relate their method(s) to their empirical material and in doing so show the richness and variety of the approaches which we have labelled 'qualitative', although 'interpretative' may be a better term to designate the subject and its practitioners. 'Interpretative' points up better the relationships between this practice in geography and in cognate disciplines where the designations interpretative sociology and anthropology already exist (e.g. Geertz, 1973; Giddens, 1976; Rabinow and Sullivan, 1979).

Interpretative geography, description and induction

What then is *interpretative* geography? Like all scientific endeavour, the aim of such a geography is to understand and explain the nature of (social) reality. But it recognizes that investigation of the social world does not construct the real world anew. In other words, order cannot simply be imposed on the world through the use of scientific methods and constructs because an 'order' already exists. As Schwartz and Jacobs (1979) graphically put it, we are in the reality reconstruction business: the tortuous business of learning to see the world of individuals or groups as they see it. The existence and relevance of the orderings and knowledge of such individuals and groups are accepted and used as the bases of examining the social world. Interpretative geography therefore accords central importance to such definitions and perceptions and how these relate to behaviour. The task of research is, therefore, to uncover the nature of the social world through an understanding of how people act in and give meaning to their own lives. As Silverman (1985) suggests, we cannot put our commonsense knowledge of social structures on the side. Thus not only do observer and observed use the same phenomena to identify meanings but we must also place these meanings at the centre of analysis. These meanings (or definitions of situations; Jackson, chapter 4, below) demonstrate the intersubjective nature of the world: that much of our experience of everyday life is shared and an investigation of this experience and world requires methods which allow the acquisition of 'insider knowledge' through interaction, observation, participation in activities and informal interviewing.

But while interpretative geography searches for and accepts the definitions and meanings of the social world as given – it reconstructs reality by revealing the taken-for-granted assumptions of individuals and groups in space – another dimension may be identified. This dimension is still concerned with the identification of meanings but does not take for granted the everyday and the commonsensical. Of course, few researchers end their endeavours with revealing the meanings of those they observe. They also order and interpret, often employing scientific constructs, deriving from previous work, theory, and the relations between theory and observation (see Ley, 1981; Eyles and Donovan, 1986), so that a scientific ordering is used to give shape to the meanings derived from everyday experience. Other researchers, however, have emphasized not the specific nature but the system of relations between words and images as sources of meaning. This approach owes much to structuralism and semiotics and is geared to the interpretation of texts in a theory-informed way because the relational nature of the system must be structured by something.

Interpretative geography is in sum concerned with the understanding and analysis of meanings in specific contexts. Its importance derives from the well-known difficulties with geography as spatial science, the critique of which is now well documented in human geography. Further, qualitative methods are not new. Such methodologies have been employed in human geography for well over ten years, particularly in humanistic geography as Ley's (1974) study of Philadelphia and Western's (1981) of Cape Town's District Six attest. Attempts have also been made to systematize method (e.g. Sayer, 1984), pointing to the importance of interpretative approaches which help focus attention on the study of specific locations. Increasingly, general theories and descriptions are being found not to apply to specific cases or places. Thus, for example, the theory of the relations between local and central states formulated largely from American experience is not so applicable to the contexts of either non-elected bodies such as British health authorities or where the local bodies have a history of vigorous independence as with the Australian states. Suggestions to study the specific are not to demand a return to the idiography of regional geography. They put forward the desire for specific descriptions from theoretically-informed positions, a strategy differing from the grand theorizing of the conceptualizers, the wide-ranging generalizations of the quantifiers, and the abstracted descriptions of the idiographers. An emphasis on methodological contributions thus focuses attention on the need for theory-informed descriptions of specific places to enhance our understandings and explanations of the world (see, for example, Massey, 1984; Harvey, 1985; Pred, 1986).

Indeed in many ways, a major task which interpretative methods try to address is, how can social reality be represented or described? To the forefront of concerns have come the problems associated with geographical description. The apparently coherent description of place by much traditional regional geography now seems shallow in that it categorizes the world into broad divisions, i.e. landforms, climate, transport, and so on, while that by locational analysts aims for the representation of the world as numerical generalizations. But the material we use to describe the world are our representations and constructions of other people's representations and constructions of what is occurring in the social world. What Geertz (1973: 10) says of the ethnographer is as apposite for the geographer:

what the ethnographer is in fact faced with – except when (as, of course, he must do) he is pursuing the more automatized routines of data collection – is a multiplicity of complex conceptual structures, many of them superimposed upon or knotted into one another, which are at once strange, irregular, and inexplicit, and which he must contrive somehow first to grasp and then to render . . . Doing ethnography is like trying to read (in the sense of 'construct a reading of') a manuscript – foreign, faded, full of ellipses, incoherencies, suspicious emendations, and tendentious commentaries, but written not in conventionalized graphs of sound but in transient examples of shaded behaviour.

For Geertz, ethnographic description, in grasping the complexities of context and the significance of local knowledge, is *thick description*. But the researcher's task does not end there. It is necessary to go on to construct a system of analysis in which 'the aim is to draw large conclusions from small, but very densely textured facts' (Geertz, 1973: 28).

This approach has much in common with induction in which generalizations are developed from information presented in case-studies using refinement, abstraction, typification and categorization. Most field researchers use analytic induction, so as to remain faithful to the data collected and avoid prior categorization of those data (see Znaniecki, 1934). Thus the 'results' at the outset of data analysis are no more than hunches to be revised and refined by repeated checking and combing through the data. The researcher must take particular notice of the data which do not fit the existing version of events. This progressive categorization and refinement end when the findings are consistent with the data. Theory is thus based on observations of one particular section of reality. Theory is conceived not in terms of logical deductions but relations between observed phenomena. It is also likely to be less grand than other propositions espoused as theory in geography, e.g. central place theory, laws of migration. This is because theory developed through induction and from thick description is general *and* contextual.

The scope and range of qualitative and interpretative methods

One way in which the researcher can try to get to grips with the complexity of the social world is by adopting a multiple research strategy. There are different types of such strategies (Burgess, 1982). First, multiple investigators can be used. They may come from different disciplines, although this may create a problem of communication. It is perhaps useful to have men and women researchers in a team. It is also useful to have researchers of different ethnic origin if the research is to deal with cultural and ethnic issues and perhaps of different ages too. The most noted bias – class – is extremely difficult to do anything about as virtually all researchers are, in terms of their class of destination at least, middle-class.

Secondly, there may be multiple theories. In this all possible theoretical propositions are used even if they are contradictory or inadequate (see Westie, 1957). For example, if we are interested in discovering the effects which state actions had on the lives of the residents in a particular district, we should utilize the varying interpretations of the role of the state, *inter alia*, as an agent of consensus; as a way of resolving competing, often equivalent claims; as a vehicle operating at the behest of the ruling class; and as an institution with relative autonomy which must though reproduce the conditions for continued capital accumulation. The researcher may then discover all the empirical relationships that pertain, interrogate these with the possible range of interpretations, identifying the degree of fit, and select those relationships where data are theory-related. Such an approach avoids empiricism and unnecessary replication. It may, however, lend itself to theoretical eclecticism; a useful if difficult to control characteristic of much human geography. The multiple theory strategy does not absolve the researcher from the need to assess the relative explanatory merits of the theories. In this assessment, it is necessary to divorce substantive considerations from assertions based not on the scientific but the apparent moral worthiness of a theory. It may, however, be argued that all social theories have a moral foundation and that scientific claims to the 'truthfulness' of their foundation are specious. Research must be theory-informed (to avoid the error of empiricism) and it must search out counterfactual cases, but the power and acceptability of its theories may eventually be based on argument and moral suasion (see Gouldner, 1967; Phillips, 1973; Eyles, 1985).

Finally, there can be multiple sets of data, requiring different methods. It is possible to obtain different data relating to different phases of the research process, different settings and different informants (see Denzin, 1970). It was indeed the early anthropologists who advocated and practised such strategies. Malinowski (1922), for example, noted the need for statistical coverage for the organization of the people under investigation; observation to discover the behaviour and conduct of individuals and collectivity; and ethnographic description based on conversation and interview to elicit the 'mentality' of the people. Thus, statistical surveys and quantitative analysis remain relevant for interpretative research. Sieber (1973) shows how the quantitative dimensions obtained from survey or sociometric analysis may be useful correctives to ideas gained from conversations in field research. They can correct the notion that all aspects of a social setting are congruent; demonstrate or refute the generality of a single observation or field observations in general; and cast new light on field observations. We should add that field research may also cast a different light on survey results. Thus, for example, the specificity of findings from such survey instruments as the Nottingham health profile and scales of health and health care satisfaction dissolves when people talk about their health and illnesses and connect them with their work, families and neighbourhoods. Perhaps, though, it is best to conclude with Trow (1957: 33) when he argued: 'different kinds of information about man and society are gathered most fully and economically in different ways. The problem under investigation properly dictates the methods of investigation' – a remark both apparently trivial and profound.

The possible range of qualitative and interpretative methods would, therefore, seem vast, and the interpretative geographer a methodological eclectic. 'The field researcher is a methodological pragmatist. He sees any method of inquiry as a system of strategies and operations designed – at any time – for getting answers to certain questions about events which interest him' (Schatzman and Strauss, 1973: 7). But the methods must be appropriate to the research problem at hand: hence, the great variety of approaches. Further, as was suggested earlier, reality is reconstructed: it is not simply there. This has, as Rock (1979: 193) points out, implications for methodology which 'neither mirrors not mines reality, it works towards its manufacture'. Such manufacture implies emerging interpretation of a changing world which has implications for the validation of such research (see below). For the present, however, we shall examine those methods that rely on interaction which individuals and groups to elicit meanings and actions and then those that are more explicitly interpretative through being textual or hermeneutic exercises.

Interacting and talking to people may take many forms, ranging from formal survey instruments with their multiple-choice checklists and closed questions to participant observation. There has been interesting recent work to rehabilitate the survey method. For example, Blaxter (1985) argues that it may be possible to develop survey instruments from qualitative research so that generalizations and policy implications may be investigated on the basis of representativeness. A spirited defence comes from Marsh (1982) who attacks the schism between two different methods appropriate to either causal explanations (surveys) or meaningful explanations (participant observation). In survey research, the process of testing causal hypotheses is often an indirect matter of drawing inferences from already existing variance in populations by a rigorous method of comparison. But while the correlations are produced by the survey, the interpretations are not. Often these are supplied by the researcher more or less systematically. Yet it seems more plausible that these interpretations should come from the data rather than outside. This has been a powerful argument for asking the people being studied to supply meanings. But does the meaning communicated demonstrate the individual's access to explanation or simply the ability to communicate? Perception geography provides an example. Do the images of places elicited show the significance of spatial cognition in decision-making or the ability to read a map or recognize the salient features of a colour photograph?

Further, a correlation from survey analysis may be elaborated by introducing intervening variables to show the possible effects between the initial variables. More and more refinement can be applied in the form of the researcher introducing more subtle interpretation through further intervening variables. When a plausible account of the actions involved is obtained, the process may stop. Marsh's solution is thus not a 'retreat' to participant observation, except when people are not capable of 'communicating the meaning of their actions validly' (Marsh, 1982: 124), but extensive piloting of data collection procedures and trial analysis of results. It is, however, possible to suggest that the validity of meanings is context-dependent, and while people obviously know what their actions mean to themselves, they may not always be clear on what they mean to others. To illustrate such a point we need only refer to the somewhat outmoded notion of 'latent function'. In Merton's (1968) example, were all the Hopi aware that their rain dance had the functions of ideational and social solidarity as well as of trying to make rain? Marsh's argument suggests, therefore, that we should not reject outright the survey method; rather use it in circumstances where people seem able to communicate what they are doing and what it means.

There is though a method or approach which 'lies between' the survey method and participant observation: the interview. Of course, social surveys are usually carried out by interview but there are different approaches. Moser and Kalton (1971) divide interviewing into formal and informal types. In the former, questions are asked and the answers recorded in a standardized form. It is thus assumed that the researcher knows already that which the interview is designed to uncover. With the use of this knowledge and piloting, the researcher must ensure that the questions are phrased unambiguously and that they are not intimidating to any respondent. The question must, therefore, be understandable and the standardized answers, as found in many questionnaire schedules, must be meaningful in terms of the respondents' experiences. These answers must also be mutually exclusive and cover all possible replies. While such schedules are useful in eliciting information of a routine nature, as with the General Household Survey (OPCS, 1984), they tend to force replies into particular categories which respondents may or may not have thought about. They also tend to assume an unproblematic relation between words and deeds. This relationship may be complicated by individuals wishing to emphasize their adherence to societally perceived good and minimize their commitment to what is seen as bad.

In the latter – informal interviewing – the questions asked, their sequence and wording are *not* worked out beforehand. In this case, the interviewer tries to tailor the wording of the questions to each particular individual and ask the questions in an order appropriate for the interviewee. The aims are to ensure that the questions have the same meanings for all respondents and to engage in 'conversation' to set the respondent at ease. Such interviewing requires great skill on the part of the researcher who must not only be an empathetic listener but a good conversationalist, able to keep a dialogue going; and a social theorist, linking responses and meanings to a broad body of knowledge. With informal interviewing, it is not assumed that appropriate question phrasing and style of answer are known in advance. These emerge as the interview progresses in the process of interaction between researcher and respondent. Such research is also referred to as depth interviewing and is portrayed in this volume by Porteus, Donovan and Cornwell. In it, the researcher must become sensitive to which questions are relevant and meaningful.

The researcher does not, however, approach the task without any framework. There is usually a checklist of topics to be covered by all respondents. In this sense, it is wrong to call such interviewing non-directive. The researcher must, if need be, encourage talk along certain avenues. Non-directive interviews are more the preserve of psycho-analysis than social research. Nor should such interviewing be called unstructured because, as Hammersley and Atkinson (1983) point out in their discussion of 'ethnographic interviewing', all interviews, like any social interaction, are structured by both researcher and informant. Such interaction takes the form of a conversation and this allows the researcher 'to probe deeply, to uncover new clues, to open up new dimensions of a problem and to secure vivid, accurate, inclusive accounts from informants based on personal experience' (Burgess, 1982: 101). Informal interviews allow the recording of everyday life. They allow people to describe and talk about their own lives in their own words. In introducing his talks with West Indians in Britain, Cottle (1978: 12) argues that 'without allowing people to speak freely we will never know what their real intentions are, and what the true meaning of their words might be.' People may still not tell the researcher the 'real' and 'true' as they 'really' see it. Even if the researcher and respondent gain mutual respect and recognition, it may still be thought that it is the researcher who is talking, who is in control, who is intrusive.

Another approach which also raises these issues is participant obser-vation, which is illustrated in this book by Mel Evans and Susan Smith. 'The participant observer gathers data by participating in the daily life of the group or organisation he studies. He watches the people he is studying to see what situations they ordinarily meet and how they behave in them. He enters into conversation with some or all of the participants in these situations and discovers their interpretations of the events he has discovered' (Becker, 1958: 652). There are, however, a variety of ways in which a researcher may engage in participant observation. Four ideal-types have been identified (Gold, 1958; Junker, 1960), ranging from complete participant in which the observation role is concealed; participant-as-observer, in which the relationship between the researcher and others is defined by the research (see Burgess, 1982); observer-as-participant, in which the distinctiveness of the researcher's role is made clear from the outset; and complete observer, in which there is no contact between researcher and researched. Most participant observation falls into the middle two categories, the separation of which in practice may be difficult. In fact, Gans (1982) suggests three: total participant, researcher-participant, total researcher. He goes on to say that he was almost always the researcher-participant involved in research, but not the participation: 'I played the required participant role, but psychologically I was outside the situation, deliberately uninvolved in order to be able to study what was happening' (Gans, 1982: 54). In his study of Levittown (Gans, 1967), he found it sometimes difficult not to become involved in political affairs in conversation with neighbours. The participant-observer has to be both inside and outside the group, institution or community under investigation; and must be immersed but remain a critical commentator able to see a complete pattern or process with daily or routine interactions and events. This relation between involvement and detachment (Powdermaker, 1966) is a determining factor in the nature of the research produced by participant observers. It is possible though doubtful that a forceful researcher may alter the situation being studied. Total immersion may lead to the researcher ceasing to research, while many pieces of such research usually have appended what Schwartz and Jacobs (1979) cruelly call a methodological confession which may throw doubt on the reported findings. But participant observation can bring a neighbourhood studied by survey analysis to life. (Remember too, it is possible to check the results from participant observation by survey analysis.) It provides an insider's account with an outsider's detachment. In concentrating on a small place or a few individuals or households, participant observation is a case-study approach, allowing theoretical generalizations to emerge from its detailed investigation of a selected dimension of reality. The case study (Cornwell, chapter 12, this volume) shows well some of the main features of the qualitative approach, namely that typicality and representativeness are unimportant and that the validity of interpretation depends on 'the cogency of the theoretical reasoning' (Mitchell, 1983: 207).

In many cases of depth interviewing or participant observation, other data are sought, analysed and interpreted. Documentary evidence, to build up a picture of the relevant past (see Jackson, chapter 4, this volume), or to obtain statements, views and meanings unobtainable through interaction, illustrated in our book by Porteous with planning documents, and David Evans with community newspapers, may also be used, although they do present particular problems concerning their authenticity, availability, selectivity and meaning. One particular type of document is the life history which is the account of a life, completed or ongoing, the use of which can present an individual's evaluations of experiences and give the context of experience (see Mandelbaum, 1973; Hägerstrand, 1982; Plummer, 1983). Thus far, its main (and then still limited) use in human geography has been in an autobiographical way as part of self-reflection to expose the values on which life and work are based (see, for example, Buttimer, 1974; 1983; Eyles, 1985).

The use of documentary evidence points also to the more explicitly interpretative approaches and the examination of 'texts'. While appearing to have much in common with hermeneutics, particularly as originally conceived as the interpretation and clarification of meaning through the philological analysis of texts, these approaches share elements of the structuralist perspective. Indeed, the approaches of Rose and Pickles in this volume have strong links with the hermeneutic and phenomenological traditions, while those of Burgess and Wood and Tomaselli are more closely related to structuralism and semiotics. There is of course a relation between rather than separation of phenomenology and hermeneutics and structuralism (see Gregory, 1978). This relation may lead to phenomenology being regarded as the context of method (philosophy as method) rather than a method *per se* (method as technique) (see Pickles, chapter 13, this volume).

If we turn to the structuralist–semiotic dimension, it must be noted that structuralists construct the human subject in a particular way within an interrelated system of signs and significations. These signs are dependent for their meanings on their place within an articulated system; they are not arbitrary but possess no outside origin or unity; and they bring together a concept and image. But although the system of signs is relational, the relations between signs and between signs and meanings are not fixed. Recent research has concentrated on how meanings are fixed and articulated: 'language is the domain of articulations and meaning is above all a cutting-out of shapes. It follows that the future task of semiology is far less to establish lexicons of objects than to rediscover the articulations which men impose on reality' (Barthes, 1967: 57).

This rediscovery has been based on different 'texts'. Indeed, the 'text' may be seen in dramaturgical terms (Smith, chapter 2; Keith, chapter 3, this volume). Language itself – conversation or descriptions – can be examined (Atkinson, 1981), but for the meanings of places to individuals and groups it may be that paintings and plans (Cosgrove, 1984), film (Tomaselli, chapter 8, this volume), advertising (Burgess and Wood, chapter 6, this volume) and television are as appropriate (but see Burgess and Gold, 1985). All such interpretations of meaning, however, are based on internal analyses of the 'text'. Such analysis seeks to establish and deconstruct the realities the text itself sets out. The subjects derived from such an analysis are not arbitrary or commonsensical but are determined by the text itself. As Silverman (1985: 154) comments, 'subjects are intrinsic to narratives: by analysing the construction of subjects, we get to the heart of the work of the text.' And, we could add, its meaning.

Validation and beyond

With their emphases on meaning, it is trite to say that qualitative and interpretative approaches differ from those of natural science and 'scientific' geography. This implies that the criteria of validation are also somewhat different. Interpretative geography does not stand outside its subject-matter: it is part of the investigation and of the discourse itself. This may be clearly seen with the textual-interpretative analyses. Principles of validation are internal to the discourse itself. Hirst (1979) suggests that the criteria of appropriateness and adequacy are specific to the objectives of the discourse and practice. Interpretations must be justified in terms of the presented evidence, so much depends on the coherence of argument and the reason, consistency and honesty of the theorist. The theorist, whatever his or her approach, must therefore reflect on the nature of his or her research, interpretations and role (see Smith, chapter 2, this volume). Questions of validation may thus involve ethical questions about researcher role and the purpose of the research. In any event, theoretical reasoning must be exposed to full and critical gaze to evaluate its relevance and cogency, examples being provided by Mel Evans with respect to ideology and David Evans to structuration.

We may also ask, to whose gaze should our reasoning be exposed? The conventional, often taken-for-granted, view is that the gaze belongs to the community of scholars, including the researcher. This view supposes a certain distance between the interpreter and the object of interpretation, 'as a reader might engage a text, rather than in terms of a metaphor of dialogue' (Marcus and Fischer, 1986: 29). Indeed, these authors suggest that dialogue is a more accurate reflection of how interpretation occurs in fieldwork. Dialogue suggests an insider's account or description of the social world as opposed to, or as well as, the more usual outsider's one. While interesting attempts to present accounts based on dialogue are reviewed by Marcus and Fischer (1986), little attention has yet been directed to how such descriptions may be validated.

But in qualitative approaches, the relationships between theoretical constructs and empirical observation must also be validated. As is perhaps well known, this relation is usually seen in terms of empirical indicators and theoretical concepts. Does the indicator really measure the concept it is intended to measure? While there are no unambiguous rules, three procedures are commonly discussed. First, there is face validity in that on the face of it the indicator measures the concept. This seems similar to the idea of the plausible account developed by Carrier and Kendall (1977) in the context of welfare developments. Does the relation between concept and indicator seem plausible? We may note that in essence the appeal is to a commonsensical, consensual understanding of a relationship in which these characteristics may be based on lay or scientific commonsense or rules. In all this, it is important not to suppress the evidence that does not fit: the interpretative geographer must also search for evidence that refutes the assumed relationship between phenomena, just as statistical geographers try to avoid spurious correlations. Disconfirming evidence and the search for counterfactual arguments are important procedures in the process of validation. Comparative or cross-cultural analyses may also assist in steering clear of 'easy' explanations. Secondly, there is criterion validity whereby a new indicator can be compared with an existing, generally accepted one. Such a procedure would be useful in replicating research or in refining an established relation between concept and indicator. Thirdly, there is construct validity which depends on listing whether propositions (which are assumed *a priori* to be highly likely) are confirmed when the new indicator is used. We might suggest that the addition of intervening variables (indicators) to the assessment of a relationship is an example of a search for construct validity.

Some of these claims to validity lend themselves to quantitative and qualitative research. The outlined approach to validation assumes that theory and evidence are unconnected or related in some unproblematic way. But inductive, reflexive research means that concepts and indicators are developed simultaneously. If, further, the behaviouristic assumption of standardized response to the same stimuli or events is dropped, the possibility of identifying standard indicators becomes doubtful and a search for them unnecessary. What may emerge, however, is a typology, often in the form of a set of ideal-types of, say, actions or meanings, which represents sub-types of a more general category. Ideal-types emerge from the specific case under investigation but have a more general applicability in determining the validity of theoretical concepts. Eyles (1985) produced ideal-types of sense of place (the specific) to inform on the relationship between the individual, the individual's identity and materiality, and ultimately the theory of structuration (the general). Ideal-types and typologies allow systematic thought to be addressed to the nature of each type of category and the relations between them (Hammersley and Atkinson, 1983), although they should not be pursued 'beyond' the data or their analytic value (Glaser, 1978). Part of their value, however, is that they may enable a development of alternative links to be made between theory and data. They may assist in the search for counterfactual argument or falsifying evidence to address the emerging theory. Further, the identification of ideal-types, second-order typifications, allows the employment of Schutz's postulate of adequacy for scientific knowledge. To be valid, a second-order typification must allow the observed to understand an action as it is described by the construct. This construct must also possess logical consistency and allow subjective interpretation in that the observed's ideas must be used in the model that account for the 'facts' observed: a possible means of validating insider accounts as well. These ideas are taken further and exemplified in a study of health and health care by Eyles and Donovan (1986).

It is also possible to analyse data using multiple theories, with multiple strategy becoming a basis of validation. Bensman and Vidich (1960) approached their study of Springdale by utilizing many different perspectives, each yielding different orders of data. This multiple theoretical strategy, called theoretical triangulation by Denzin (1970), is but one basis of this form of validation. All are predicated on the notion of triangulation which itself derives from an analogy with surveying. It is possible to use different research workers on the same problem or data from different sources, e.g. respondents, phases in the fieldwork, social contexts and times. Inferences from one set of data can be checked against those from others. But data from different sources do not necessarily provide a more complete picture. As Lever (1981) notes, it is not a matter of checking whether inferences are valid but of finding out which ones are. It should also be noted that differences between data-sets may be just as illuminating as similarities. Further, many of the qualitative approaches have developed their own specific criteria of validity. All rely on the significance of the 'insider account', whether theoretical or lay.

But just as we have not reviewed all the technical problems connected with how to do qualitative research – e.g. gaining access, listening and asking questions, note-taking and recording data, using documents and analysis and evaluation – because good texts already exist, we do not intend to rehearse these criteria separately because again, good sources are easily found (Silverman, 1985, chapter 8). We must note, however, that clarity as to the aims of the research will help answer questions of method (and therefore of validation), a topic addressed by Sayer (1984) in terms of intensive and extensive research. And finally, while our contributors can only largely provide snapshots of how particular research was carried out, interpretative geography is cumulative, depending on reflection on past research and roles (see Vidich et al., 1964; Ley, 1988), and the incorporation of these reflections (and the critical comments of all our audiences – peers, study populations, and so on) into future research.

References

Atkinson, P. (1981) 'Inspecting classroom talk', in C. Adelman (ed.), *Uttering, muttering*, Grant McIntyre, London.

Barthes, R. (1967) *Elements of semiology*, Jonathan Cape, London.

Becker, H. S. (1958) 'Problems of inference and proof in participant observation', *American Sociological Review* 23, 652–60.

Bensman, J. and A. J. Vidich (1960) 'Social theory in field research', *American Journal of Sociology* 65, 577–84.

Blaxter, M. (1985) 'Self-definition of health status and consulting rates in primary care', *Quarterly Journal of Social Affairs* 1, 131–71.

Burgess, J. and J. Gold (eds) (1985) *Geography, the media and popular culture*, Croom Helm, London.

Burgess, R. G. (ed.) (1982) *Field research*, Allen & Unwin, London.

Burgess, R.G. (1984) *In the field*, Allen & Unwin, London.

Buttimer, A. (1974) *Values in geography*, Resource paper 24, Association of American Geographers (AAG), Washington.

Buttimer, A. (ed.) (1983) *The practice of geography*, Longman, London.

Carrier, J. and I. Kendall (1977) 'The development of welfare states', *Journal of Social Policy* 6, 271–90.

Cosgrove, D. (1984) *Social formation and symbolic landscape*, Croom Helm, London.

Cottle, T. J. (1978) *Black testimony*, Wildwood House, London.

Denzin, N. K. (1970) *The research act*, Aldine, Chicago.

Eyles, J. (1985) *Senses of place*, Silverbrook Press, Warrington.

Eyles, J. and J. Donovan (1986) 'Making sense of sickness and care', *Transactions, Institute of British Geographers* 11, 415–27.

Gans, H. J. (1967) *The Levittowners*, Free Press, New York.

Gans, H. J. (1982) 'The participant observer as a human being', in Burgess (ed.), *Field research.*

Geertz, C. (1973) *Interpretation of cultures*, Harper, New York.

Giddens, A. (1976) *New rules of sociological method*, Hutchinson, London.

Glaser, B. (1978) *Theoretical sensitivity*, Sociology Press, San Francisco.

Gold, R. L. (1958) Roles in sociological fieldwork, *Social Forces* 36, 217–23.

Gouldner, A. W. (1976) *Enter Plato*, RKP, London.

Gregory, D. (1978) 'The discourse of the past', *Journal of Historical Geography* 4, 161–73.

Hägerstrand, T. (1982) 'Diorama, path and project', *Tijdschrift voor Economische en Sociale Geographie* 73, 323–39.

Hammersley, M. and P. Atkinson (1983) *Ethnography*, Tavistock, London.

Harvey, D. (1985) *Studies in the history and theory of capitalist urbanisation* (2 vols), Basil Blackwell, Oxford.

Hirst, P. A. (1979) *On law and ideology*, Macmillan, London.

Junker, B. H. (1960) *Fieldwork*, University of Chicago Press, Chicago.

Lever, J. (1981) 'Multiple methods of data collection', *Urban Life* 10, 199–213.

Ley, D. (1974) *The black inner city as frontier outpost*, AAG, Washington.

Ley, D. (1981) 'Behavioural geography and the philosophies of meaning', in K. Cox and R. Golledge (eds), *Behavioural problems in geography revisited*, Methuen, London.

Ley, D. (1988) 'Interpretive social research in the inner city', in J. Eyles (ed.), *Research in human geography*, Basil Blackwell, Oxford.

Malinowski, B. (1922) *Argonauts of the western Pacific*, Routledge & Kegan Paul, London.

Mandelbaum, D. G. (1973) 'The study of life history', *Current Anthropology* 14, 177–96.

Marcus, G. E. and M. M. J. Fischer (1986) *Anthropology as cultural critique*, University of Chicago Press, Chicago.

Marsh, C. (1982) *The survey method*, Allen & Unwin, London.

Massey, D. (1984) *Spatial divisions of labour*, Macmillan, London.

Merton, R. K. (1968) *Social theory and social structure*, Free Press, New York.

Mitchell, J. C. (1983) 'Case and situation analysis', *Sociological Review* 31, 187–211.

Moser, C. A. and G. Kalton (1971) *Survey methods in social investigation*, Heinemann, London.

OPCS (Office of Population, Census & Surveys) (1984) *The general household survey 1982*, HMSO, London.

Phillips, D. (1973) *Abandoning method*, Jossey-Bass, London.

Plummer, K. (1983) *Documents of life*, Allen & Unwin, London.

Powdermaker, H. (1966) *Stranger and friend*, W. W. Norton, New York.

Pred, A. (1986) *Place, practice and structure*, Polity Press, Cambridge.

Rabinow, P. and W. Sullivan (eds) (1979) *Interpretive social science*, University of California Press, Los Angeles.

Rock, P. (1979) *The making of symbolic interactionism*, Macmillan, London.

Sayer, A. (1984) *Method in social science*, Hutchinson, London.

Schatzman, L. and A. L. Strauss (1973) *Field research*, Prentice-Hall, Englewood Cliffs, NJ.

Schwartz, H. and Jacobs, J. (1979) *Qualitative sociology*, Free Press, New York.

Sieber, S. D. (1973) 'The integration of fieldwork and survey methods', *American Journal of Sociology* 78, 1335–59.

Silverman, D. (1985) *Qualitative methodology and sociology*, Gower, Aldershot.

Trow, M. (1957) 'Comment', *Human Organization* 16, 33–5.

Vidich, A. J., J. Bensman and M. Stein (eds) (1964) *Reflection on community studies*, Harper, New York.

Western, J. (1981) *Outcast Cape Town*, Allen & Unwin, London.

Westie, F. R. (1957) 'Toward closer relations between theory and research', *American Sociological Review* 22, 149–54.

Znaniecki, F. (1934) *The method of sociology*, Farrar & Rinehart, New York.

2

Constructing Local Knowledge
The Analysis of Self In Everyday Life

Susan J. Smith

Introduction

A number of authors have commented on an image of urban life in Britain's inner cities in which the problem of crime has been woven into the tenor of race relations (see also chapter 3). This symbolic association between 'race' and crime in Britain has a long history. It is a link steeped in the imagery of the 'culture conflict' theories of early twentieth-century North America (epitomized in the writings of Sellin, 1938), and one whose stereotypes and prejudices are periodically resurrected and reworked. During the 1970s, for instance, Britain's 'mugging' panic attached the stigma of (potential) criminality to large sections of the country's Afro-Caribbean youth (see Hall et al., 1978). No less invidious is the criminality attributed via the mass media to an undifferentiated Asian community, in the form of veiled allegations of illegal immigration, factional and interfamilial violence, and bungling fraudulence (see S. J. Smith, 1985). Inflated by a largely unsympathetic press, these labels linking criminality with racial stereotypes have tended to stick, despite the virtual impossibility of assessing their legitimacy (see S. J. Smith, 1982a).

The research discussed in this chapter explored the social reality of the image linking 'race' and crime in part of inner city Birmingham (England). The study was not conceived as an investigation of criminality (the usual focus of the 'race and crime' debate as outlined by Lea and Young, 1984), but as an inquiry into the plight of (actual and potential) victims and as an assessment of public reactions to the perceived threat of crime. While some basic findings concerning victimization and fear are written up elsewhere (S. J. Smith 1982b, 1983), the discovery most relevant to the present discussion concerns the local salience of the 'race and crime' image: it proved impossible to consider the *effects* of crime –

fear, protective behaviours, avoidance strategies – without encountering, in all sections of the community, enduring stereotypes linking 'racial' attributes with degrees of criminality or respectability.

Though drawing on these results, the followng analysis of the image fusing race-related and crime-related issues is primarily methodological. It does not, therefore, concern itself centrally with the political and economic construction (and reconstruction) of 'race' during colonialism and following the post-war sequence of labour and refugee migrations from the New Commonwealth and Pakistan to Britain (this process is well documented by Miles, 1982 and Rich, 1986). Neither is the politics of law and order, that so excites the mass media and provides governments with an appealing electoral platform, subject to detailed scrutiny (but see Chibnall, 1978; Hall et al., 1978). Nor shall I focus directly on links between national politics, the racism of a provincial press and local interpretations of deviance (though this is the topic of other papers on a similar theme, e.g. S. J. Smith 1984b; 1985). My interest is rather in establishing just *how* a local (in this case, urban) image can legitimately be investigated. The aim is to draw attention to the analyst's role in interpreting – indeed constructing – urban imagery. The argument is that no analysis of public perceptions is complete until it includes an understanding of the active role of the analyst's *self* which is exercised throughout the research process: in the choice of a problem and a methodology; in relating to and acting with a studied public; and in negotiating the legitimacy of a project by subjecting procedures and findings to the (formal and informal) vetting of intellectual peers.

In effect, therefore, this chapter is an attempt to establish just what a local (urban) image is by the time it reaches the printed page. Broadly, the argument is that *what* an image is depends on *how* it is studied. More specifically, I contend that while the use of qualitative methods can provide some of the most authentic representations of public perceptions, the validity of such research depends on a more rigorous and self-conscious sequence of investigative procedures than is usually recognized. I am not claiming to have approached my own research with quite the degree of sensitivity I now argue to be important. My hope is that a retrospective view of what occurred fortuitously – as well as of opportunities missed – will provide the beginnings of a more purposive framework for future projects.

Investigating an image

Geography's major contribution to an understanding of urban imagery has been through the medium of perception studies. Such research is premissed on the ability of studied individuals to objectify what lies in their mind's eye and express it in a form suitable for measurement. Generalizations about shared perceptions and group identities are subsequently inferred on the basis of the similarities amongst an aggregate of individuals' images. Such an approach has provided novel and illuminating insights concerning class- and race-related differences in the subjective availability of urban space (Lynch, 1960; Francescato and Mebane, 1973; Ley, 1974), and, in drawing attention to the importance of the legibility of urban environments, it has significant (if largely unrealized) implications for public policy.

There is, however, another route into the world of public perceptions and behaviour. It is based on the subjective understanding of a participating observer, rather than (or in combination with) the formal schedule of a visiting interviewer. Such a route has found legitimacy hard to win, battling, as it has, with the conceptual imperialism of the quantitative revolution and with a conception of 'science' epitomized in the language of inferential statistics. Nevertheless, it can be argued that experiential research is quite as rigorous and demanding as the techniques of empirical-analytical science (a contention elucidated in S. J. Smith, 1984c); and the logical consistency required to validate case analyses is just as scrupulous as the demands of statistical inference and experimental replication (as shown by Mitchell, 1983).

Amongst many arguments for and against the merits of qualitative research, there are two which speak overwhelmingly in favour of adopting such an approach to investigate urban imagery. The first seeks to rectify a sustained imbalance in the kinds of knowledge pursued by social science. In the rush to produce immediately policy-relevant findings (from research ripe for cost-effective funding), we are in danger, especially with politically salient topics like 'race' and 'crime', of forgetting that an important aim of inquiry must be to capture something of the *meaning* of life in particular social settings. There are elements of this that simply cannot be grasped other than through the analyst's direct experience. Moreover, contrary to the opinion of some sceptics, the rationale for gaining such experience lies not simply in the thrill of the exotic or the fun of the unusual; it is grounded, rather, in a long philosophical tradition asserting the primacy of 'commonsense' understanding as the foundation of all more formal systems of knowledge.

Secondly, in the wake of what Pred (1981) terms a new consensus in social theory (which directs attention to the 'concrete situations of everyday life' where society is reproduced and individuals are socialized), it is disturbing that the empirical evidence needed to sustain the conceptual leaps associated with it remain very thin on the ground. There is still a conspicuous lack of information as to how the 'generation of and consequences of particular everyday individual practices *at specific temporal and spatial locations* fit into the continual workings and transformation of society' (Pred 1981: 7; his emphasis). Although Giddens (1984) might be justified in claiming that the concept of routinization grounded in practical consciousness (the realm of tacit knowledge that is skilfully but uncritically applied) is vital to the theory of structuration, we know relatively little about how people construct and live their routines, let alone how they use them to challenge, sustain or mediate the structures of society in which they are embedded. Experiential research is one (necessary but not, of course, sufficient) strategy required to satisfy these new demands of social theory. Subjective understanding will not conform to *a priori* categories, much less settle comfortably into the coding boxes of a questionnaire; but it is the necessary means of divining (both through the experiential process itself, and by communicating it to others) a *social* understanding about how societies work that is constructed from the 'bottom up' rather than from the 'top down'. Such a strategy will rarely appeal to policy-makers, and it is unlikely to wed big business to the ideals of academia. At a practical level, however, it allows local publics to define local problems; and this, at a theoretical level, might begin to forge some much-needed links between the interpretative-hermeneutic sciences and critical theory.

Emphasizing, therefore, the importance of what Habermas (1968) terms the 'practical' interests of the hermeneutic sciences (as distinct from the technical interests of empirical-analytical research), this chapter considers the contribution of qualitative research to the analysis of an urban image. The argument draws on ethnographic fieldwork collated during two years' residence in north central Birmingham; it relies, therefore on 'data' subject to selective abstraction and subjective interpretation rather than to formal measurement, statistical manipulation and empirical generalization. This account of public perceptions of 'race' and crime is concerned not so much with the 'reality' of the image as with the practical and theoretical consequences of myself, the analyst, having *lived* it. Since other contributors to this volume outline and evaluate the technique of participant observation, my final comment on the terms of reference for this experiential study concerns the chosen means of conceptualizing the data of subjective experience and empathetic encounter.

First, I follow Nisbet (1976) in regarding sociology as an art form. This is not to argue that such an art stands apart from, or in opposition to, scientific inquiry. It is, rather, to draw attention to the often neglected fact that both the physical and social sciences take their impetus from 'precisely the same kinds of creative imagination which are to be found in such areas as music, painting, poetry, the novel, and drama' (Nisbet, 1976: 9). Art and science are both concerned to illuminate reality and explore the unknown. Both are experimental, but whereas artists self-consciously exploit their creative imagination to bring renown, intellectual convention places the imagination of the scientist at the margins of academic respectability. Yet, as Harvey (1985: xv) acknowledges, even though science approaches the world with finely-tuned investigative procedures, there are always 'moments, events, people and experiences that impinge upon imagination in unexpected ways, that jolt and jar received ways of thinking and doing, that demand some extra imaginative leap to give them meaning'. I shall argue that no knowledge, but least of all knowledge about the social world, arises apart from the creative imagination of both participants and observers. To this extent, participant observation is an 'art' that is fundamental to the development of human geography as a social 'science'.

This established, a question arises concerning how to express the message of such an art form. Fortunately, anthropologists and social psychologists have already given this some consideration. It is part of the 'reconfiguration of social thought', so cogently outlined by Geertz (1983), that 'analogies drawn from the humanities are coming to play the kind of role in sociological understanding that analogies drawn from the crafts and technology have long played in physical understanding' (1983: 19). The most prominent of such analogies are those which liken social life to a game, a drama or a text, so illuminating the strategies of face-to-face encounter, the performance skills involved in collective behaviour, and the hidden meanings of social jokes or local gossip (see also Harré, 1978; Abelson, 1981; Hare, 1985).

These three analogies are used to structure the discussion which follows, and they affirm that it is in qualitative research that the analyst's role in constructing a studied 'reality' is most starkly exposed. Although it will be argued that this is less of a problem – or at least a different kind of problem – than is usually supposed, the primary aim of the chapter is to use the above-mentioned analogies in a sequence to stress that, in studying the imagery of daily life, a participant observer must be concerned with monitoring not one but three levels of social interaction: negotiations between the analyst and those studied; interactions amongst the members of a studied community; and debate – both formal and informal – between analysts and their intellectual peers (these three levels are also discussed by Phillips, 1978). Relating these levels of interpretation to the game, drama and text-interpretation analogies, respectively, the rest of this chapter considers the role of the – my – self, in conjunction with those it influences and is influenced by, in the construction of the image linking criminality with racial stereotypes in north central Birmingham.

Research strategies: Applying the rules of the game

Any attempt on the part of an analyst to enter the life-world of others is, above all, strategic. However laudable the aims, such research begins with a deliberate and calculated decision to participate in someone else's daily round. This raises important ethical questions and I hope that what follows will not be read without a sense of unease. At a personal level, it is easy to submerge the instrumental and exploitative elements of participant observation beneath a wave of altruistic intent. I shall argue, however, that it makes both moral and analytical sense to expose the power relations inherent in ethnography at an early stage of the research.

Experiential research, as Giddens (1984, chapter 2) points out, involves more than passively sifting information from a readily available pool of events. Access to the raw material of experiential research involves not detached observation but purposive entry into a stream of social encounters. At this level, the analyst is involved above all in a process of *negotiation* to gain access to established conventions and procedures in order to come to grips with the practical knowledge required to partici- pate in local life. The aim is not, however, simply to discover the 'rules' of the social game, but to become conversant with them to the extent that one feels safe angling for advantage and seeking privileged access to information. The relationship to be monitored in this context is that between the observer and the observed. Such interaction is both risky and strategic, and the game analogy offers the most appropriate form in which to play out, and convey, the process.

The negotiations to be made in north central Birmingham concerned the entry of a white East Midlands woman into the culturally mixed milieu of a West Midlands inner city and into the male-dominated world of the local police. I recognize now, though my understanding of the process was much more scanty then, that the outcomes of such nego- tiations depend crucially on how the presentation of 'self' is handled. My discussion of this process therefore includes not only an account of some strategies required to begin to 'play the game' of participant observation or action research, but also an assessment of the effects of such strategies on the subject-matter of the enquiry.

Much of the initial part of the discussion can be illustrated with reference to a local 'community lunch' – a regular but informal lunchtime meeting of residents and workers, attracting 'gatekeepers' from all walks of local life. The attendance varied from month to month but would include community nurses and health visitors, members of residents' associations, people from pensioners' clubs, teachers, community liaison police, church-leaders, advice centre workers, and so on. Such meetings were to be the key means of gaining an introduction to the many local residents I would not normally routinely encounter. It was from this setting that the local salience of the 'race and crime debate' first emerged, and it was my credibility in dealing with this that would condition the success of subsequent research.

Stacking the odds

Gatherings like the community lunch encapsulate many of the 'rules of the game' so crucial to experiental research. By bringing together the different social worlds of a neighbourhood, such venues provide analysts with their greatest opportunities (both to meet a broad spectrum of local interests, and to see, in microcosmic form, the development and dissolution of the alliances and conflicts that give local life its dynamic), and also their greatest risks (in that access must be negotiated to all parts of the local world, and reputation must be preserved at the same event amongst diverse groups whose interests often conflict). It is probably through the insights of Erving Goffman, master of the 'interaction ritual', that aspiring ethnographers can best come to grips with the strategies of face-to-face interaction required to manage such delicate encounters.

Goffman (1967) draws attention to the importance in managing social interaction not just of conversation, but also of glances, gestures, positionings and verbal statements. His writing argues for the difference that even 'the fleeting facial move an individual can make in the game of expressing his alignment to what is happening' (Goffman, 1967: 1). Vindicating this assertion, experimental and personality psychology has more recently developed an understanding of people's capacity to develop not only acute sensitivity to the social and interpersonal cues that signal appropriate behaviour in different settings, but also high degrees of self-monitoring to ensure personal compliance with these 'micro-norms' of social interaction (see Shaver, 1985). When relying on the 'snowball effect' of heterogeneous venues like the community lunch it is crucial that the ethnographer develops these skills to the full. In Snyder and Cambel's (1982) terms, participant observers must develop an identity that aligns more with a model of the flexible 'pragmatic self' than with that of a dogmatic 'principled self'. In Goffman's (1967) terms, they must be good at 'face-work'.

It is face-work which, more than any other strategy, forms a basis for the self-monitoring required to win an entry to community life. 'Face' is 'an image of self delineated in terms of approved social attributes' (Goffman, 1967: 5). Although face can usually be defined and presented in a manner finely tuned to the context in which an encounter takes place, in a setting like the community lunch, where a variety of group norms and expectations are brought together, one's confidence in face can easily be undermined. This happened a number of times during my attempts to negotiate an introduction to the lives of the individuals and groups represented at the noon forum: when a police officer intervened in a conversation with a volunteer from the neighbourhood advice centre, my sympathies with the problems of law enforcement almost compromised my access to a rich world of locally-defined problems; when an evangelistic Christian confided his concerns about the 'threat' of the Muslim faith, the topic of religion had to be sacrificed altogether; when sustaining a conversation with an elderly white pensioner and a black representative of the local youth opportunities scheme, my decision to 'sit on the fence' precluded a further appointment with either of them.

In such circumstances, the need for 'face-work' – the means of counteracting events and statements whose symbolic effect is a threat to face – is very high. Over time, such face-work will require the researcher to set up – through attitude, gesture and demeanour – a reputation. Its nature, as the above examples suggest, will partly condition the outcome of the inquiry. A number of strategies routinely employed to develop a reputation are outlined by Jones and Pittman (1982), and some are more appropriate than others to the role of the participant observer. In opting for one rather than another, it is important to recognize that whatever impression one's more or less self-consciously constructed reputation creates, it revolves around an interest in realizing, augmenting or maintaining the balance of power in a relationship. It is for this reason that it is important for the participant observer to choose a strategy purposively, rather than to allow power to be abstracted and manipulated in ways that are unanticipated and unacknowledged.

Jones and Pittman's (1982) first type of reputation – intimidation – is obviously inappropriate for the ethnographer if any kind of empathetic relationship is ever to be sustained. Ingratiation (the appearance of wanting to be liked), though inevitable to an extent, is equally to be avoided, in that it demands all kinds of compromises that could verge on the deceitful. Resorting to self-promotion or exemplification (seeking to impress others with either professional competence or moral worthiness) are strategies that can be very successful in securing both data and prestige. They may, however, result in the kind of knowledge that lacks authenticity, in that appeal to professional or moral superiority begins to distance the observer, excluding him or her from the most intimate meetings and activities. The remaining option – supplication – is the impression that is at once the most risky in terms of one's reputation, but also most desirable because it leaves the bulk of the power of a relationship in the hands of those being studied. As a strategy, supplication involves the exploitation of one's own weakness. It requires explicit acknowledgement of one's dependence for information and guidance on those (the studied public) with superior resources (in this case, knowledge about the commonsense wisdom surrounding the 'race and crime' debate).

Ideally, the strategies outlined above are the means to an end (that of gaining an insider's access to local life). They should not, in theory, become factors shaping that end. Face-work, for instance, should simply be a way of dealing with the lottery of unexpected and undesirable events punctuating daily routine. However, the participant observer is more vulnerable than most to the unexpected because he or she is unable to assent to the half-truths, illusions and rationalizations that usually account for the smooth running of a social world. Though people generally cooperate to avoid confrontation and save face, 'finding that there is much to be gained from venturing nothing' (Goffman 1967: 43), this is not a luxury for the ethnographer whose very task is to probe the taken-for-granted and explore the undisturbed. This raises an important question concerning just what the consequences of self-conscious self-presentation and impression management are. Does the analyst's peculiar role unduly influence the studied subjects? Through strategies invoked to increase the odds of success, does the participant observer or action researcher so change the rules of the game that the play is no longer a valid object of enquiry?

Playing the game

Experiential research is often criticized on the grounds that the analyst could – deliberately or unsuspectingly – 'contaminate' or manipulate the social setting under study. Simply by being there, it is argued, the researcher is bound to influence the kinds of thing that people say and do. This is undoubtedly true, and there are two common responses. On the one hand, observers have sought to make themselves as unobtrusive as possible (minimizing 'participation' and maximizing 'observation'); on the other hand, analysts have viewed their role as an active one, *shaping* events, where possible, to further the interests of the researched population (the emphasis here being on 'action research' rather than passive spectating).

Both responses have their pros and cons, but neither confront nor question the validity of the charge that the presence of an analyst can damage or distort the data. My argument is that this assumption must be challenged, on at least two levels. *Intuitively*, personal experience suggests that it is I rather than the setting that changes during fieldwork. To explain this *theoretically*, I contend that fears concerning the analyst's ability to contaminate the data of experience are based on pre-nineteenth-century ideas about the nature of the self. Expanding this reasoning below, it is suggested that with a greater theoretical understanding of the self, the extent of the analyst's intervention is immaterial so long as it is clearly acknowledged and built into the analysis.

Before the late nineteenth century, ideas about the self reflected theological conceptions of the separation of soul and mind: they assumed a distinction between persons and things; they stressed the personal nature of identity; and they were founded on a set of social mores which assigned responsibility for the social consequences of action to the individual (Johnson, 1985). However, as Rosenberg and Gara (1985) point out, a major turning-point occurred with the publication of William James' *Principles of Psychology* (1890), with George Herbert Mead's attempt to elaborate a theory of intersubjectivity that would conceive of the self as socially originated (see Joas, 1985), and with the airing of related work by Josiah Royce and Charles Peirce (see Miller, 1975). In the literature of symbolic interactionism which these early thinkers inspired, the self attained unprecedented significance, not as something innate to the individual, but as the socially constructed focus round which all other social processes revolve (see Rock, 1979: 102–77). So conceived, the concept found its way rapidly into the quantitative analyses of experimental and personality psychology (see Shaver, 1985), but curiously, it has rarely been a central concern of those involved in experiential sociology and humanistic geography.

The crucial significance of the pragmatists' redefinition of self for the oral ethnographic tradition of inquiry is apparent from Mead's (1927) class lectures in social psychology. Accounts of the consequences of participatory research must be radically revised when it is recognised that the self (including that of the analyst) 'exists only in relationship with other selves and cannot be reached except through other selves' (1927: 155). The self is, moreover, 'continuously coming into existence, like the rest of experience; it shifts and changes with the social situation' (1927: 42). Indeed, 'one cannot exist as a self without the universal, the group, that makes the self possible' (1927: 164). The self in the pragmatic sense is not originally given to actors: it is, rather, the product of a complex of social relationships (Joas, 1985) – indeed, it can be conceived of as 'culture internalised' (Fallding, 1982). From such a perspective, current conceptions of the self portray it as social and symbolic (i.e. not the sum of discrete and immutable attributes or traits), multidimensional, situational and transactional (Johnson, 1985).

It is not surprising, then, that my impression at the end of two years' fieldwork is that *I* changed. (I would have changed wherever I was, of course, but not in the same way.) This might have affected my interpretations of the subject matter, but it would be arrogant to suppose it affected the course of local life. In fact, in so far as the pragmatic notion of the self is authentic, the issue for participant observers is not whether their presence contaminates a social setting, but rather the converse. The analyst must reflect on those elements of the social world that shape the self responsible for research. For the analyst's self is not a coherent, static assemblage of personality traits that is able to observe without absorbing. Instead, it is continuously redefined in interaction with others to become 'a special mirroring and incorporation of the social processes in which it is embedded' (Rock, 1979: 146). As analysts live local activity, they become part of local place (a process discussed in general terms by Soja, 1985). As much of what a study is to reveal will be etched into the self as will be written into a notebook, and by reflecting on self, to reveal something of the nature of culture and group identity, the participant observer can begin to analyse the social world in which he or she is immersed. As M. B. Smith (1985) points out, people's theories about *themselves* are important for their interpretations of social life, and the findings of experiential research are not fully analysed until the implications of this are acknowledged. This is an important touchstone for any attempt to negotiate an entry into different worlds of lived experience, but it is equally significant once the 'rules of the game' have been mastered and full participation in the drama of local social life begins.

On stage: Rehearsing the drama

The procedures outlined above draw attention to the importance of the self in all interpretations of social life. Subjecting the self to scrutiny, however, carries a further implication for the oral-ethnographic method. It emphasizes the extent to which public selves can be a variable reflection of private identities. There is a distinction between the inner 'I' and the public 'me' (see Rock, 1979; Joas, 1985) that suggests that, while self-scrutiny must give helpful clues about the nature of the social worlds under study, scrutiny of *other* selves is virtually impossible, in view of the layers of presentational strategy masking the private being of the individual. This is not, however, a disadvantage when experiential research turns for inspiration to the analogy of social life as drama.

To illustrate the point, this section is concerned with how to analyse relationships at the second conceptual level distinguished in the introduction, concerning socializing *within* a studied community. Addressing this task, Geertz (1983: 70) has argued that 'accounts of other people's subjectivities can be built up without recourse to pretensions to more-than-normal capacities for ego effacement and fellow feeling.' His own studies in Java, Bali and Morocco show that, ideally, the observer's strategy is not so much that of entering another's self as that of 'grasping a proverb, catching an allusion, seeing a joke' (Geertz, 1983: 70). From this perspective, the analyst can glean much by entering local life in his or her own right rather than by attempting to emulate others, though the process still depends on techniques 'more like the skills of literary and dramatic criticism and of poetics than the skills of physical scientists' (Harré, 1978: 52).

The social analogy perhaps best able to convey the symbolic meaning of the events and imagery of the world of lived experience is that depicting social life as drama or dramatic ritual. The dramaturgical perspective is part of a long anthropological tradition, tacitly drawn upon in masterpieces of interpretative understanding like that attained by Gluckman (1940) in his observations at the opening of a bridge in 'Zululand', and by Mitchell (1956) in his account of the Kalela dance. Recently, however, the dramatic analogy has been applied much more systematically, and the line between drama as analogy and drama as 'reality' – or at least as the only way of conceiving and living reality – has become (quite legitimately) blurred (see Hare, 1985).

The drama of social life can be appreciated most immediately in crowd behaviour: in the vibrance and colour of carnival (Cohen, 1980); in the violent exchange of riot; in the ritual of institutionalized ceremony (Geertz, 1983: 26–30). But the dramatic analogy is equally relevant for an appreciation of the minutiae of routine encounters that overlap and interlock during the everyday performances that form and re-form group boundaries, and so sustain, dissolve or deny the lines of power and authority on which a social fabric hangs.

Erving Goffman excels in this arena, too, even though the dramaturgical perspective hinges more on the notion of performance than on that of strategic negotiation. By relating the concepts of performance, frontstage and backstage behaviour to social life, by showing how people variously present themselves in order to control both their own image and the overall theme of an episode of interaction, Goffman (1959) laid the groundwork of much that was to follow. However, it is Hare (1985) who has pushed the analogy to its logical conclusion, formalizing a range of interpretative devices such as image, theme, plot, script, roles, protagonist, audience, and so on. Without labouring in quite the same way to achieve congruence with all things theatrical, I suggest that a focus on plot, script and performance is helpful in understanding the nature and consequences of the image linking crime and race in north central Birmingham.

The 'plot' has to be understood at the level of national ideology and politics. It revolves around tensions between the 'stick and carrot' of immigration control and race relations legislation; it reflects friction caused by the assignment of responsibility for illegal immigration and overstaying to the police; and it embraces the progressive marginalization and criminalization of the black population in political rhetoric, judicial opinion and police practice. (For some amplification of these themes, see Hall et al., 1978; Nugent and King 1979; Gordon, 1983; Lea and Young, 1984.)

This 'plot', abstractly linking race relations issues with a moral panic over law and order, provides a pool of ideas around which the 'script' appropriate to a particular event or locality is constructed. Abelson (1981) argues that all public life is based on the scripts that people possess to guide their behaviour in different kinds of social interaction. In an inner city neighbourhood where the crime rate is relatively high and fear of crime is widespread, the 'script' most frequently and routinely drawn upon is that relating to the management of danger and uncertainty. The skeleton of such a script is fleshed out as the mass media translate broad 'plots' into a form more immediately accessible and utilizable by the general public. The process is particularly effective for sensational and newsworthy topics like crime and race relations, and the anxieties each generates are often conflated.

In north central Birmingham, the majority of public information about crime is gleaned from the mass media and from hearsay. Less than 5 per cent of the population claim to have any other source of knowledge about local crime rates, and as Piepe et al. (1978) have shown, it is the provincial rather than the national press that is the most effective source of such local wisdom. Moreover, I have shown elsewhere (e.g. S. J. Smith, 1985) that the 'script' put together by the provincial press in the West Midlands is one that fuses images of deviance with racial stereotypes, presenting black people in the inner city as a threat rather than as a cultural resource. These images are not, of course, received uncritically.

The press does not dictate *what* people think and do; rather it indicates what they might think *about* and how they might ascribe meaning to events. The news helps people work out what to expect as the consequence of their actions by providing a public record of what has happened, or what is thought to have happened, before. The script, then, is an unfinished checklist of cues providing the public with a basis from which to extemporize. In north central Birmingham, this basis is the image linking 'race' and crime. Such a script contains the necessary prompts to guide performance in times of uncertainty, but it also leaves much to the actors' imaginations: it is less a prescription for behaviour than a source of inspiration for the improvised drama of everyday life.

Plots and scripts may be deduced from surveys and secondary sources, but performance can only be assessed through observation and participation. To this end, participant observation and action research must be selective (socially, spatially and temporally). The consequence, as Kirk and Miller (1986) explain, is that experiential data can only be reported in terms of some explicit or implicit theory. At the broadest theoretical level, the Birmingham case study, like most observational research, was framed by the ontological presuppositions of interactionism which assume that 'structure is animated by the everyday behaviour of people, not by an immanent and *sui generis* logic of its own' (Rock, 1979: 146). More specifically, the research was oriented around the (initially tacit) question concerning: How and why are the racial categories and stereotypes that arise as a contingency of national politics and international economy sustained and reproduced in a *local* structure of social relations? The 'raw data' of such a study are not, therefore, neutral. Rather, as Harré (1978: 16) observes, they flow from the interaction of theory with experience 'in the course of which the matter under study is selectively perceived and interpreted'. Fieldwork in north central Birmingham thus focused on those dramatic interludes that helped account for the salience of 'race' as a principle of social action. Had a different 'plot' and 'script' been adopted as a starting-point, the focus could equally have been on the salience of age, class, gender or any other socially and politically recognizable attribute.

Having established a set of selective principles, it became apparent that the interludes with the most consistent bearing on the local salience of 'race' in Birmingham related to the definition and subsequent avoidance of danger and uncertainty. Ideas about danger flowed both from public speech and social action, and the significance of each is considered in turn.

Gossip and rumour about deviance in north central Birmingham tended to draw on, and thereby 'confirm', the association between criminality and racial stereotypes forged by the provincial press (see S. J. Smith, 1985; 1986: 121–8). Such conversations helped people articulate their fears, enabling them to define danger easily and unambiguously (though not necessarily accurately). Analyses of forms of talk therefore proved important to the task of understanding the construction and utilization of urban images. Through talk, as Bourdieu (1972: 189–90) points out, what begins as private speculation can, as discussion proceeds, assume hitherto unrealized legitimacy. In Rock's (1979: 112) terms, words objectify: they 'prise objects out of the stream of immediate experience and award them structure and enduring identity.' The act of speech makes people take sides and express an opinion to which they must adhere, if only fleetingly. The consequences are well illustrated in the West Midlands case-study. There the analysis shows how, through gossip and rumour, uninformed speculation is articulated in terms of a prevailing wisdom linking race and crime. In north central Birmingham, with a plot and script that takes for granted the nature of deviance, little could be uttered on the topic of crime without some allusion to the racial identity of criminals. Constantly reaffirmed, such stereotypes shape attitudes and inform behaviour and so play their part in guaranteeing the salience of 'race' in the structuring and restructuring of social relations.

Talking about danger, however, is only one way of defining it, and urban imagery penetrates far beyond the spoken word. One device useful in monitoring and analysing the infusion of danger in and out of particular social encounters is what Goffman (1974) terms 'frame analysis'. Its efficacy depends on detailed observations of how the mood of an encounter can change from one 'frame' to another as the terms of an episode of interaction are defined. For example, one quiet afternoon along the Lozells Road, the orientation towards 'fun' of an ebullient group of black youths eating the fares of 'Dolly's Takeaway' encountered the 'leisured' frame of two police officers approaching from the opposite direction. A chain of subtle gestures was observed as the two parties became aware of each others' approach. An almost imperceptible sequence of exchanges provided enough impetus to transform the episode from one frame (fun and leisure) to another (danger and suspicion). The sequence was as follows.

The police officers seemed to stiffen their walk and move closer together. One twitched his hand towards what might have been a radio, and both fixed their eyes on the oncoming group with the consequence that their subsequent conversation spilled melodramatically from the sides of their mouths. The effect was to reframe a leisurely stroll into a display of professionalism. The youths, in turn, exaggerated their usual bounce into what could have been construed as a swagger. They talked more loudly and gesticulated more often. A frame oriented towards fun slipped into one characterized by ritual demonstration. At the same time, the reserved window-shopping of two elderly white pensioners became an expression of passive solidarity as they linked arms and drew their bags to their bodies. This became, too, an expression of deference, as they crossed the road to remove themselves from the path of the encounter. However, as the groups moved closer and one officer's request for a chip was laughingly answered with the flash of an empty packet, a friendly shrug of the shoulders was sufficient to dispel the atmosphere of confrontation and replace it with one of amiable sparring. Such switching of frames is achieved through what George Herbert Mead has termed a 'conversation of gestures', and this silent exchange is as significant for an understanding of urban imagery as is the gossip and rumour described above.

Avoidance behaviour, however, entails more than simply defusing a situation defined as dangerous. It entails, too, the deliberate exclusion of potentially dangerous areas and people from one's daily round. In the Birmingham example, reliance on racial stereotypes to this end occurred primarily when some major adjustment of behaviour was required to minimize the high levels of fear that accompany acutely perceived threat. The salience of people's appearance or cultural symbols in the management of danger varied according to how dramatic a response was required to cope with the advance of the unexpected. (This is discussed in Smith (1984a), where it is suggested that whenever and wherever risk seems acute, reactions to crime tend to reflect and reconstitute 'racial' categories as a principle of social action.)

This brief sketch of how speech and action are directed towards the management of danger in Birmingham begins to indicate how, in the drama of daily life, the 'plot' and 'scripts' concerning 'race' and deviance that are nationally and ideologically constructed, tend to be locally accepted. These terms of reference are not seized upon uncritically, and they are extensively reworked, redefined and improvised upon, according to the specific needs of a particular 'performance'. But for the most part, the effect of such reworking is to ensure that the local reproduction of social relations sustains the racial categories set up nationally and internationally. As far as the public are concerned, such a 'production' is acceptable because it works: plot and script offer a pragmatic basis on which to conduct everyday life in an uncertain environment. In this sense, the drama of social life in north central Birmingham is more than a metaphor: it is the way things are. The analyst, however, must retain the ability to leave the theatre.

Interpreting the text: Finding or creating meaning?

Qualitative research involves more than negotiating an entry into communal life and participating in the drama constructing urban images. Crucially, the role of the analyst is to translate and interpret this image. Experiential research differs from the process of living as a non-researcher in that it requires not just participation, observation and description, but also abstraction, contemplation and selective communication to academic (and other) peers. This is the point at which research moves beyond the level of what Giddens (1984) terms discursive and practical consciousness, to gain access to information about the sources and consequences of social action that are not immediately apparent to other actors. In drawing on such information, a third level of interaction requires analysis during qualitative research – that between researchers and their intellectual 'community of interest'. When this is incorporated, it is text interpretation rather than gaming or performance that provides the most appropriate analogy for the research process.

In so far as the analyst's mandate includes interpretation and communication, one of the most underplayed advantages of participant observation is the very fact that researchers usually begin as outsiders, whose experiences and presuppositions differ from those possessed by the 'target' community. Since knowledge is both historically and geographically specific, and because what people know is a constraint on what they can think and do (Thrift, 1985), it is not arrogance but realism to suppose that the researcher will have access to some kinds of information not possessed by those under study and that this will have a bearing on subsequent analysis. In the same vein, as Bauman (1978) observes, since the meanings associated with other cultures can only be grasped in relation to the meanings of one's own culture, the latter might be thought of more as an asset than a liability.

This reasoning suggests that a certain amount of detachment is necessary to achieve subjective understanding, and it follows that analysts' *over*-identification during participant observation can be as much of a problem as under-involvement and insensitivity. The role of the analyst is finely balanced and the problem of understanding is that of how to 'produce an interpretation of the way a people lives which is neither imprisoned within their mental horizons, an ethnography of witchcraft as written by a witch, nor systematically deaf to the tonalities of their existence, an ethnography of witchcraft as written by a geometer' Geertz (1983: 57). One has to be close enough to grasp the significance of commonsense perceptions and behaviours – the cement of cultural systems that 'lies so artlessly before our eyes it is almost impossible to see' (Geertz, 1983: 92). One must move far enough away to provide a conceptual understanding of this world.

Elsewhere, I have illustrated the effects of analytical 'closeness' and 'distance' on conceptions of social relations, arguing that the image linking race and crime in north central Birmingham can be interpreted not only as a perception acknowledged and utilized by residents, but also as an abstraction with more relevance to the cumulative task of social theory than to the immediate contingencies of a daily routine (see Smith, 1986). The 'race and crime' image *can* be described in terms of its role at the level of commonsense understanding (where it provides a pragmatic, if not necessarily rational, guide to the routine activities of daily life) but it can also be analysed in terms of its significance for an understanding of the distribution and manipulation of power (in that it guarantees that 'race', rather than any other social attribute becomes the criterion by which privilege is defined and status maintained).

What must be stressed, however, is that in developing such an argument – that is, in sketching a conceptual understanding of the world of common sense, in presenting for academic scrutiny just one interpretation of a text rich in symbols and signs – the role of the analyst's *creativity* is central, though it is very rarely acknowledged. One might not agree with Ricoeur (1971) that judgement concerning interpretation is guesswork, but one cannot deny the power of his argument that validation in this context is more indebted to the logic of probability than to the logic of empirical verification. For where meaning is concerned, the concept of *accuracy* of representation is redundant. The meanings associated with everyday life, like those associated with literary texts, are inherently unstable. Thus as Menzel (1978) points out, meaning is never dictated unambiguously by what is observed, by the testimony of actors, or by any other data. No action or event has *a* meaning and 'in most instances, the determinants of the meaning of an act requires a heavy dose of researcher input' (Menzel, 1978: 156).

People and events only seem coherent because we imagine them to be so, and because, in representing them, we find acceptable ways of smoothing over the incoherence, miscalculations and uncertainties that our inherently partial understanding of the world contains. This process is unavoidable. It does not so much contaminate the raw data of experience as render it understandable in the light of whatever set of pre-suppositions the communicator adopts. Moreover, such 'smoothing over' is not just an academic exercise. It is an inevitable facet of the way in which life is lived and knowledge is constructed, and it requires analysis in just the same way as any other part of the process of experiential research. In view of this, most errors relating to the use of subjectively experienced data lies not in being 'creative' as a social analyst, but in failing to recognize the leaps of imagination required to apprehend the world and in insisting on excluding them from analysis.

It is, then, the researcher who takes the initial responsibility for assigning meaning to the lives of those written about. However, the legitimacy – indeed, the very nature – of such assignations will be determined in large part by the vetting procedures invoked by the analyst's intellectual peers. As Gergson (1982: 145) observes, with a frankness rarely encountered in the literature: 'the manner in which the social scientist interprets behavior, the manner in which data are employed for purposes of defending or criticizing a theory, and one's confidence in the validity of a theory are principally dependent on and limited by the social support systems operating within the sciences themselves.'

The 'art' of qualitative research depends on a creativity sanctioned not only by what is given in the chaos of subjective encounter but also by what is assigned legitimacy by the social and professional worlds in which the analyst participates. The authenticity of experiential research rests as much on the dictates of an intellectual 'interpretative community' as on direct encounter with a public; and interpretation, like experience, is a social and political act. The key methodological shortcoming of qualitative research is not, I contend, a consequence of dealing with the 'soft' data of experience but of appearing content to have discovered the rules of the game between researcher and researched, and feeling satisfied having reviewed the drama of local social life. The third level of interaction – that between analysts and academic peers, concerning the meaning and interpretation of observations – is crucial. It, too, must be analysed, for our insights into this process are our only clues as to why we have come to know what we think we have found out.

Conclusion

A new series of monographs on qualitative methods has recently been launched in the wake of concern that those pursuing experiential research are less able than other scientists to 'talk about what it is they do' (Kirk and Miller, 1986). This chapter suggests that such discourse is impossible unless analysts also converse about 'who it is they are'. Self-consciousness is a fundamental precondition of oral-ethnographic research if the tacit pressures, presuppositions and biases that condition all perception and experience are to be 'controlled for' in the quest for interpretative understanding. To argue this point, I have, in considering the construction of an urban image linking 'race' and crime, drawn upon three common symbolic analogies of social life, portraying it as a game to be played, a drama to be acted and a text to be interpreted. These analogies are used to illustrate the importance of analysing subjective experience in terms of relationships between observer and observed, in terms of the interplay of actors within a studied locale, and in terms of a researcher's relationship with the wider academic community. It is important that qualitative research moves forward on each of these conceptually (but not ontologically) distinct levels if it is to develop the analytical procedures and validity checks necessary for the art of experiential research to contribute fully to the development of human geography as a social science.

References

Abelson, R. P. (1981) 'Psychological status of the script concept', *American Psychologist* 36, 715–29.

Bauman, Z. (1978) *Hermeneutics and social science*, Hutchinson, London.

Bourdieu, P. (1972) *Outline of a theory of practice*, trans. R. Nice, Cambridge University Press, Cambridge.

Chibnall, S. (1978) *Law and order news*, Tavistock, London.

Cohen, A. (1980) 'Drama and politics in the development of a London carnival', *Man* 15, 65–87.

Fallding, H. (1982) 'G. H. Mead's orthodoxy', *Social Forces* 60, 723–37.

Francescato, D. and Mebane, W. (1973) 'How citizens view two great cities; Milan and Rome', in R. M. Downs and D. Stea (eds), *Image and environment*, Aldine, Chicago, 131–47.

Geertz, C. (1983) *Local knowledge. Further essays in interpretive anthropology*, Basic Books, New York.

Gergsen, K. J. (1982) 'From self to science: what is there to know?', in J. Suls (ed.), *Psychological perspectives on the self*, volume 1, Lawrence Erlbaum, New Jersey and London, 129–49.

Giddens, A. (1984) *The constitution of society*, Polity Press, Cambridge.

Gluckman, M. (1940) 'Analysis of a social situation in modern Zululand', *Bantu Studies* 14, 1–30, 147–74.

Goffman, E. (1959) *The presentation of self in everyday life*, Doubleday, New York.

Goffman, E. (1967) *Interaction ritual*, Penguin Books, Harmondsworth.

Goffman, E. (1974) *Frame analysis: an essay on the organization of experience*, Harper and Row, New York.

Gordon, P. (1983) *White law*, Pluto, London.

Habermas, J. (1968) *Knowledge and human interests*, trans. J. J. Shapiro, Beacon Press, Boston.

Hall, S., Critcher, C., Jefferson, T., Clarke, J. and Roberts, B. (1978) *Policing the crisis*, Macmillan, London.

Hare, A. P., (1985) *Social interaction as drama*, Sage, Beverly Hills and London.

Harré, R. (1978) 'Accounts, actions and meanings', in M. Brenner, P. Marsh and M. Brenner (eds), *The social contexts of method*, Croom Helm, London, 44–65.

Harvey, D. (1985) *Consciousness and the urban experience*, Basil Blackwell, Oxford.

Joas, H. (1985) *G. H. Mead. A contemporary re-examination of his thought*, trans. R. Mayer, Polity Press, Cambridge.

Johnson, F. (1985) 'The Western concept of self', in A. J. Marsella, G. De Vos and F. L. K. Hsu (eds), *Culture and self. Asian and Western perspectives*, Tavistock, New York and London, 91–138.

Jones, E. E. and Pittman, T. S. (1982) 'Toward a general theory of strategic self-presentation', in J. Suls (ed.), *Psychological perspectives on the self*, Volume 1, Lawrence Erlbaum, New Jersey and London, 231–62.

Kirk, J. and Miller, M. L. (1986) *Reliability and validity in qualitative research*, Sage, Beverly Hills and London.

Lea, J. and Young, J. (1984) *What is to be done about law and order?*, Penguin Books, Harmondsworth.

Ley, D. (1974) *The black inner city as frontier outpost*, Association of American Geographers, Washington.

Lynch, K. (1960) *The image of the city*, MIT Press, Cambridge, Mass.

Mead, G. H. (1914) 'Class lectures in social psychology', in D. L. Miller (1982) *The individual and the social self. Unpublished work of George Herbert Mead*, Chicago University Press, Chicago and London, 27–105.

Mead, G. H. (1927) 'Class lectures in social psychology', in D. L. Miller (ed.) (1982) *The individual and the social self. Unpublished work of George Herbert Mead*, University of Chicago Press, Chicago and London, 106–175.

Menzel, H. (1978) 'Meaning – who needs it?', in M. Brenner, P. Marsh and M. Brenner (eds), *The social contexts of method*, Croom Helm, London, 140–71.

Miles, R. I. (1982) *Racism and migrant labour*, Routledge & Kegan Paul, London.

Miller, D. L. (1975) 'Josiah Royce and George H. Mead on the nature of the self'. *Transactions of the Charles S. Peirce Society* 11 (2), 67–89.

Mitchell, J. C. (1956) *The Kalela dance*, Manchester University Press, Manchester.

Mitchell, J. C. (1983) 'Case and situation analysis', *The Sociological Review* 31, 187–211.

Nisbet, R. (1976) *Sociology as an art form*, Oxford University Press, New York.

Nugent, N. and King R. (1979) 'Ethnic minorities, scapegoating and the extreme right', in R. Miles and A. Phizacklea (eds), *Racism and political action in Britain*, Routledge & Kegan Paul, London, 28–49.

Piepe, A., Crouch, S. and Emerson, M. (1978) *Mass Media and Cultural Relationships*, Saxon House, Westmead.

Phillips, D. L. (1978) 'Hierarchies of interaction in sociological research', in M. Brenner, P. Marsh and M. Brenner (eds), *The social contexts of method*, Croom Helm, London, 210–36.

Pred, A. (1981) 'Social reproduction and the time-geography of everyday life', *Geografiska Annaler* 63B, 5–22.

Rich, P. (1986) *Race and empire in British politics*, Cambridge University Press, Cambridge.

Ricoeur, P. (1971) 'The model of the text: meaningful action considered as a text', *Social Research* 38, 529–62.

Rock, P. (1979) *The making of symbolic interactionism*, Macmillan, London.

Rosenberg, S. and Gara, M. A. (1985) 'The multiplicity of personal identity', *Review of Personality and Social Psychology* 6, 87–113.

Sellin, J. T. (1938) 'Culture conflict and crime', *SSRC Bulletin No. 41*, Report of the sub-committee on personality and culture, SSRC, New York.

Shaver, P. (ed.) (1985) 'Self, situations and social behaviour', *Review of Personality and Social Psychology* 6 (whole issue).

Smith, M. B. (1985) 'The metaphorical basis of selfhood', in A. J. Marsella, G. De Vos and F. L. K. Hsu (eds), *Culture and self. Asian and Western Perspectives*, Tavistock, New York and London, 56–88.

Smith, S. J. (1982a) 'Race and crime statistics', *Background Paper No. 2* Board of Social Responsibility, Race, Pluralism and Community Group, London.

Smith, S. J. (1982b) 'Race and reactions to crime', *New Community* 10, 233–42.

Smith, S. J. (1983) 'Public policy and the effects of crime in the inner city', *Urban Studies* 20, 229–39.

Smith, S. J. (1984a) 'Negotiating ethnicity in an uncertain environment', *Ethnic and Racial Studies* 7, 360–73.

Smith, S. J. (1984b) 'Crime and the structure of social relations', *Transactions, Institute of British Geographers* NS9, 427–42.

Smith, S. J. (1984c) 'Practising humanistic geography', *Annals, Association of American Geographers* 74, 353–74.

Smith, S. J. (1985) 'News and the dissemination of fear', in J. Burgess and J. Gold (eds), *Geography, the media and popular culture*, Croom Helm, London, 229–53.

Smith, S. J. (1986) *Crime, space and society*, Cambridge University Press, Cambridge.

Snyder, M. and Cambel, B. H. (1982) 'Self-monitoring: the self in action', in J. Suls (ed.), *Psychological perspectives on the self* Volume 1, Lawrence Erlbaum, New Jersey and London, 185–207.

Soja, E. W. (1985) 'The spatiality of social life: towards a transformative retheorisation', in D. Gregory and J. Urry (eds), *Social relations and spatial structures*, St Martin's Press, New York, 90–127.

Thrift, N. (1985) 'Flies and germs: a geography of knowledge', in D. Gregory and J. Urry (eds), *Social relations and spatial structures*, Macmillan, Basingstoke and London, 366–403.

3

Racial Conflict and the 'No-Go Areas' of London

Michael Keith

Carrying out research into the violent clashes between the police and the black community in London in the early 1980s, it was considered essential to attempt a reconstruction of the local histories of those areas in which the confrontations had been most marked. This was achieved principally through extensive interviews with local residents and participant observation work and interviews with the Metropolitan Police.

One phenomenon that recurred in the research was the predominance of a very small number of sites in which violent clashes between police and the local community were common and had been common since at least the early 1970s. A conflict that had a national character appeared to have specific local manifestations. It was noticeable that the reputation of these locations differed completely between different interest groups. There was never a single, discernible 'sense of place' but instead a series of competing interpretations.

A second theme that recurred in the mid-1980s was the repeated use in the press and in political discourse of the term 'no-go area', a phrase that had leaked from Northern Ireland, a phrase that implied that there were parts of British cities which the police were unwilling or unable to patrol. These two themes were connected and it seemed important to try to distinguish between the use of a lexical item in political rhetoric and the development of significant social patterns. In so doing it is not intended to discredit political discourse or to distract from the broad social context in which such micro-scale processes are set.

The argument of this chapter rests on one premise – that meanings and values which are tied to particular locations are not immanent properties of those locations yet may be communicated by them in the same manner as all sign systems.

Defining a methodology as 'qualitative' perhaps makes sense only in implied opposition to a quantitative alternative. The methodology and the explanatory model used in this chapter depends on the value of the linguistic metaphor in explanation of the social world. Whether these linguistic roots are themselves drawn from a discipline that is 'ideographic' or 'nomothetic' is similarly a desiccated dualism, for the prime benefit of the linguistic metaphor lies not in a reconciliation of such oppositions but from the possibility of incorporating the problem of intentionality into an explanation rather than hiding it in statistical generalization or camouflaging it in humanistic obscurantism.

The myth

If the 'no-go area' is to find a place in the tainted vocabulary that structures public debate of policing issues, it might be useful to untangle some of the mystification that surrounds the term. It appears to be used at present pejoratively, as a classification of those parts of British cities where relations between the police and the, almost invariably black, community are so poor as to result in a distinctive form of policing. Two fallacies seem particularly pervasive; one that this phenomenon is new to mainland Britain, the other that it is causally related to the number of crimes committed by black people.

In a non-utopian society a police force will at best be the upholders of a transparently flawed status quo. It is this defence that creates the genuine distinction between law and order, the police are simultaneously both 'crime fighters' and enforcers of one particular social and moral order, a dichotomy that echoes in the tension between the privacy that exemplifies the freedom of the city and the anonymity that generates criminal opportunity; the tension between a community of interest in combating certain offences and a common ambivalence towards a great many of the laws that define such 'crimes'. The mismatch between what is criminal in law and criminal in sentiment, the folk distinction between the rogue as underdog and the 'real' villain, exemplifies this ambiguity. Such opposing trends must be reconciled in reality rather than in any official rule-book, if the routine practice of police work is to be sustained without ceaseless confrontation. The ostensibly contradictory image of the British 'bobby' as both law enforcer and social worker was the successful product of such a compromise. Ignatieff has pointed out that this was first achieved in the context of the singularly divisive status quo of nineteenth-century Britain. Through spatial differentiation, in those areas where these contradictions were most profoundly felt, where social injustice was manifest, the police negotiated a complex, shifting, largely unspoken 'contract'. They defined the activities they would turn a blind eye to, and those which they would suppress, harass or control. This 'tacit contract' between normal neighbourhood activities and police objectives was sometimes oiled by corruption, but more often secured by favours and friendship. This was the microscopic basis of police legitimacy and it was a fragile basis at best. (1979)

Spatially sensitive policing was as much a successful instrumental ploy to win the local support needed for the flow of information that is the *sine qua non* of crime detection as it was a pious condition of action.

Today's conflict between the police and black people is also histori- cally mature in all but its most lurid manifestations. It is a conflict that is specifically not the *product* of disproportionate involvement of black people in crime. As a House of Commons Select Committee in 1972 made clear, relations between police and young 'West Indians' could by that time already be described as 'explosive'. They also stated categorically that

Of all the police forces from which we took evidence not one had found that crime committed by coloured people was proportionately greater than that by the rest of the population. Indeed in many places it was somewhat less.

On the evidence of the police themselves the conflict with black people pre-dates any allegations of black criminality. The historical maturity of this conflict has itself prompted many black communities to question the justice of British law enforcement, frequently rendering implausible notions of 'policing by consent'. When consent is withdrawn by a large section of the black community (not just by a neat social problem category, 'black youth') then the flow of information to police dries up, and it becomes impossible to solve many crimes committed by black people. Whether this minority element is relatively larger or smaller than that in socially comparable white groups is of only peripheral significance to the issue of police/black conflict, as for that matter is also the precise nature of the intangible connection between deprivation and delinquency (even if both of these issues are of major import in related social and criminological analysis).

'Places' as 'signs'

In reality, behind the issue of 'no-go areas' in London lies the evolution of what are now officially referred to by the Metropolitan Police as 'symbolic locations', which have frequently provided an arena in which general trends of social conflict are realized in specific forms of popular protest and violent confrontation. These locations are also often referred to as *front lines* and regularly witness the rejection of the traditional police/policed power relation. This is the internal relation between police and public, ultimately founded on the potential use of legitimate force by the police. The power relation which is taken for granted across other parts of the city is challenged as a matter of *practice* within a particular context, the ultimate authority of the police force is disputed. Resistance to arrest and attacks on police officers become commonplace. Understanding these clashes demands not only reference to local history but also an analysis of the affective associations tied to particular places that condition social action on such evocative 'stages' for conflict.

The work of Goffman (1963; 1971; 1972), much favoured in humanistic geography and symbolic interactionist sociology, provides an obvious theoretical grounding for this analysis. Yet one of the dangers of stressing the dramaturgical metaphor Goffman employs is that space and particular places will be seen as explicitly communicative settings for social action. I would suggest that this is very far from the case. The institutional settings of much of Goffman's analysis provide clearly defined scenes and boundaries that are not always replicated throughout the social world. Places act as signs but the symbolism is read in very different ways by those deciphering the 'spatiality' of social life (Soja, 1985). Put another way, many symbolic keys and cues are tied to a limited set of locations in the spatial realization of social form, producing not a problem of ambiguity in the reading of the social world (cf. Olssen, 1978) but an example of the proliferation of meaning. This can be reconciled with dramaturgical analysis by borrowing some of the concepts developed in the field of continental structuralism and semiology (Barthes, 1967; 1979; Eco, 1979).

A *place* can be defined in terms of its location in the communicative networks that are the basis of semiological analysis. '*Places*' form part of our cultural shorthand. Expectations of particular patterns of behaviour are contextualized by location, each location may have certain historical associations, trigger a Proustian process of recall. Significantly, in such 'readings' of the social world the tension between *individual apprehension of* and *socially given* meaning is as problematic in Vidalian studies of 'a sense of place' as in other studies of human behaviour (cf. Buttimer, 1974; Gregory, 1978; 1981). Just as a word in language has a conventional definition but is used in an idiosyncratic coinage, places signify both societal and personal experiences. The memories bound up in a particular place may be the property of one, two or a handful of people. The significations of the Somme battlefield may be vicariously accessible to Western European culture generally, tied by the experiences of real and imagined relatives, whilst the symbolic power of Hiroshima is self-evidently universal. Places may act as signs, but the messages they communicate will not be the same for everybody who reads them.

'Symbolic locations', front lines and social conflict

Three of the most well-known sites of conflict between the police and the black community in London are All Saints Road in Notting Hill, Railton Road in Brixton and Sandringham Road in Hackney. All three 'places' have witnessed collective disorders or uprisings that have subsequently been described as 'riots' (1976, 1977 in the former case; 1981 in the latter two cases). All three 'places' have subsequently been described as 'no-go areas' in which the police are afraid to act (see Keith, 1986), a simplistic classification that glosses over local history and social reality. These are 'places' where the role of black people in Britain is acted, re-enacted, defined and re-defined every day. An integral part of that role is the relationship with the police, which has deteriorated steadily for more than thirty years through the combined influences of racism, economic marginalization, stereotypical labelling and criminalization. The fundamental point to grasp about the front line is not that police/black relations are worse on All Saints Road, Railton Road or Sandringham Road than anywhere else in the surrounding area: it is rather that these are the sites at which *resentment* of power relations is transformed into *resistance* of power relations. Resistance to those arrests that do occur in these three locations is common.

It is at this point that linking theory and observation, semiology and social reality, is so helpful in understanding the realization of social conflict in space. There are two principal dimensions of linguistic symbolism; the metaphoric (paradigmatic) involving relations of similarity and the metonymic (syntagmatic) involving relations of continuity. In the social semiology of Roland Barthes those dimensions are most readily understood in terms of varying components of behavioural sets that can individually be referred to as languages. Hence in the clothing language (see figure 3.1) three items which are mutually interchangeable are tied metaphorically (e.g. blazer, suit, dinner jacket), whilst each item of clothing will be linked metonymically both to complementary sets of clothing and, quite possibly, a socially correct behavioural repertoire for a particular combination in the clothing language.

Similarly, place names evoke very different emotional reactions from different individuals. This phenomenon is accentuated when these names are replaced by normative nomination, the power of naming. The front

CLOTHING:

	Metaphoric	**Metonymic/syntagmatic**
	Blazer	
	Suit jacket	
	Dinner jacket	(a) A 'piece' in the garment code, a part that is symbolically tied to the whole, i.e. bowtie, dress shirt, etc.
		(b) Symbolically tied to a social protocol, i.e. the appropriate behaviour of somebody in a dinner jacket

SPATIAL SEMIOLOGY:

	Metaphoric	**Metonymic/syntagmatic**
'Front lines', united by similarities, distinguished by differences, but broadly interchangeable	All Saints Road	
	Railton Road	
	Sandringham Road	
		(a) Locales signifying an appropriate repertoire for a set stage: the appropriate behaviour at a particular 'place'
		(b) An individual incident as a 'part' symbolizing a whole history of police/black relations in a particular place.

Figure 3.1   Two dimensions of linguistic and symbolic representations
Source: Barthes, (1967).

line, the ghetto, the inner city. These terms may refer to specific locations, these terms may be objectively defined, but they are always more than simple classifications because their very coinage and usage endows them with a significance that extends beyond academic discourse. Language is not innocent.

In terms of the linguistic paradigm the three 'symbolic locations' can be seen as metaphorically linked. They are not precise replications of each other, but in terms of the sign systems involved they are almost mutually interchangeable (see figure 3.1). But it is the property of metonymy that most clearly renders comprehensible the set of actions that recur when police authority is challenged. For many black people who live in Notting Hill, Brixton and Hackney any police action at all will trigger off a set of mental associations about the relationship between black people and the police, when *any police action at all* is set in the context of front line, the signification is that much more powerful, the sense of injustice at the 'different reality' of black Britain (see Bhavnani et al., 1986) is overwhelming. For black communities in particular parts of London, that reality is bound up in particular locations, history is deeply imbedded in the places in which that history was enacted. Violent resistance to arrest can be understood only in terms of the whole history of black Britain, not from the forensic minutiae of an individual incident.

For the police, a completely different set of codes and messages is based on exactly the same set of locations. All Saints Road and Railton Road have a renown that stretches throughout the Metropolitan Police, the 'canteen mythology' of Notting Hill that a senior officer there described in a personal interview (Keith, 1986). For junior officers, these places are the sites of regular 'attacks' on the police by black people. Such associations may or may not be rationalized in terms of racist 'folk psychology', depending on the individual; significantly, these *rationalizations* (both the racist and non-racist ones) may well not alter police behaviour on these 'stages' when this behaviour is itself structured by the anticipation of real confrontation, not the ideologies that are employed to 'make a sense' out of these clashes. Moreover, even for those individuals keen to learn, the rapid three-year turnover rate of senior officers in each police division will frequently constrict any understanding of local history among senior management. For all ranks, the sedimentation of history in particular places remains of little interest.

Thus, in terms of social theory, a distinction could be made between the metonymic[1] (historical) and the syntagmatic[2] (operating *principally* in the present) modes of linguistic symbolism. Black perceptions are constructed as a form of local knowledge (cf. Geertz, 1973; 1982) and are fundamentally metonymic in the reading of the social world; the police action seen by a local community as part of a historical whole, invoking a 20–30-year history of black experience in a particular 'place'. For the police, operational goals have priority and 'place' as a sign is read syntagmatically; the action as part of an expected sequence, an anticipated repertoire of behaviour that occurs wholly in the present and characterizes a particular location. It is this very structure of police practice in such areas that guarantees that the policing institution acts as a 'machine for the suppression of time', history is lost. In the daily round, in the rush to handle today's problems, the past is either forgotten or remains unlearnt.

It is important to acknowledge that such symbolism, such evocative properties of places, are not 'summoned up' by the individual. As Goffman and many others (e.g. Marsh et al., 1978; Harré, 1979) have demonstrated, the reading of spatial signs is not reflexively monitored but is either part of subconscious or 'practical conscious' apprehension of the world in which we live. Such powerful affective connections between places and our understandings of those places are inseparable, precisely because we internally *define* these places by this set of mental cross-references. Like a word and its meaning a place is tied to its own signification.

Police on patrol in these sensitive locations *are* discouraged by senior officers from making inflammatory arrests, a policy often greatly resented within the lower ranks of the Metropolitan Police (Keith, 1986). Consequently, front line areas have often gleaned a form of privileged status, a status at times exploited by exponents of both petty and serious crime *subsequent* to the collapse of policing by consent. Yet, far from constituting a wholesale withdrawal of police, the differential policing of London's front lines in Notting Hill, Brixton and Hackney has involved the introduction of supplementary policing strategies that include 'symbolic location' monitoring by Special Branch, targeting and surveillance, special foot patrols and the presence of a mobile reserve strength to handle any violent clashes that may occur (Keith, 1988). The anticipation of violent conflict is built into policing priorities, often superseding problems of law enforcement. Not only are places stigmatized with negative imagery (Burgess, 1985) but also the conflict with the black community becomes part of the routine of policing (the *durée*); a facet of institutional practice, not the product of a social pathology of racist police officers.

In methodological terms, spatial semiology is not hostile to dramaturgical analysis; at least in part the humanist/structuralist opposition in social geography is illusory. In practical terms, the subjective understanding of particular places mediates social conflict. Actions relate to the codes communicated by location and these messages will vary between individuals and social groups. It is possible that a single agent may read these messages at many different levels, desirable to deconstruct the coding process in order to reveal the relationship between stages, actions and 'the naming of places'.

When social relations in space are classified in terms of 'no-go areas' the phrase assumes connotations that are highly normative. The role of the medium of space is itself interpreted and deployed to rhetorical effect

(Keith, 1987). Public debate tends to be constructed around a tapestry of assumptions and myths concerning the history of the British police. The reality of the so called 'no-go area' is just one place where the seam that holds this tapestry together begins to show.

Notes

1 Metonymy: 'substitution of the name of an attribute or adjunct for that of the thing meant (e.g. crown for king, turf for racing).' (*Concise Oxford Dictionary*)
2 Syntagm: 'Word or phrase form in syntactic unit; orderly collection of statements' (ibid).

References

Barthes, R. (1967) *Elements of semiology*, Jonathan Cape, London.
Barthes, R. (1973) *Mythologies*, Paladin, London.
Barthes, R. (1979) *The Eiffel Tower*, Hill and Wang, New York.
Bhavnani, R., Cooke, J., Gilroy, P., Hall. S., Ouseley, H. and Vaz, K. (1986) *A different reality*, West Midlands Council, Birmingham.
Burgess, J. (1985) *'News from Nowhere'*, in Burgess, J. and Gold. R. (eds) *Geography, the media and popular culture*, Croom Helm, London.
Buttimer, A. (1974) *Values in geography*, Association of American Geographers, Washington.
Eco, U. (1979) *A theory of semiotics*, Indiana University Press, Bloomington, Indiana.
Geertz, C. (1973) *The interpretation of cultures*, Hutchinson, London.
Geertz, C. (1982) *Local knowledge*, Hutchinson, London.
Goffman, E. (1963) *Stigma*, Penguin Books, Harmondsworth.
Goffman, E. (1971) *Relations in public*, Basic Books, New York.
Goffman, E. (1972) *Interaction ritual*, Allen Lane, London.
Gregory, D. (1978) *Ideology, science and human geography*, Hutchinson, London.
Gregory, D. (1981) 'Human Agency and Human Geography', *Transactions, Institute of British Geographers* 6, 1–18.
Harré, R. (1979) *Social being*, Basil Blackwell, Oxford.
House of Commons Select Committee on Police Immigrant Relations (1972) Report, HMSO, London.
Ignatieff, M. (1979) 'Police and the people: the birth of Mr Peel's blue locusts', *New Society* 30 August 1979.
Keith, M. (1986) 'The 1981 riots in London', Unpublished DPhil thesis, Oxford.
Keith, M. (1987) 'Something happened', in Jackson, P. (ed.), *Race and racism* Allen and Unwin, London.
Keith, M. (1988) 'Riots as a social problem in British cities', in Herbert, D. T. and Smith, D. M. (eds), *Social problems and the city* (forthcoming).

Marsh, P., Rosser, E. and Harré, R. (1978) *The rules of disorder*, Routledge & Kegan Paul, London.

Olssen, G. (1978) 'Of ambiguity', in Ley, D. and Samuels, M. (eds), *Humanistic geography*, Croom Helm, London.

Soja, E. (1985) 'The spatiality of social life', in Gregory, D. and Urry, J. (eds), *Social relations and spatial structures*, Macmillan, London.

Thackrah, J. (ed.) (1987) *Contemporary policing*, Police College, Bramshill.

4

Definitions of the Situation
Neighbourhood Change and Local Politics
in Chicago

Peter Jackson

Introduction

According to the sociologist William Isaac Thomas (1863–1947), a situation defined as real is real in its consequences. Irrespective of their inherent truth or falsity, people's subjective 'definitions of the situation' significantly influence their behaviour. This chapter explores the implications of Thomas's observations for an understanding of the process of neighbourhood change in Chicago where alternative 'definitions of the situation' are often violently opposed and bitterly contested.

The present chapter also has something in common with Thomas's empirical concerns, for his concept of the 'definition of the situation' was first elaborated in a monumental study of *The Polish peasant in Europe and America* (1918–20) which he wrote jointly with Florian Znaniecki. Thomas and Znaniecki employed a variety of documentary methods in their work including the judicious use of several hundred letters that Polish immigrants in America wrote home to their families in Europe.[1] This chapter similarly relies on a range of documentary methods including published Census data and electoral returns and previously unpublished archival material. These sources are further supplemented by a series of interviews with key informants conducted during the course of six months' fieldwork in Chicago in 1983. (A note on the methods used in this study is included as a brief Appendix to the text.) The chapter can therefore be read as a contribution to the recent revival of interest in ethnographic research documented by Hannerz (1980), Jackson (1985), and others. This tradition of ethnographic research stretches back to the pioneering work of the 'Chicago school' (Bulmer, 1984) of which Thomas and Znaniecki were founder members.

Inspired by Robert E. Park's commitment to first-hand knowledge 'not as a substitute but as a basis for more formal and systematic investigation' (Park, 1950), much of what Thomas and Znaniecki wrote about the adaptation of Polish immigrants to American life was based on their own observations of the Polish community in Chicago, for Chicago then boasted the largest concentration of Poles in America (*Polonia Amerykanska*). The word *Polonia* itself was commonly used to refer to a particular geographical concentration of Polish-Americans such as could be found in several Chicago neighbourhoods at this time. By far the greatest single concentration occurred in the West Town 'community area' on Chicago's Near West Side, also known as 'Polish Downtown' (see table 4.1).[2]

The West Town neighbourhood, which forms the basis for this study, is depicted in figure 4.1. Since its strongly developed associations with the Polish population in the early years of this century, West Town has subsequently gone through a process of very rapid ethnic 'succession' and is now predominantly black and Hispanic.[3] The ecological literature suggests that rapid neighbourhood change automatically leads to widespread 'social disorganization', a phrase that Thomas used in the context of his work on Polish immigration to refer to 'the decrease in the influence of existing social rules of behaviour upon individual members of the group' (Thomas and Znaniecki, 1918, vol. II: 1128). More commonly, however, the phrase has been used to refer to a range of 'social pathologies' such as high and rising crime rates; physical dilapidation, including housing decay, abandonment and arson; political alienation and a general sense of powerlessness to control the neighbourhood's destiny.[4]

Table 4.1 Polish population in Chicago, 1910 and 1930

	Total population	Polish birth & parentage	% Polish
Chicago			
1910	2,185,283	213,776	9.8
1930	3,376,438	401,316	11.9
'Polish Downtown'			
1910	203,505	96,243	47.3
1930	187,292	91,697	49.0

Source: Kantowicz (1975), Tables 2 and 26.

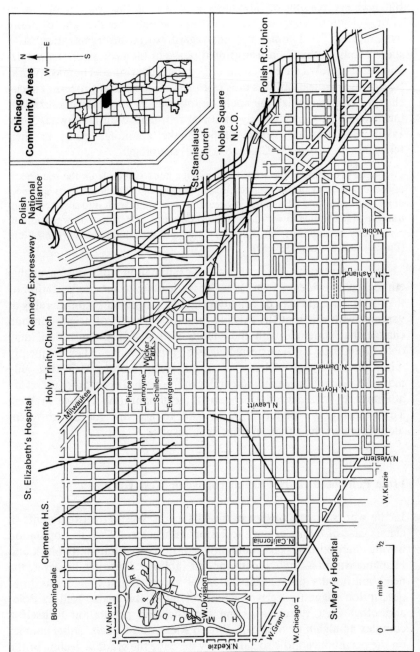

Figure 4.1 West Town community area, Chicago

Many of these features seem at first sight to be found in West Town. But a closer reading of Thomas's own use of the concept of 'social disorganization' suggests that the term should be thought of more dynamically, for Thomas did not regard 'social disorganization' as a static condition but as a transitional phase in the process of 'reorganization'. As Janowitz argues in his critical introduction to Thomas's work, 'social disorganization' was only one phase of a broader process of social change: social organization could be followed by social disorganization, but it could in turn give way to social reorganization (Janowitz, 1966: xxxii). Burgess and Bogue (1964) make a similar point in their retrospective survey of 'Chicago school' sociology:

> . . . social disorganization needs to be studied not so much from the standpoint of social pathology (although that also requires certain attention) but as an aspect of an interaction and adjustment process that eventually leads into social reorganization. Many trends in social disorganization lead to personal disorganization, community breakdown; but others are attempts at community reorganization. (Burgess and Bogue, 1964: 10)

These observations prompt a re-examination of the available ethnographic evidence from West Town leading to an interpretation of the social consequences of neighbourhood change that is considerably at variance with much of the existing literature. Studies of neighbourhood change that conclude with the charge of 'social disorganization' may only be reacting to the external signs of rapid change. They frequently miss the underlying evidence of an emerging 'moral order' that only more detailed ethnographic research can uncover. This chapter therefore attempts to document the process of neighbourhood change in West Town during the period 1920–80 and to account for the different 'definitions of the situation' that have resulted.

From Polonia to Barrio: Ethnic change in West Town

In the words of one observer, the history of West Town represents 'a classic case of ethnic group succession' (Bachelor, 1976), its population having changed from predominantly Polish to predominantly black and Hispanic within a single generation. As table 4.2 confirms, however, the neighbourhood's population history is more complex than this brief description suggests. Early residents included Italians as well as Poles and other East Europeans, and the Hispanic population is itself a complex amalgam of Mexican, Puerto Rican and Cuban. Other sources on the neighbourhood's social history describe the gradual decline of the

Table 4.2 Ethnic change in West Town, 1920–80

	1920[a]	1930[a]	1940[a]	1950[a]	1960[b]	1970[b]	1980[c]
Total	232,653	187,292	169,924	161,620	139,657	125,120	96,428
Poland	46,196	36,992	27,801	19,087	34,224	17,769	N.A.
USSR	20,387	9,424	5,360	4,663	8,336	4,910	N.A.
Italy	8,978	8,290	6,776	4,843	7,556	4,388	N.A.
Germany	7,429	3,276	1,988	1,367	5,971	2,840	N.A.
Austria	4,371	1,853	1,555	911	1,433	718	N.A.
Hungary	3,163	1,285	865	499	565	333	N.A.
Norway	2,384	1,484	793	492	533	N.A.	N.A.
Czechoslovakia	2,132	2,175	1,310	937	1,326	664	N.A.
Lithuania	1,132	1,089	821	601	N.A.	N.A.	N.A.
Greece	556	673	642	1,200	N.A.	N.A.	N.A.
Black	308	841	695	2,263	2,366	5,518	8,671
Puerto Rican	N.A.	N.A.	N.A.	N.A.	7,948	33,166	28,469
Mexican	N.A.	N.A.	N.A.	N.A.	2,232	7,335	23,477
Cuban	N.A.	N.A.	N.A.	N.A.	N.A.	490	376

Notes
a Foreign birth only.
b Foreign stock (birth and parentage).
c Race and Spanish origin (ancestry).
Source: US Census of Population and Housing

Russian Jewish population formerly concentrated around Humboldt Park in the 1920s (Kitagawa and Taeuber, 1963). German and Scandinavian settlers also left their mark in the street names and 'historic homes' of Wicker Park (Sommers, 1979). A Ukrainian 'village' maintains a vestigial presence on Chicago Avenue centred on the Ukrainian-American Civic Centre and Democratic Organization, located in adjacent buildings between Western and Leavitt Avenues. But it is undoubtedly the Poles who are most closely associated with West Town's recent past.

In the 1930s and 1940s people of Polish descent comprised over 50 per cent of the neighbourhood's population. Chicago was the informal capital of the nation's Polish-American community and the Poles were the city's largest ethnic group. Although there were Polish-American communities elsewhere in Chicago (notably in Bridgeport, Back-of-the-Yards and South Chicago), West Town was the undisputed centre of Chicago's 'Polish Downtown'.

According to some observers, Chicago's *Polonia*, West Town, was 'a classic ghetto' (Kantowicz, 1977) with ward-level indices of dissimilarity in the 50s throughout the early decades of this century. The same authority describes West Town in terms of 'institutional completeness' with a full range of Polish churches, schools and ethnic businesses. Four Polish-language daily newspapers were published in Chicago, together with several others published less frequently. Like other Catholic immigrant groups at the turn of the century, *Polonia* was organized into national parishes with the first Polish Roman Catholic church, St Stanislaus Kostka, established in West Town in 1867. Others soon followed (see table 4.3). Over 35,000 children were enrolled in Polish parish schools in Chicago in the 1920s and the community supported 2500 grocery stores owned or run by Poles, 150 Polish restaurants, 250 Polish undertakers, and countless small stores catering to predominantly Polish tastes (Lopata, 1954; Parot, 1981).

Polish-American solidarity was based on two cross-cutting loyalties, towards Church and state, represented respectively by the Polish Roman Catholic Union and the Polish National Alliance (see figures 4.2 and 4.3). These two city-wide fraternal organizations were supported by the 4000 or so Polish-American voluntary organizations that flourished in Chicago up until the 1950s. The most persistent symbol of Polish religious solidarity was, and still remains, St Stanislaus Church (see figure 4.4). Threatened with demolition in the 1950s by the construction of the Kennedy Expressway, the parish rallied round and, with the help of the neighbourhood's powerful Congressman, Daniel Rostenkowski (whose house was threatened with demolition alongside the church), the

Table 4.3   Polish Roman Catholic churches in 'Polish Downtown'

	Year founded	Total parishioners in 1918
St Stanislaus Kostka	1867	30,000
Holy Trinity	1872	25,000
St Josaphat	1884	9,000
St Hedwig	1888	20,000
St John Cantius	1893	25,000
St Mary of the Angels	1897	12,000
Holy Innocents	1905	15,000
St Helen	1913	7,000
St Szczepan	1919	—
St Fidelis	1920	—

Sources: Kantowicz (1975), table 1; Parot (1981), 227–8, 234–8.

Figure 4.2   Headquarters of the Polish Roman Catholic Union (founded 1880)

Figure 4.3   Offices of the Polish National Alliance's daily newspaper, *Dziennik Zwiazkowy*, on Milwaukee Avenue ('Polish Broadway')

community succeeded in having the expressway re-routed to avoid demolition of the landmark building.

Politically, the Polish community in Chicago has always been staunchly Democratic. From the founding of the Polish-American Democratic Organization in the 1930s, the Poles became an archetypal ethnic voting bloc, their strategy of separate development and internal solidarity explaining both their loyalty to the Democratic machine and their failure to reap the richest rewards of city government. To do so would have demanded that they play coalition politics as the Irish were later to do so effectively under Mayor Daley.[5] Daniel Rostenkowski's father, Joseph, who was elected 32nd Ward alderman in 1931 and later became Mayor Daley's unofficial legislative representative in Congress, was perhaps the only Polish-American in Chicago ever to have been capable of launching a successful mayoral bid himself.[6] Instead, he turned down the opportunity to seek higher office, preferring the local arena where his son continued the tradition by representing West Town in Congress.

Figure 4.4   St Stanislaus Kostka church (founded 1876)

Gradually, West Town's Polish population began to decline as immigration from Europe waned and as older immigrants and their families made the move to the suburbs. They were replaced in the 1960s and 1970s by a growing black and Hispanic population who gradually began to challenge the white ethnic population for political power, culminating in the election of Harold Washington as the first black mayor of Chicago in 1983.[7]

Ethnic politics in West Town

As the electoral data in tables 4.4 and 4.5 suggest, West Town's white ethnic groups have retained power longer than their purely demographic predominance might suggest. Local representatives from other ethnic groups have made relatively little impact on city politics. Those Hispanics who attained office in the 1970s, for example, did so as pawns of the Democratic machine, which remained securely under the control of the Irish and East Europeans. Not surprisingly in such circumstances

Table 4.4   Aldermanic elections in West Town, 1975–83

Year	Ward 26		Ward 31	
1975	Sydlo	7,814	Keane	8,093
	LoGalbo	3,786	Velazquez	3,638
	Diaz	879	Smetters	1,446
1979	Nardulli	unopposed	Kula	7,536
			Figueroa	4,881
1983	Nardulli	unopposed	Santiago	6,848
			Goltia	3,272
			Truman	1,551
			Pruitt	1,306

Year	Ward 32		Ward 33	
1975	Gabinski	unopposed	Mell	5,977
			Galvin	5,731
1979	Gabinski	unopposed	Mell	unopposed
1983	Gabinski	12,077	Mell	10,320
	Manning	2,867	Rodriguez	2,070
	Fabecich	1,100		

Source: *Chicago Tribune*, 26 February, 1975; 1 March, 1979; 23 February, 1983.

of entrenched political power, West Town has a long history of 'alder-manic arrogance and neglect' (Bachelor, 1976: 118), epitomized by the enforced resignation of Alderman Thomas Keane in November 1974 following his conviction on federal charges of mail fraud and conspiracy. While Keane was sentenced to five years in jail and was fined $27,000, his power-base was such that his wife replaced him as alderman for the 31st District, gaining two-thirds of the vote.

The political strength of West Town's older (white ethnic) population is also revealed in their resistance to the repeated threat of urban renewal. Because of its proximity to the Loop, a variety of city agencies and private redevelopment corporations have from time to time advanced proposals for urban renewal in West Town (see, for example, *Chicago Tribune* 1 March 1964; Marciniak, 1977; Walton, 1981). On each occasion these plans have been greeted with suspicion and hostility by local residents who fear being displaced from their homes or being

Table 4.5   Congressional elections in West Town, 1974–82

Year	District 7		District 8	
1974	Collins (Dem)	63,962	Rostenkowski (Dem)	75,011
	Metzger (Rep)	8,800	Oddo (Rep)	11,664
1976	Collins (Dem)	88,239	Rostenkowski (Dem)	105,595
	Ward (Rep)	15,854	Urbaszewski (Rep)	25,512
1978	Collins (Dem)	64,716	Rostenkowski (Dem)	81,457
	Holt (Rep)	10,273	Lodico (Rep)	13,302
1980	Collins (Dem)	80,056	Rostenkowski (Dem)	98,524
	Hooper (Rep)	14,041	Zilke (Rep)	17,845
1982	Collins (Dem)	102,845	Rostenkowski (Dem)	113,536
	Cheeks (Rep)	15,350	Hickey (Rep)	21,717

Source: American Votes Vols 11–14 (1974–80); updated from *Chicago Tribune*, 4 November, 1982.

forced to accept 'undesirable' neighbours. As a result, only one publicly subsidized redevelopment has taken place in West Town – at Noble Square – leaving much of the remaining housing stock old and dilapidated. Residents have fiercely opposed the construction of public housing in West Town on the grounds that it will lead to racial change.[8] Their fears explain the anomalous position of West Town among Chicago's community areas where it ranks high in terms of poverty and other measures of 'need', but low in terms of the number of public housing units whose availability is supposedly based on these criteria (Warren, 1980).

Housing is perhaps the most contentious political issue in West Town. The total number of housing units has fallen by 24 per cent between 1950 and 1980 (from 49,000 to 37,000) and while the total population has fallen by 40 per cent over the same period (from 160,000 to 96,000), the number of households has declined much less rapidly. As a result, the number of vacancies (excluding dilapidated and uninhabitable units) has remained almost constant. Housing is therefore an extremely scarce resource, particularly for members of the lowest income groups, such as the blacks and Hispanics. (Median family incomes for all ethnic groups in West Town were in any case only just over $8000 in 1970.)

Like other reasonably central low-income neighbourhoods, however, West Town has not been immune from the recent gentrification trend that has swept America (Laska and Spain, 1980; Smith and Williams, 1986). The area around Wicker Park, with its historic 'mansion' houses

(Sommers, 1979), has proved particularly popular. While at present only around 20 per cent of West Town's housing is owner-occupied, the gentrification trend is perceived as a genuine threat by those organizations that represent low-income groups, such as Northwest Community Organization and the Wicker Park Neighborhood Council. Groups favouring gentrification, such as the Old Wicker Park Committee who supported the neighbourhood's designation as an Historic District in 1976, approach the issue of neighbourhood change with extreme caution. According to their minutes, the Old Wicker Park Committee was established in 1973, expressing its concern over 'the condition of Chicago's inner city and the flight to the suburbs by many valuable residents'. The Committee therefore sought, in its own words, to 'stabilize' the population around Wicker Park and 'to promote racial and ethnic harmony'. Opponents of gentrification, such as the Wicker Park Neighborhood Council, have devoted much of their energy to exposing the 'unacceptable real estate practices' that gentrification seems to attract. (For details see *Circa*, a Wicker Park Newsletter, December 1981.)

As well as resisting unwanted changes in the neighbourhood's housing market, some West Town residents have sought to oppose changes in the local school system. In 1982, West Town's public school population was 76 per cent Hispanic, 14 per cent black and less than 10 per cent white (Chicago Board of Education, 1982). However, more than one-third of the neighbourhood's elementary schools and two-thirds of the high schools were Catholic parish schools outside the City-controlled public sector. Available evidence (e.g. Walton, 1981) suggests that the parish schools have a much higher proportion of white pupils (26 per cent) than the public schools. Inter-ethnic conflict regularly occurs in both public and private sectors, particularly over the issue of bilingual/bicultural education which is bitterly opposed by many non-Hispanic parents.

Local community organizations reflect similar tensions arising from the neighbourhood's internal ethnic diversity (cf. Bachelor, 1976; Marciniak, 1977). West Town's foremost voluntary organization, Northwest Community Organization (NCO), was founded in 1963 under the professional guidance of radical community organizer Saul Alinsky. Indeed, it can be argued that NCO owes its enduring success to the fact that it has always sought to emphasize *territorial* issues rather than making inevitably divisive appeals to particular ethnic groups. Even so, its territorial basis and deliberate focus on 'small winnable issues' (Alinsky, 1969) has benefited some groups more than others, notably (white ethnic) home-owners rather than (predominantly black and Hispanic) tenants. One practical outcome of this complex interplay between class, tenure and and ethnicity was the secession from NCO of an explicitly Hispanic organization, West Town Concerned Citizens Association, led by Jorge Morales, in 1977.

Given these circumstances of rapid neighbourhood change and the evidence of conflicting interests at the institutional level, one might predict the occurrence of widespread 'social disorganization' at the level of interpersonal relations. The next section uses ethnographic evidence to evaluate such an interpretation.

Reactions to neighbourhood change

The principal material on which this analysis rests was culled from the unpublished files of a five-year study of neighbourhood reactions to crime, undertaken by members of Northwestern University's Centre for Urban Affairs (1975–80), supplemented by my own fieldwork in West Town (January–July 1983). The Northwestern study involved a comparison of ten neighbourhoods in three US cities of which the area around Wicker Park in West Town was one. The study found that Wicker Park was the most 'fearful' of the ten neighbourhoods in terms of people's subjective feelings, even though it did not register the highest levels of actual victimization (Lewis and Maxfield, 1980). This pervasive fearfulness is amply borne out by the ethnographic data presented below which have been transcribed directly from the project's files.[9] While it is not possible to provide a full ethnographic picture of the West Town neighbourhood from the material available in the project files, a rich series of qualitative accounts can none the less be abstracted with a reasonably satisfactory amount of contextual detail. The files give an indication of each individual's age, sex and ethnicity with additional information, such as occupational status, in many cases. This material allows us to make a number of inferences about people's reactions to neighbourhood change and to challenge the conception of 'social disorganization' employed elsewhere in the literature.

There is, at first sight, much evidence of 'social disorganization' in the West Town material. To some extent this impression is exaggerated by the fact that the Northwestern study relates specifically to residents' fears about crime in the neighbourhood, the subject of the research project for which the data were originally collected. For some residents, fears about crime in the neighbourhood are easily extended to encompass practically the whole of the city. As one resident complained:

St Elizabeth's Hospital is pretty rough; Hoyne and Pierce are bad. Old Town is worse than around here. Cabrini Green is worse, Woodlawn is worse, Marquette

Park is really bad, Back-of-the-Yards is no good, Englewood is all bad and all black. The Loop is dangerous, Comiskey Park, Wrigley Field are both no good. There are no parts of Chicago which are safe. It is pretty dangerous all over. It's all about the same.

For most residents, however, neighbourhood fears are much more localized and seem to be governed by a number of implicit principles. Not all areas are regarded with equal suspicion, although some are almost universally stigmatized. The area around Humboldt Park, for example, is regarded by many as quite impenetrable: 'they will kill you there for nothing.' It is also alleged that police officers avoid certain areas around Wicker Park because of the neighbourhood's reputation for danger. Most residents have an extremely detailed knowledge of their immediate environment but a very hazy notion of what lies beyond the periphery of their own immediate locality. Many people therefore feel relatively safe in their own community but use territorial markers, such as railroad tracks and other landmarks, to steer a safe passage through less familiar areas.

Neighbourhood fears vary temporally as well as spatially. As one elementary school principal argued:

The community in the day time is fairly safe – everyone knows where they are supposed to be. But at night it is different; it is terrible. The gangs come out. There are killings. There was one down by the Polish taverns. . . . It is very dangerous at night.

Adaptation to fear and uncertainty takes a variety of forms. One woman, who feared that 'something can happen' every time she left her house and who described the neighbourhood as a jungle, planned to leave West Town altogether. Others who work in West Town would not live there because of its fearful reputation. An employee of a local community centre who lived elsewhere described the neighbourhood as very dangerous: 'There are robberies, assaults, and murders almost every day.' Besides moving out altogether, other common strategies include the avoidance of areas that are perceived to be particularly dangerous.[10] Another woman described how she and her daughter had seen five Puerto Rican boys sitting across from her house, blocking the sidewalk. She walked twelve blocks out of her way to avoid the risk of a confrontation even though she was only half a block from her house. Many people similarly avoided certain street intersections (such as Damen and Pierce) because of their fearful reputation ('a hotbed for drug traffic and mugging').

Residents generally felt that crime and violence had increased in recent years. To many people these changes were disconcerting and largely incomprehensible. In searching for an explanation, West Town residents commonly attributed blame to the neighbourhood's recent history of ethnic change:

Until the wrong elements arrived a person could walk the streets and use everything, day or night, without fear. But those days are gone.

In the absence of 'hard' information, residents tended to rely on gossip and other informal channels of communication for news of local events.[12] No better example could be found of the circumstances in which rumour flourishes. For, as Shibutani (1966) argues, rumours emerge in ambiguous situations where there is an unsatisfied demand for information. For example, youth gangs represent a source of particularly acute local concern for many West Town residents. Accurate information concerning the gangs is highly elusive so rumours flourish. According to one person, there are four or five different gangs in the Wicker Park area; according to another there are about eight; and according to a third there are 29 gangs in West Town's 14th police district alone.

   Different sources of information make different claims to authenticity. For example, a police lieutenant states that there were two major gangs in and around Wicker Park – the Latin Kings and the Spanish Cobras – their presence and mutual hostility confirmed by the evidence of local graffiti (cf. Ley and Cybriwsky, 1974) (see figure 4.5). Others, however, with no less conviction, affirm the existence of two different gangs, the (Spanish) War Lords and the (black) Vice Lords. Shibutani suggests that rumours are often directed at groups who are considered to be outside the majority community's moral order and that the content of such rumours is consistent with the presuppositions of the people among whom the rumour circulates. In situations of inter-group conflict, an 'enemy' is constructed with an array of despised attributes which serve to support the morale of one group by deprecating the qualities of another (cf. Damer, 1974). In such cases, stereotyped opinions about different ethnic groups are invoked to rationalize behaviour and to give vent to anxieties and apprehensions. The following two instances can be interpreted in this way:

Most of the neighbors are Puerto Ricans and they don't care. Puerto Ricans, Mexicans, and blacks make up the neighborhood. They throw garbage out of the windows, sit and drink beer, and throw beer cans out on the street, and then they move.

The Puerto Ricans are dirty, they throw garbage out the windows and don't put trash in the trash cans. They don't keep up their alleys, neighborhood, their property. It used to be a beautiful neighborhood but now it's changed.

Figure 4.5   Gang-related graffiti in Wicker Park

It is much harder to identify why particular stereotypical attributes are associated with a particular ethnic group. To some extent, of course, stereotypes are self-reinforcing as people actively seek out evidence of behaviour or attitudes that conform to a pre-existing stereotype. On the other hand, there may be definite contextual reasons for the association between a particular group and a particular set of attributes. For example, the growth of the Puerto Rican population in Chicago coincided with a period of retrenchment in city services associated with the city's fiscal problems. Street-cleaning services were among those cut back leading to greater accumulations of garbage on the streets. Accompanied by the general poverty of the Puerto Ricans, the decaying nature of the neighbourhood's housing stock and the severely diminished local employment opportunities, the precise nature of the stereotypical features attributed to the Puerto Ricans in West Town (as in the previous two quotations) is not altogether surprising. This is certainly not to condone the practice of ethnic stereotyping but simply to highlight the need to examine the material circumstances in which such practices occur.

Nostalgic feelings for a lost and better past are also a common reaction to neighbourhood change. Such feelings do not always rely on ethnic stereotypes but they are often at least implicit as in the following example:

It used to be you knew everyone, everybody felt comfortable. It's not like that anymore. People don't want to be anything like that anymore. Even in church hardly anyone comes to the things they have. The neighborhood has changed, a lot of people left . . . because strange people had moved in.

Occasionally, people's memories are less deceptive: 'The kids and groups of young men hanging around is nothing different from what they used to have . . . there has always been change in the neighbor-hood.' These opinions, though relatively rare, are sometimes extremely perceptive:

Opportunists start stories. Sure there's crime. There is crime everywhere; there always has been and always will be. We're not going to stop crime. We can reduce it but these people make citizens more afraid than they need to be. Gang trouble is more rumor than fact.

Local expressions of concern about arson are almost as frequent as rumours about gang violence in West Town. Both can be interpreted as evidence of 'social disorganization' but both also reveal much about the underlying moral or social order of the slum, to use Suttles' (1968) memorable phrase. Arson is a common occurrence in West Town, some 300 separate fires having taken place within a 32-block area near Humboldt Park in the course of a single year according to the Chicago Daily News (6–8 September 1975). Explanations for such incidents vary widely, however, reflecting different definitions of the situation. According to some sources, for example, teenagers are paid to burn down houses in order that their owners can collect the insurance. These same sources argue that in general 'people know who is responsible for the arson but are reluctant to get involved; they may get excited if the building is next door, but if it's on another block they don't care.' Others argue that city officials and private developers use arson in a deliberate and malicious way to push through their renewal plans in the face of community opposition. By extension, some people have argued that arson directly benefits those who gain from a neighbourhood's sub-sequent gentrification:

There was an article last week that Wicker Park was a good place to invest your money. Some of the areas which were burned out are almost like they were intentionally cleared out to form a border to protect the nice areas. There seem to have been a lot of transactions and speculations going on in the burned out areas.

Finally, of course, there are rumours that associate arson directly with inter-ethnic conflict. A local insurance adjuster epitomizes this position:

The clashing of different ethnic groups in the area might give rise to much of the tension which results in the burnings. . . . . The old Polish population resents the Latino invasions, the Latinos don't like the old Poles, the young people don't like the old people and, therefore, since the neighborhood is so diverse and changes so rapidly there are bound to be extraordinary tensions. These sometimes find their way into action.

In such circumstances, every fire is attributed to arson even in the absence of any direct evidence.

It should be clear from the evidence presented so far that most West Town residents have definite opinions about the social consequences of neighbourhood change even if their experience is limited to their own immediate surroundings. In some cases this local knowledge is both detailed and specific. Many people know that different ethnic groups patronize different stores, that Mexican and Polish-American youth gangs hang out on different corners, and that most gang violence is directed towards rival gangs rather than towards ordinary people. As one resident explains:

Each gang has its own special turf sometimes as small as two blocks on two consecutive streets. Turfs may overlap if the gangs are both Latin, but not if they are black and white.

Academic interpretations are as diverse as residents' local knowledge. In contrast to the literature on 'social disorganization' with its generally derogatory, moralizing tone, for example, several authors have used ethnographic evidence to support a sub-cultural theory of deviance arguing that much apparently 'deviant' behaviour can be interpreted as a rational strategy for seeking status in the deprived world of the inner city where conventional avenues to the acquisition of status are severely curtailed (cf. Cohen 1955; Cloward and Ohlin, 1960; Fischer, 1975). Similar interpretations have been advanced to account for street-corner gangs, small-time racketeering and community politics (e.g. Thrasher, 1927; Whyte, 1955; Ley, 1974).

The evidence from West Town is amenable to a similar interpretation. As one informant argues, membership of the Latin Kings is 'an identity thing': 'it makes you feel that you can fight back against the system; they can't push you around any more.' Another member of a Latino gang talks in terms of gaining prestige in the eyes of his friends having been excluded from more conventional and legitimate means of achieving status:

It's easy to take the wrong path in life if you're poor. I started cutting school and hanging around on the corner, they were the hip group. They were ripping off quick money in their pockets, smoking dope, dropping pills. Made it all very easy for me to steal; whenever I wanted something I'd go rip something off. I started with hub caps and then took the whole car. Things they took got bigger and that just put more money in the pocket. I wanted to be one of the boys and I wanted to be accepted. The parents couldn't give me anything at home.

Other gang members put the matter more succinctly: 'If you were a member of a gang, other people respected you. It gave you status.' For others, gang membership offered a solution to very specific problems of personal identity:

I came to Chicago when I was nine and I've been involved with gangs ever since. I was leader of several gangs such as the Latin Kings. I was the first Puerto Rican in the Black Nation. What drove me there was that I was a black Puerto Rican. I joined because I wanted to feel like I belonged to something. As a black Puerto Rican I wanted an identity. The gang gave me love and attention.

While the actions of gang members may be regarded as misguided or aberrant, the preceding material suggests a possible rationale for their behaviour and hints at the existence of an emergent moral or social order underlying the superficial evidence of chaos and disorder. Indeed, one is tempted to remark that many contemporary social scientists seem to share the failings of the early 'Chicago school' sociologists who have been criticized for their tendency to regard everything but conformity with the standards of conventional middle-class society as a matter of 'disorganization' (Hannerz, 1980: 56).

Conclusion

In describing the process of neighbourhood change in West Town, it is clear that different people employ different 'definitions of the situation' and that these subjective definitions have practical social consequences. Interpretation of the ethnographic evidence allows one to appreciate the significance of these differences by providing a more detailed under-standing of the material circumstances of people's everyday experience. It also reduces the risk of applying inappropriate moral standards to forms of conduct that may be tolerated locally but appear unacceptable by external, 'middle-class' criteria. To understand the apparent failure of the Hispanic population to engage in city politics, for example, requires an explanation that is couched in terms of their systematic exclusion from positions of power within the Democratic party machine rather than an analysis of their supposed linguistic 'disadvantage'. To put it more abstractly, the ethnographic interpretation of urban life must always be balanced by an understanding of the contextual features that structure people's experience. Thus, one cannot understand the history of ethnic politics in West Town without an adequate conception of the local consequences of federal and city budget cuts which have decimated the level of available resources, leaving each group competing for the remaining spoils. Inevitably, in these circumstances, local groups come to see each other as rivals, and few organizations achieve sufficient material gains to ensure their long-term viability. Moreover, local groups see little prospect for changing the rules of national or city politics in order to improve their situation.

These contextual features are crucial to our understanding of neigh-bourhood change despite their frequent omission from conventional 'community studies' and even from more recent ethnographic work. This omission has led some authors to criticize residents for failing to identify their common interests, blaming the local environment for problems that are structural in origin. For example, Ley (1974) found that crime (particularly juvenile and gang crime) was the major concern of residents in the black inner city area of Philadelphia which he studied. Residents made no mention of economic, family, educational or physical problems from which he inferred that they were guilty of 'misidentifying' their environment. Similarly, Katznelson (1981) found that residents in the Washington Heights-Inwood district of northern Manhattan identified as 'major problems', crime, dirty streets, a dilapidated environment, decaying housing and drug addiction rather than unemployment, poverty or other fundamental questions of political economy. From this he concluded that the territorial nature of local political organization served to dissolve the potential for major social change. Finally, Susser (1982) argues that race and ethnicity have 'interfered with' the development of a sense of common purpose between different groups in the Williamsburg-Greenpoint section of Brooklyn, an argument that she does not extend to gender where her analysis is considerably more subtle.

The present study suggests the need for greater caution before dis-missing the significance of residents' local knowledge. The ethnographic evidence from West Town shows that many residents accurately recognize their own interests and understand the root cause of their problems even if they are not able to act on this knowledge for structural reasons that are beyond their control. One Puerto Rican man provides a good example of this in his analysis of neighbourhood crime.

Crimes in this community are the product of this society's inequality. If Puerto Rican people were given an opportunity to participate in American society, then the crime rate would be radically changed. Since society cannot afford to offer the Puerto Rican an educational opportunity most of them end up unemployed. The main problem in Wicker Park is economic.

If residents sometimes appear to be ignorant of the underlying causes of local problems, the reason may lie in their tacit awareness of their inability to solve these problems at the wider institutional level. In defining the situation at the neighbourhood level they locate their problems in the immediate environment over which they feel themselves to retain some degree of direct control. When even this degree of local autonomy is threatened, the level of neighbourhood 'incivility' increases (Lewis and Maxfield, 1980) and 'social disorganization' may result. An appreciation of the social significance of alternative 'definitions of the situation' demands sensitive interpretation based on detailed qualitative research at the local level combined with an understanding of the structural roots of neighbourhood change. This is the kind of interpretative understanding towards which urban ethnography can make a distinctive contribution.

Appendix
On the Methods Used in This Study and the Problem of Ethnographic Description

While much of this study depended on published sources such as Census and electoral records and on the unpublished archives of Northwestern University's 'Fear of Crime' project, it was possible during a relatively brief period in Chicago (January – July 1983) to combine these sources with my own personal observations and fieldwork. The West Town neighbourhood was selected because of its recent history of rapid ethnic 'succession', and because of its location, in the neighbourhood immediately adjacent to the site of Gerald Suttles' celebrated study of ethnicity and territoriality in the inner city (Suttles, 1968). Comparison with other neighbourhoods was possible through casual observations of my own and through conversation with various graduate students who were themselves engaged in ethnographic studies at Chicago and Northwestern Universities. The closest parallel to West Town was provided by the multi-ethnic, steelmill community of south Chicago, originally studied by William Kornblum (1974) and conveniently re-studied as part of Richard Taub's recent comparative project on neighbourhood change in Chicago (Taub et al., 1984). The significance of my own case-study of neighbourhood change and local politics was greatly enhanced by the fact that it coincided with the mayoral election in which a black candidate, Harold Washington, defeated his white ethnic opponents after an often bitter campaign. As a result, the whole city's attention was focused on the same issues that occurred in microcosm in West Town. Newspapers and other media provided parallels to the events that took place on a daily basis in the course of my own fieldwork.

Fieldwork began by traversing the area several times on foot, mapping the visible signs of neighbourhood change and community conflict (graffiti, vacant buildings, store signs, construction and demolition work, etc.). I then visited several of the area's principal institutions (libraries, hospitals and schools), made contact with various community organizations (Northwest Community Organization, the Old Wicker Park Committee, etc.) and arranged to interview their representatives. More informal conversations occurred as opportunity arose by pursuing introductions and following up other contacts. Many of the issues with which I was concerned (ethnic 'succession', fear of crime, graffiti, arson, gentrification, etc.) were manifested in the area around Wicker Park which therefore became the focus for the rest of my inquiry. This decision was reinforced by the discovery of Northwestern University's archive of ethnographic material on West Town much of which also concentrated on the Wicker Park area. If I had intended to undertake a full-blown 'community study', this is the area where I would have taken up residence. Because the present study was more limited in scope, I chose not to move to Wicker Park but to continue to make regular visits from my base at the University of Chicago. The limitations of this strategy are, however, freely admitted.

Fieldwork continued over a period of seven months during which time I accumulated a considerable amount of material from interviews, observations, newspaper files, school records, official City records, and so on. I began to write up the study while I was still collecting new material and while I continued to research the area's history through the analysis of Census data, consultation of Local Community Fact Books and visits to institutions like the Polish Museum of America. The problems of writing ethnography – the actual construction of a particular ethnographic text – are of sufficient interest currently to warrant more lengthy discussion.

Whereas most recent accounts of the problem of ethnographic description are concerned with questions of representation, textual strategy and poetics (Marcus and Fischer, 1986; Clifford and Marcus, 1986), the production of this particular ethnography involved rather more severely practical problems. My initial intention had been to write two separate papers, one dealing with the 'formal' level of electoral politics and with the changing place of West Town in the City's various redevelopment plans, the other dealing with the 'informal' level of people's responses to these changes 'on the ground'. Both papers were to have been informed by my reading of the 'Chicago school' authors, particularly W. I. Thomas, on 'social disorganization' and 'moral order'. After several false starts, it proved impossible to write these papers separately. The 'formal' and 'informal' were too closely interwoven to make such an analytical separation possible. And while I was able to clarify my interpretation of the 'social disorganization' issue at a theoretical level (Jackson, 1984), it proved equally impossible to apply these abstract ideas directly to the West Town material. There were also practical problems of juxtaposing my own ethnography with the archival material from the Northwestern study and of combining qualitative and quantitative data.

These problems were finally resolved by abandoning the attempt to describe 'formal' and 'informal' responses to neighbourhood change in two separate papers and by employing another of W. I. Thomas's concepts, the 'definition of the situation', as the organizing principle around which to construct the ethnography. Rather than writing up the empirical material as a 'community study' and only then drawing out its theoretical significance, it became possible to handle the theoretical and empirical aspects of the argument concurrently. In other words, the ethnography was not a purely descriptive exercise from which theoretical principles could be derived. The very act of constructing the 'description' was only possible once the theoretical argument was clearly established. It was then possible to employ the ethnographic material as a commentary on and a qualification of Thomas's theoretical arguments and as a means of criticizing some of the more questionable inferences in the current ethnographic literature. Writing this case-study confirmed my judgement on several questions whose significance I had previously only grasped in the abstract (cf. Jackson, 1985), namely the necessity of placing ethnographic material in a broader structural context and the vital significance of 'local knowledge' (about which academics are all too often patronizing or dismissive).

Notes

The research on which this chapter is based was undertaken while the author was an American Studies Fellow of the American Council of Learned Societies at the University of Chicago. The author is most grateful to Mr Chuck Prentice of Northwest Community Organization for sharing his knowledge of the area and to the following for their comments on earlier drafts of the paper: Derek Gregory, Albert Hunter, Dan Lewis, Gerald Suttles and members of Sandra Wallman's City Workshop at University College London.

1   For a discussion of the documentary methods employed by Thomas and Znaniecki, see Plummer (1983: 39–42). Selections from their original 'methodological note', together with a commentary, are included in Bierstedt (1969).

2   Chicago's 'community areas' were originally designated by the sociologist E. W. Burgess in the 1930s. Despite their academic origins and administrative contrivance, these areas have over time taken on the characteristics of subjectively meaningful communities as Hunter's subsequent investigations have confirmed (Hunter, 1974).

3   There is a voluminous ecological literature on ethnic 'succession' which dates back to the classic statement by Park (1936). It is reviewed most usefully by Aldrich (1975). Despite all the objections that have been raised against the application of ecological concepts to the study of urban life, the terminology is still in current use as a recent study of neighbourhood change in Chicago confirms (Taub et al., 1984).

4   For a recent discussion of the concept of 'social disorganization' in the context of Chicago sociology, see Jackson (1984).

5   The definitive account of Polish-American politics in Chicago is Kantowicz (1975). For an insider's account of the Daley machine, see Rakove (1975).

6   Kantowicz describes how restricted the elder Rostenkowski's strength was outside his own local milieu: 'Somewhat limited in intelligence, cunning, blunt, straightforward, and emotional, he was as strong as a feudal lord in

Polish Downtown but was not the man to appeal to respectable America, any more than the other ward bosses of Polonia's capital were' (Kantowicz, 1975: 211).

7   For an analysis of the basis of Washington's electoral victory, including a commentary on the significance of the black and Hispanic coalition, see Marable (1985: 191–246).

8   Throughout the City, tenants in Chicago's public housing projects are almost exclusively black. High-rise projects such as Cabrini Green and Robert Taylor Homes are stigmatized as 'ghetto housing' by the City's white residents who have regularly resorted to violent methods to maintain the racial 'stability' of their communities. For descriptions of this process, see, among others, Philpott (1978), Hirsch (1983) and Taub et al. (1984).

9   I am most grateful to Professor Dan Lewis for providing unrestricted access to this valuable material and for permission to quote freely from it.

10   A similar tendency has been reported in other stressful inner city areas as far apart as Philadelphia (Ley, 1974) and Birmingham (Smith, 1984).

11   In a recent comparative study of race and crime in eight Chicago neighbourhoods, Taub et al. (1984) noted a similar tendency to 'encode' a neighbourhood's future in racial terms. They argued that the relationship between crime and neighbourhood deterioration is a complex one: 'crime rates function as symptoms and symbols of the general decline of a neighborhood when residents have other reasons to fear that the area has begun to skid. Many of these fears are linked to the issue of racial change' (Taub et al., 1984: 15).

12   For an analysis of neighbourhood fears about crime and the quality of locally available information in inner city Birmingham, see Smith (1985). For a general review, see Smith (1987), also chapter 2 of this volume.

References

Aldrich, H. (1975) 'Ecological succession in racially changing neighborhoods: a review of the literature', *Urban Affairs Quarterly* 10, 327–48.

Alinsky, S. (1969) *Rules for radicals*, Random House, New York.

Bachelor, L. W. (1976) 'The community organization as a political representative', Unpublished PhD dissertation, University of Chicago.

Bierstedt, R. (ed.) (1969) *Florian Znaniecki on humanistic sociology*, University of Chicago Press, Chicago and London.

Bulmer, M. (1984) *The Chicago school of sociology*, University of Chicago Press, Chicago and London.

Burgess, E. W. and Bogue, D. J. (eds) (1974) *Contributions to urban sociology*, University of Chicago Press, Chicago and London.

Chicago Board of Education (1982) *Racial/ethnic survey of students*.

Clifford, J. and Marcus, G. E. (eds) (1986) *Writing culture: the poetics and politics of ethnography*, University of California Press, Berkeley.

Cloward, R. A. and Ohlin, L. E. (1960) *Delinquency and opportunity*, Free Press, Glencoe, Illinois.

Cohen, A. K. (1955) *Delinquent boys*, Free Press, Glencoe, Illinois.

Damer, S. (1974) 'Wine Alley: the sociology of a dreadful enclosure', *Sociological Review* new series 22, 221–48.

Fischer, C. (1975) 'Toward a subcultural theory of urbanism', *American Journal of Sociology* 80, 1319–41.

Hannerz, U. (1980) *Exploring the city*, Columbia University Press, New York.

Hirsch, A. R. (1983) *Making the second ghetto: race and housing in Chicago, 1940–1960*, Cambridge University Press, Cambridge.

Hunter, A. D. (1974) *Symbolic communities*, University of Chicago Press, Chicago.

Jackson, P. (1984) 'Social disorganization and moral order in the city', *Transactions, Institute of British Geographers* new series 9, 168–80.

Jackson, P. (1985) 'Urban ethnography', *Progress in Human Geography* 10, 157–76.

Janowitz, M. (ed.) (1966) *W. I. Thomas on social organization and social personality*, University of Chicago Press, Chicago and London.

Kantowicz, E. R. (1975) *Polish-American politics in Chicago, 1888–1940*, University of Chicago Press, Chicago and London.

Kantowicz, E. R. (1977) 'Polish Chicago: survival through solidarity', M. G. Holli and P. d'A. Jones (eds), *The ethnic frontier*, William B. Eerdmans, Grand Rapids, Michigan.

Katznelson, I. (1981) *City trenches: urban politics and the patterning of class in the United States*, University of Chicago Press, Chicago and London.

Kitagawa, E. M. and Taeuber, K. E. (1963) *Local community fact book: Chicago metropolitan area 1960*, Chicago Community Inventory, Chicago.

Kornblum, W. (1974) *Blue collar community*, University of Chicago Press, Chicago and London.

Laska, S. B. and Spain, D. (eds) (1980) *Back to the city: issues in neighborhood renovation*, Pergamon Press, New York.

Lewis, D. A. and Maxfield, M. G. (1980) 'Fear in the neighborhoods: an investigation of the impact of crime', *Journal of Research in Crime and Delinquency* 17, 160–89.

Ley, D. (1974) *The black inner city as frontier outpost: images and behavior of a Philadelphia neighborhood*, Association of American Geographers, Monograph No. 7, Washington, DC.

Ley, D. and Cybriwsky, R. A. (1974) 'Urban graffiti as territorial markers', *Annals, Association of American Geographers* 64, 491–505.

Lopata, H. Z. (1954) 'The function of voluntary associations in an ethnic community: "Polonia"', Unpublished PhD dissertation, University of Chicago.

Marable, M. (1985) *Black American politics: from the Washington marches to Jesse Jackson*, Verso, London.

Marciniak, E. (1977) *Reviving an inner city community*, Loyola University Discourse series, Chicago.

Marcus, G. E. and Fischer, M. M. J. (1986) *Anthropology as cultural critique*, University of Chicago Press, Chicago and London.

Park, R. E. (1936) 'Succession: an ecological concept', *American Sociological Review* 1, 171–9.

Park, R. E. (1950) *Race and culture*, Free Press, New York.

Parot, J. J. (1981) *Polish Catholics in Chicago, 1850–1920: a religious history*, Northern Illinois University Press, DeKalb, Illinois.

Philpott, T. L. (1978) *The slum and the ghetto: neighborhood deterioration and middle class reform, Chicago, 1880–1930*, Oxford University Press, New York.

Plummer, K. (1983) *Documents of life*, George Allen & Unwin, London.

Rakove, M. (1975) *Don't make no waves, don't back no losers: an insider's account of the Daley machine*, Indiana University Press, Bloomington, Indiana.

Shibutani, T. (1966) *Improvised news: a sociological study of rumor*, Indiana University Press, Indianapolis, Indiana.

Smith, N. and Williams, P. (eds) (1986) *Gentrification of the city*, Allen & Unwin, London.

Smith, S. J. (1984) 'Negotiating ethnicity in an uncertain environment', *Ethnic and Racial Studies* 7, 360–73.

Smith, S. J. (1985) 'News and the dissemination of fear', in J. Burgess and J. R. Gold (eds) *Geography, the media and popular culture*, Croom Helm, London, 229–53.

Smith, S. J. (1987) 'Fear of crime: beyond a geography of deviance', *Progress in Human Geography* 11, 1–23.

Sommers, N. (1979) *The historic homes of Wicker Park*, Old Wicker Park Committee, Chicago.

Susser, I. (1982) *Norman Street: poverty and politics in an urban neighborhood*, Oxford University Press, New York.

Suttles, G. D. (1968) *The social order of the slum*, University of Chicago Press, Chicago and London.

Taub, R. P., Taylor, D. G. and Dunham, J. D. (1984) *Paths of neighborhood change: race and crime in urban America*, University of Chicago Press, Chicago and London.

Thomas, W. I. and Znaniecki, F. (1918–20) *The Polish peasant in Europe and America*, 5 vols, R. G. Badger, Boston, Mass.

Thrasher, F. M. (1927) *The gang*, University of Chicago Press, Chicago.

Walton, P. A. H. (1981) Community and the parochial school in the inner city. Unpublished PhD dissertation, Northwestern University, Chicago.

Warren, E. (1980) *Subsidized housing in Chicago*, Center for Urban Policy, Loyola University Urban Insights series.

Whyte, W. F. (1955) *Street corner society*, 2nd edn, University of Chicago Press, Chicago.

5

Topocide: The Annihilation of Place

J. Douglas Porteous

People of earth, your attention please . . . This is Prostetnic Vogon Jelz of the Galactic Hyperspace Planning Council . . . As you will no doubt be aware, the plans for development of the outlying regions of the Galaxy require the building of a hyperspatial express route through your star system, and regrettably your planet is one of those scheduled for demolition. The process will take slightly less than two of your Earth minutes. Thank you.

There's no point in acting surprised about it. All the planning charts and demolition orders have been on display in your local planning department in Alpha Centauri for fifty of your Earth years, so you've had plenty of time to lodge any formal complaint . . .

What do you mean you've never been to Alpha Centauri? For heaven's sake, mankind, it's only four light-years away, you know. I'm sorry, but if you can't be bothered to take an interest in local affairs that's your own lookout . . .

Energize the demolition beams!

Douglas Adams, *The Hitch Hiker's Guide to the Galaxy* (1979)

In Adams' telling satire, Earth is duly demolished to make way for the planned expressway. In more sombre tones, George MacKay Brown's *Greenvoe* (1976) recounts the story of a fictionalized Orkney island evacuated and made uninhabitable in favour of a military installation. These are two examples only; a considerable body of imaginative literature is concerned with topocide.

The theme of topocide (the deliberate annihilation of place) has rarely attracted geographers, although other social scientists, as well as planners, have agreed that 'the metaphor of death can appropriately be applied to communities' (Adams, 1980). Yet there is overwhelming evidence that grandiose modern planning projects, from Third World 'resettlement' schemes to western urban renewal, have had deleterious effects on impacted social groups and can readily lead to the destruction of places ranging in size from a home or a neighbourhood to a village or small town.

Reactions have included a literature of 'planner-bashing' which rarely deals with the complete annihilation of places and often ignores the roles of private enterprise and politicians (Porteous, 1977). In contrast, this study examines the processes by which industrialists and politicians, as well as planners, are currently engaged in the topocide of the village of Howdendyke, East Yorkshire.

Methods

The purpose of this chapter is to elicit the reactions of the inhabitants of Howdendyke to the continuing annihilation of their village, and to compare these with the points of view of those responsible for this radical change. Whereas the material in the following 'backgrounding' section was derived chiefly from a variety of documentary sources (local newspaper reports, planning applications and reports, the minutes of local government bodies), the bulk of the chapter is based on lengthy depth interviews with Howdendyke residents, and shorter, more formal interviews with politicians, planners and the directors of private enterprises.

Topocide is an emotional issue; quantitative research procedures were clearly inappropriate. Depth interviewing (Jones, 1985) was selected as the method most likely to elicit residents' feelings. Depth interviews typically involve an initial period of introduction, followed by several separate interview sessions, usually in the respondent's home, using both tape-recording and notepad methods of recording information. Interview sessions are unstructured; every attempt is made to avoid leading questions and to promote the respondent's self-definition of the issues to be discussed. Subsequently, notes are rewritten and tapes transcribed.

One of the most difficult problems in depth interviewing is that of establishing a rapport between respondent and interviewer. In this case no rapport problems were experienced, for I was a resident of Howdendyke village during my first 21 years (1943–64) and all but one of the 22 interviewees had known me since childhood. I was clearly regarded as an 'insider' by interviewees, which facilitated disclosure and reduced inhibitions. Indeed, so eager were interviewees to air their views of the contemporary state of Howdendyke that little time was left for another part of my interview task, the collection of oral history material. The latter material was also difficult to elicit because respondents expected that I 'knew it already'.

As an 'insider', researching my own former village, I must state my biases. My biases are in favour of the planned-for (Porteous, 1971). I am naturally distressed that a place that has great meaning for me is being erased (cf. Berman, 1982), and I feel with some passion that ordinary people deserve, at least, an opportunity to tell their own stories (see Rowles, 1978).

To counteract this deviation from academic detachment, an experiment in consultation was conducted. An earlier version of this chapter was sent in April 1986 to all those residents and officials mentioned therein, drawing attention to their statements, and soliciting their comments. Subsequently, most of those who did not reply were contacted and re-interviewed in July 1986.

The replies of officials form an interesting counterpoint to the points of view of residents and to my own interpretations. Although this procedure is virtually unknown in geography, it comes close to Jackson's (1980) call for geographers to distinguish between 'folk' and 'academic' definitions of a situation (see also chapter 4 in this volume), and approaches Giddens' (1976) concept of the 'double hermeneutic'. The result is research which is reflexive, committed, and yet as fair as possible to all parties involved in the controversy. (For a much fuller theoretical and methodological discussion, see Porteous, 1988.)

A village planned to death

Howdendyke is a small riverport lying 50 miles from the sea on the Yorkshire Ouse. The vista is Dutch: flat arable land, still subject to inundation with exceptionally high tides. A hamlet of sailors and small entrepreneurs was transformed in 1857 by George Anderton, an entrepreneur who built an agricultural fertilizer factory, developed a river fleet, and purchased both farms and housing in the village. In the course of the next century the previously 'open' village was transformed into a 'closed' one almost wholly owned by a single family firm.

Fundamental changes began in the late 1960s. By 1954 Anderton's owned every non-council dwelling in the village except seven. Whether the intention was personal aggrandizement on the part of the family or a shrewd step towards industrial expansion is not known. But by 1960 the family had died out and the firm passed from paternalistic local control to that of Hargreaves Fertilizers, a far-off conglomerate whose chief concern was cost-efficiency.

In 1960 also the East Riding Development Plan designated 11 acres at Howdendyke (the Anderton works) as industrial land. All other land remained as unallocated 'white land' and industrial expansion was expected to take place in towns.

By 1967 Hargreaves had begun to rationalize their branch plant. Vehicle and vessel fleets were sold, twelve company houses sold to tenants, and two large tracts of farmland, which together almost surround the village (figure 5.1) were given up. These two greenfield sites were each equal in size to the whole village of 1967. Given the above, the following series of events does not appear coincidental.

In 1968 Hargreaves applied to build a 200 ft river jetty, on a scale never before seen in the area. When the application was withdrawn, it was replaced by an almost identical one on the part of Humberside Sea & Land Services (HS & L), a cargo-importing firm. About the same time an application of the local Rural District Council for the two greenfield sites (24 acres) surrounding Howdendyke to be designated as 'industrial land' was approved by the county. Villagers were soon surprised to find a glucose factory being built by Tate & Lyle on the upstream site, and a HS & L cargo-handling facility on the downstream site. With the subsequent failure of the glucose factory both sites came into the hands of HS & L and both are now used for cargo handling and warehousing.

The planning context of Howdendyke's topocide since 1968 can be summarized as follows:

1 Given the existence of an M62 motorway exit close to deep water, Boothferry Borough Council designated Howdendyke as an industrial estate.
2 The Humberside Structure Plan (1979), however, permits non-urban industrial expansion on the river only if the industry is river-related. Cargo handling should occur at existing ports such as Goole, only five miles upstream.
3 The Structure Plan designated Howdendyke as a 'non-selected settlement', meaning that no new residential development (except for infilling or replacement) would be permitted.

Given these planning parameters, one would predict a stable residential village with some river-related industrial growth. By 1985, however, the residential village had been more than half-destroyed and the new industrial sites housed not industry but import cargo-handling operations directly competing with existing ports nearby.

This 'planning anomaly' or 'exception', as it has become known to county planners, has occurred because of the actions (whether independently or collusively cannot be ascertained) of industrialists, local politicians, and planners:

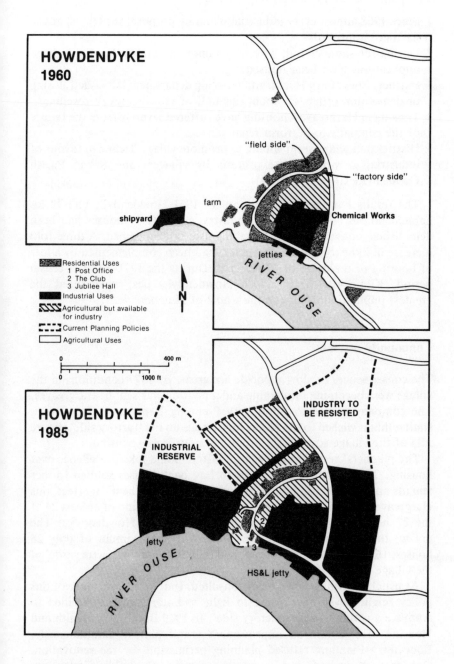

Figure 5.1   Howdendyke in 1960 and 1985

1 Since 1968 almost every industrial planning proposal for Howdendyke has been approved.
2 During the same period, with only minor exceptions, housing-related applications have been refused.
3 Further, Boothferry Health and Housing department has issued closing or demolition orders on about one-half of Howdendyke's dwellings.
4 Tenants in Hargreaves' housing have suffered severely from the failure of the company to perform repairs.
5 District politicians seem willing to promote village decline in favour of industrial growth, despite protests by villagers and Kilpin Parish Council (KPC).

The results have been devastating. In 1961 Howdendyke had 72 inhabited houses and 11 acres of industry. By 1985 39 houses had been demolished, converted to non-dwelling uses or condemned. A three-fold increase in industrial space, therefore, had been complemented by a loss of housing of the order of 53 per cent. During the 1971–81 inter-censal period, Kilpin parish, in which Howdendyke lies, experienced the greatest population decline in the whole of Humberside.

Community reactions

The consequences of slow topocide are great. By 1977 conditions in the village were becoming intolerable and a petition was sent to Hargreaves. The company turned to Boothferry Planning Department for advice, stating that it wished to use all the house-sites on the 'factory side' (figure 5.1) of the village street for a proposed industrial expansion.

The planners' response was that industry should take precedence over housing. They advised Hargreaves to buy back houses sold to former tenants and to demolish houses rather than renovate them. In effect, this Hargreaves–Boothferry policy sanctioned the demolition of at least 24 of the 27 houses remaining on the 'factory side' of Howdendyke. The policy, then, envisaged a future village with a maximum of only 28 houses, 16 of them council-owned, and only three on the 'factory side' of the village street.

As usual, the villagers were not consulted. Indeed, the existence of this policy might never have come to light had not someone decided to renovate a cottage on the 'factory side'. In 1979 Boothferry Health and Housing offered him an improvement grant; almost simultaneously, Boothferry Planning refused planning permission for the renovation. Only in such ways do hidden agendas come to the public's attention. Thus was revealed, to Howdendyke's startled population, the vision of a future Howdendyke largely devoid of residents.

Since 1980 an unevenly matched battle to save the village has been in progress. The remaining residents and KPC (both with no significant power) face the big guns, Boothferry Council, Boothferry Planning, and two business corporations whose subsidiaries operate at Howdendyke as Hargreaves (now BritAg) and HS & L.

Boothferry Council is the ultimate decision-taker. Pressed by KPC, the Council queried its chief planning officer about structure plan contraventions. The planner replied that the plan was 'very flexible' and that 'there are different ways of interpreting [it] in different circumstances.' The planning department was 'duty-bound' to promote industrial development. Further, the planner argued that the continued existence of 'factory-side' houses could be detrimental to industrial expansion as residents might be able to prevent such expansion on the grounds of nuisance! Given this advice, Boothferry Council agreed to the abandonment of at least half of Howdendyke village.

Statements by two councillors appear to have carried the day against Howdendyke residents and KPC. The member for the ward containing Howdendyke was strongly in favour of industrial development there. He stated that his council was 'at the mercy of Hargreaves', that 'the houses . . . are unrepairable and need demolishing', and that this was 'the only sensible way to tidy up the boundaries and make a proper building line.' The member for the adjacent ward stated categorically, although wholly erroneously: 'It might be difficult to accept for the people of Howdendyke, but this village has been running itself down for the last thirteen years to my certain knowledge.' To this councillor (later Mayor of Boothferry), Howdendyke seemed to be disappearing of its own volition, rather than as the result of industrialists' 'cost-efficiency,' planners' 'flexibility', and the vigorous promotion of industrial growth by borough politicians.

Dismayed, Howdendykers made various responses. Some owner-occupiers tried to sell their houses. Others protested to the local Tory MP, who proved ineffectual. KPC organized petitions and formulated a policy supporting the continued coexistence of industry and housing. Yet some residents still felt an appeal to reason and justice could save their community, as the following letter extract indicates:

Boothferry Council has put a cloud over our long-established community . . . The Council appears to want to demolish . . . half the village, so that possible industry may be given priority. [Yet Howdendyke's dwellings] would have potential if their occupiers were allowed planning permission and grants for improvements.
   So come on, Boothferry Council and Hargreaves, by all means tidy up the village, but don't exterminate it. Is there really any need to spoil our village with speculative planning?

It was to no avail. In late 1985 BritAg planned to demolish the Club, the village social centre. This closely followed a Boothferry Health directive to the Club membership to make good certain deficiencies or face closure. The Club members asked BritAg, as landlord, for assurances that the building would remain standing once they had improved it. These were refused: Catch 22. Almost simultaneously, a BritAg/HS & L planning application sought permission to develop most of the remaining vacant land in the village, including the Club site, as a lorry park and storage area.

In the early 1980s protest letters to the local newspaper had been captioned: 'The village that will not die.' By 1985 the typical byline had become: 'Another nail in the village's coffin.' Perceptive residents in nearby villages readily penetrated to the heart of the matter: 'Howdendyke is a classic example of "planning blight". It is NOT dying. It is slowly being killed off by piecemeal development.' And again, on the 'stealthy' process of village murder:

I say 'stealthy' because the closure [of the Club] is not accidental or indeed inevitable, but is the product of business interests working against the community to acquire land for their use . . . whatever the industries say, they are apparently only interested in the demolition of the whole village.

On blockbusting: Residents speak

Blockbusting is an American term which originally referred to the process whereby speculators circulate rumours that 'undesirable minorities' will soon overwhelm a neighbourhood, thus precipitating panic sales and a buyer's market (Abrams, 1971). In the case of Howdendyke, blockbusting does not appear to be so deliberate, but has come about as a by-product of corporate operations. It has, rather, involved: (i) air, noise and other pollution by HS & L, along the residential waterfront; and (ii) neglect of housing, with the creation of an atmosphere of uncertainty, by Hargreaves, in the remainder of the village. From a large body of material, two interviewees have been selected to illustrate these twin processes at the macro-and micro-scales.

Blockbusting the waterfront

Joe Apthorpe bought a house on the edge of Howdendyke in the early 1970s. Subsequently, HS & L erected its large jetty nearby. By the early 1980s Joe and his neighbours had fled, and their houses had become HS & L offices. Joe recalls the process:

Humberside Sea & Land's jetty creates a lot of noise. First, ships coming upriver turn round by dropping anchor and swinging round on their anchor-chains, all to instructions on a loud-hailer. Then they draw back their metal hatches with a clatter. Ships have to come up with the tide, so these intolerable noises often go on in the middle of the night. Sleep is impossible.

The jetty cranes produce noise from their heavy engines and the rattling of unloading cargo. Some cargo goes into the warehouse yard, which is another source of noise. This comes from mechanical shovels arranging bulk cargo, from lorries, and from the foul language of lorry drivers. The drivers have to shout to make themselves heard. You can only appreciate the sound of metal ingots being dropped into a metal lorry if you've heard it for yourself. And the jetty works a seven-day week, so there's no rest from the noise even on Sundays.

Although noise pollution seems to be the major evil, many other irritations led to Joe's decision to leave:

The road's so narrow and there's an endless stream of lorries to and from the jetty. They can't pass properly so they destroy the footpaths, and they often park on the road, making it even narrower. The road's unsafe for pedestrians, especially children and pensioners going down to the Post Office. And the ships and the jetty leave their spotlights on all night. The light comes right through our curtains and makes sleeping difficult. And the lights dazzle motorists and make the road even more unsafe.

Air pollution is a third hazard:

These ships unload a lot of bulk powder cargoes. The dust covers on the grabs just aren't effective. On windy days you can see the dust blowing and coating the roads, the verges, the hedges, windows, even gardens. Fruit is unfit to eat, and vegetables. We don't know whether the dust is toxic. All the windows and paintwork need cleaning much more often than normal. And lorry drivers don't sheet their loads, so the dust streams off the backs of the lorries. There's sometimes so much dust in the air you can actually taste it.

Little was said about visual pollution, although Joe noted that HS & L had ignored conditions imposed upon them by previous planning permissions. For example, a belt of trees around the warehouse site, which would at least screen its ugliness, had not materialized. Throughout the village, especially in the riverfront zone, similar complaints were made. Widows living alone were not the only inter-viewees to complain of harassment by drunken foreign sailors. Some spoke of continual nervous stress.

By the mid-1980s this waterside problem has been 'solved' by the removal of both the inhabitants and their dwellings. Of 22 inhabited riverside houses in 1960, only six remained inhabited in 1985, and one of these, the Club, was under threat of demolition. Joe recalls his difficulties in trying to sell his house in the late 1970s:

I felt bitter. I had my house on the market for years. The stumbling-block was always Humberside Sea & Land's jetty and storage yard. One lady came to see the house but backed off when she heard the noise. Another said, 'I couldn't live with that noise.' Another sale was almost clinched when the buyers heard that Humberside Sea & Land were asking for an extension to the jetty. Even a group of county planners were disgusted by the noise. . . .

Joe was eventually liberated by HS & L themselves, who bought up the small block of houses and converted them to offices.

Blockbusting terraced housing

Along the village street leading from the waterfront, blockbusting has occurred mainly on the 'factory side', and has taken a more passive form. For an understanding of this process, we turn to other testimony.

Annie Westoby, twenty years a widow, has lived in the same house for over forty years. The house has rich meaning for her as her married home and as the repository of memories of her dead husband. 'I'd never move,' she says, 'this is where we were happy.'

Annie lives in a row of houses already more than half-empty. In the early 1980s there was considerable demand for these empty houses, but Hargreaves refused either to let or sell. To one company director, these houses were merely 'hovels'. Blockbusting, in this case, consisted of malign neglect, expressed in a variety of forms.

One of the results of partial evacuation of a terrace is the imposition of higher costs on those who remain: 'There's one empty on this side and three on that, and hence I'm spending a mint in fuel to keep it all aired and warm'. Unchecked vandalism and poor boarding-up create more problems:

So you get the weather blowing in next door and everything is dreadfully damp. The damp comes through the wall and I've to have constant fires. If I go away for the weekend the house becomes dreadfully cold and a musty smell comes through from next door. It's not very pleasant.

As houses deteriorate, company failure to make repairs becomes critical:

Not that they ever refuse . . . not actually refuse. But you ask for things and nothing happens, and it goes on and on and on until you think they've forgotten. So you've asked several times and you just come to the conclusion that nobody wants to know and you try and help yourself. But it comes to a point where it's a man's work and you can't do it yourself so it just has to go.

In one case, only with the stimulus of an external public authority, ('someone with a bit more push than I had') did Hargreaves make a crucial repair, and even then 'it's a botch job'.

Annie feels that her predicament is rooted in deliberate policy: 'As far as Hargreaves are concerned, they haven't any property.' And she finds the company's attitude difficult to bear:

It's the indecision of everything. You feel so frustrated and you feel people are used and unkindly used. Why should they be allowed to play ducks and drakes with people's lives? Granted they can't turn people out without suitable [alternative] accommodation. But it's the indecision, not knowing when and how. If only they would come and talk to us.

But 'they' don't, and tenants' questions are fielded quite unsympathetically. As Annie comments: 'And I hate being talked down to.' The end result of these multiple frustrations is that tenants give up the struggle. The company 'Wait for people to go out, and the people go out five times out of ten through frustration, because they're so sick and tired.' Annie sadly envisages the future of her terrace to be that of houses previously demolished by Hargreaves:

You see these houses flattened and then for years brick rubble and the land left desolate and nothing done. It's a wicked shame, especially when people want to stay.

And they do wish to stay, and have signed several almost-unanimous petitions declaring this. Despite a general air of resignation after nearly twenty years of industrial expansion and residential decline, some residents still express strong feelings:

I think the village has had it. They're trying to make an industrial place of it. They've even got planning permission to put warehouses in the field at the bottom of our garden. But they won't shove me out. I was born and bred here, and here I'll stay. I'm stopping here and they can't put me out. I'm staying where I am.

The problem with such sentiments is that blockbusting has already succeeded against people with similar feelings, and that both planners and politicians have consistently refused to listen.

An experiment in consultation

One of the major faults common to the power elites involved in Howdendyke's topocide is their lamentable failure to consult with the impacted population. In contrast, one of the ethical imperatives of qualitative social research is the need to give one's informants the right to comment upon and criticize one's interpretations. Accordingly, a first draft of the earlier part of this chapter was sent for comment to all those persons specifically quoted or referred to in the text. These comprised directors of HS & L and BritAg, the Chief Planning Officer (CPO) and the director of Health and Housing for Boothferry Borough, two Boothferry Council members, one of whom was mayor, one resident and two ex-residents of Howdendyke, and a resident of a neighbouring hamlet.

Response was mixed. The politicians did not reply, nor did the Health and Housing director. Only brief acknowledgements of receipt emanated from HS & L, BritAg and the CPO. In contrast, three of the four residents replied immediately, supporting the report and offering positive comments. I am pleased to quote from Annie Westoby's response. She commends

the way you have been able to explain the feelings which we *all* have regarding the unfeeling and uninterested way we have all been treated . . . 'they' call it progress and creating jobs but it is so wicked to have everything cut and dried for themselves and . . . we are not given an opportunity to state our feelings . . . I wonder to myself, how, if the positions were reversed, would they feel? . . . in every context of the word . . . they have murdered our village. . . .

It is such comments which make the difficult work of committed qualitative research worthwhile.

Despite further reminder letters, no other responses appeared. In late summer 1986, therefore, personal interviews were conducted with directors of HS & L, the CPO, the Director of Health and Housing and the mayor of Boothferry. The responses follow.

The director of BritAg spoke of the world glut of fertilizers which rendered the rationalization of British plant imperative; statements made in 1977 regarding probable expansion at Howdendyke were related to possible closures elsewhere. A 1982 proposal to turn the Howdendyke factory into a mere storage facility was an attempt to expand company options in rapidly changing circumstances. The sale or lease of land and jetties to HS & L was a rational use of resources, given the current improbability of chemical factory expansion, and the reduction of the Howdendyke workforce by more than half in later 1985.

The BritAg spokesman agreed that the initial sale of tied housing at Howdendyke was an error, and admitted, to some extent, that the company had been insensitive to local wishes. He noted, however, that 'progress means that someone always gets hurt.' Further, he explained that, in trying to keep the Howdendyke plant viable, Tunisian raw materials had to be imported. These, being very dusty, caused pollution and complaints. In trying to combat pollution, the plant entered the down-spiral of decreasing cost-effectiveness and increasing likelihood of closure. This was yet a further argument for the separation of people from industry, especially as people's desired environmental standards had risen drastically since the 1950s.

The spokesman discounted any notion of an agreement with HS & L to get rid of Howdendyke village; events and circumstances change too quickly for the formulation of such a strategy. In terms of this account, then, the destruction of Howdendyke appears to be a logical inevitability, the sad outcome of a tragic unfolding, but of no great importance in the general scheme of things.

A director of Humberside Sea & Land Services agreed that BritAg did not have a close relationship with his firm: 'we are just tenants who pay a royalty for every ton we carry over their land.' There is a much stronger link with TR Chemicals (on the former Tate & Lyle site), for the site is jointly owned by HS & L, and Tinoverman Ltd, which does the shipping work for TR Chemicals, is an HS & L 'shell company'. HS & L, indeed, is a large firm with sixteen 'trading arms' in Humberside. It was formed in the 1960s as a reaction to the 'endless delays and labour disputes at registered ports'. And despite the fact that HS & L workers at Howdendyke are unionized, 'there has been never a day's stoppage here.' This was attributed to good pay, considerable 'identity' between workers and management, and a 'small, intimate, family atmosphere', which has even extended to taking on certain Anderton-like traditions, such as sending Christmas hampers to Howdendyke pensioners.

The spokesman agreed that this paternalistic stance did not offset the nuisance and noise caused by HS & L in the village, and admitted that one of HS & L's own workers, an owner-occupier in Howdendyke, was suing the company for loss of amenity and potential loss of housing value. The director expected that, at the very least, the company would be asked either to buy out some properties close to its operations or to double-glaze the windows of some of the village houses.

Attention was then drawn to the positive achievement of directly providing about 200 jobs, not to mention scores of independent lorry drivers and haulage firms. Allowing for BritAg's decline, this meant that HS & L and its associates had more than doubled the employment available at Howdendyke since the 1960s. Nor was this achieved by taking trade from the port of Goole, for the low-value high-bulk cargoes handled by Howdendyke were unsuited to the slow turn-around of registered docks. No immediate expansion of HS & L was envisaged, but should trade ever increase, Howdendyke was capable of doubling its current capacity.

Boothferry Health and Housing was represented by its director, the Chief Housing and Environmental Services Officer. He affirmed that in condemning Howdendyke houses he was merely performing his statutory duty, housing deterioration 'having become evident' or 'been brought to our attention', though not, apparently, by Hargreaves/BritAg. The synchronicity of a Health and Housing inspection of Howdendyke Club and HS & L's application to place a lorry park on its site elicited the reply: 'It is unfair to talk of anything but coincidence in this case: life is full of coincidences.'

When asked about the possibility of rehousing people from condemned houses by building new housing in Howdendyke, a scheme perfectly permissible under Structure Plan guidelines, the director replied that first, the Council were no longer building council houses except for old people, and second, that old people require services which are not available at Howdendyke. He also expressed astonishment that his department had placed closing orders on as many as 'thirty-odd' houses in Howdendyke.

The Chief Planning Officer (CPO) of Boothferry Planning Department was appointed only in 1974 and thus was able to say little about earlier policies. With regard to the crucial decision to industrialize Howdendyke that was made in 1968, he suggested that the former County Council had prepared a policy report recommending port-related industry at Howdendyke, even though it may have been against the County Plan, that a petition was received from local people, and that the Secretary of State was referred to, but did not intervene. When I asked for the names of the chief local architects of this plan, I was told that they were either dead or had moved away. The CPO then offered to send me a copy of the 1968 report; I have not received it.

The CPO affirmed that all major planning applications for Howdendyke had been advertised in the local press, and that 'even neighbour notification may have taken place.' When asked why public meetings had never been held in Howdendyke, he confirmed that he had the discretion to hold public meetings, but stated, 'it was not usual to hold public meetings unless creating a Local Plan.' Given manpower problems, Howdendyke does not qualify for a Local Plan, for these are being generated only to cope with the pressing problems of expanding 'key settlements'. Finally, given the 'obvious' need for private wharves in Boothferry, Howdendyke is the most suitable place in terms of river frontage and road access.

The CPO stressed that all planning recommendations and political decisions in Boothferry have been legal and procedurally correct. Howdendyke has been long considered a 'special case' exempt from Structure Plan guidelines. He agreed with the BritAg spokesman that it is ridiculous to replace houses which are at the end of their structural life, which do not qualify for local authority grants, and which are close to noxious industry.

Of two politicians approached, the one whose ward includes Howdendyke refused to speak with me ('I've nowt to say'). In a brief telephone conversation, however, he noted: that Howdendyke is an industrial area; that Howdendyke's houses were 'in a bad state' and rightly condemned; that there have been no complaints from anyone moved out; and that 'what I want for this area is jobs, and more jobs.'

In contrast, the Mayor of Boothferry, a retired industrialist, spoke with me at length. He commended HS & L's provision of jobs at Howdendyke, spoke strongly in favour of further industrial expansion, asserted that Hargreaves' expectations of expansion in 1977 were made in good faith, confirmed that there was no need for a special plan for a non-selected settlement of low planning priority, and noted that failure to place closing orders on manifestly unfit housing could have led to charges of neglect of duty.

He stressed the 'ridiculousness' of renovating houses so close to industry, and noted that Howdendykers had a 'mentality' that led them to refuse offers of good housing in nearby towns. When I spoke of place loyalty, he said that the council could not 'compensate for sentiment'. Finally, he stressed that job generation was of the utmost importance, that the Council had always proceeded legally and according to due procedure, that all decisions were made democratically, and that 'there can be no progress without some discomfort'.

From the above interviews it would appear that Howdendyke, as a residential village, has been written off. The common emphasis on 'due procedure', however, does suggest that a degree of uneasiness lurks behind assurances that a wider vision of progress and betterment demands the sacrifice of a small place and its people's place loyalties. Little sympathy was expressed for the plight of Howdendykers.

When asked directly what were their visions of Howdendyke's future, interviewees made fairly consistent replies. BritAg saw little hope for the expansion of its factory and wished to terminate, when possible, the tenancies of its four remaining tied houses. HS & L felt the residential village, ultimately, had no future. While Health and Housing 'couldn't imagine' that the whole village would disappear, I was asked to remember that the majority of houses there were now Council-owned, and that half of these were built in 1936, and the other half were 'Airey houses' which elsewhere had developed structural problems too expensive to repair. The CPO would not express an opinion, but reiterated the theme that 'the location of the village was poor in terms of living conditions' because of the proximity to industry. This statement, common to several of the interviewees, is at best unhistorical, the village having preceded most of the industry.

Only the Mayor bluntly spoke his mind. 'I would like to see the whole village go', he said, 'and become an industrial area. I'd like to clear it and compensate house-owners and rehouse tenants elsewhere.' Clearly, in the eyes of planners, politicians and private enterprise, the future of the village of Howdendyke is to become a resident-free Howdendyke Industrial Estate.

Apparent confirmation of this appeared at the time of the final interviews in summer 1986, when Boothferry Borough approved an HS & L/BritAg plan for the vacant land on the 'factory side' of the village to be used as an HS & L lorry park and storage area. This involves the closure of the Jubilee Hall and the Club (two of the three village social centres), although a replacement Club is promised on a different site.

This development will effectively extend the current high levels of noise and vehicle nuisance from the waterfront to the whole of the remainder of the residential village. It is likely that this will elicit further complaints from the remaining villagers and may result in their eventual evacuation. Alive to this possibility, Howdendyke's inhabitants drew up two almost unanimous petitions and wrote several letters of protest. The phrases below are typical, rather than extreme, examples of residents' current feelings about this latest blow to the integrity of their community:

It seems that certain people in high places are doing their utmost to drive us out . . .

The two major companies in Howdendyke [are] bent on the virtual destruction of the remains of this tiny village.

The village was here before the factories. We wish to stay here, not to be hounded out by the industries around us.

We feel we are being squashed out of existence from the place we have lived in all our lives.

Please help us.

No help was offered. Unfortunately, politicians, planners and the directors of private enterprise are not yet legally required to live with the nuisances they have generated before taking decisions to augment those nuisances.

Conclusion

The village of Howdendyke seems doomed to eventual extinction. Unfortunately for its residents, the process by which such topocide takes place is not apparent, for most inhabitants have no clear understanding of the planning process or of the effective relationship between private enterprise, politicians, and bureaucrats. And little attempt has been made by any of these groups to provide information to residents. So whereas individuals clearly understood the processes whereby they were personally induced to move (Joe Apthorpe) or made uncomfortable (Annie Westoby), no resident was able to explain to me how it was that 'they' were legally able to continue with their slow but inexorable topocide.

Although the Structure Plan dutifully emphasizes the importance of public participation in planning, Boothferry authorities have made little attempt to ascertain the desires of Howdendyke residents, let alone accommodate these. Indeed, the official attitude might well be summed up by Boothferry Borough's latest brochure, *Opportunities for Development* (1986), which notes:

The Council has an impressive record in dealing with planning applications for industrial and commercial use – over 89% were approved in the 10 years up to 1984. In 1985 the record touched 95%.

Without irony, the brochure goes on to laud the district's 'picturesque villages'.

Nor is there any effective grass-roots counterweight to the powerful politician–planner–industrial complex. Resistance, ill-organized, ill-informed and largely based on non-quantifiable attachment to place, has little effect. Successful community defence against the planning juggernaut is invariably led by middle-class people (Cybriwsky, 1978); Howdendyke is almost wholly working-class and current policies prevent in-migration.

In sum, the conditions for the topocide of Howdendyke seem to be: a wholly working-class population, largely tenants, with little knowledge of the planning process and no tradition of dissent; control of land and employment by distant, profit-oriented corporations; planners willing to ignore their own guidelines and unwilling to engage in public participation processes; local politicians bent on development at almost any cost; and a certain deafness and lack of compassion on the part of all these authorities. And topocide is even easier when the policies of planners, politicians, and industrialists dovetail so precisely.

Should these processes continue, even optimistic scenarios (Table 5.1) point to a housing loss over the period 1960–99 of between two-thirds and three-quarters of all housing. No once-vibrant community can survive such losses and live.

The word most commonly used by interviewees to describe these activities is 'wicked'. I endorse these sentiments. Howdendyke residents

Table 5.1 Housing loss scenarios, 1960–99

Scenario	Houses occupied 1960	Houses occupied 1985	Houses occupied 1999
1 (probable)	72	34 (53% loss)	25 (65% loss)
2 (likely)	72	34 (")	20 (73% loss)
3 (possible)	72	34 (")	4 (94% loss)
4 (pessimistic)	72	34 (")	0 (100% loss)

Scenario 1: loss of nine remaining units on 'factory side' of village.
Scenario 2: further loss of five remaining waterfront units.
Scenario 3: demolition of sixteen council houses; tenants relocated.

and their parish council representatives have invariably taken a reasonable approach, always involving compromise, when dealing with bureaucrats, politicians and industrialists. The responses have been wholly unreasonable and perhaps reflect the inhuman face of capitalism so common in Britain today. On this general theme, I shall let Berger (1984) have the penultimate word:

During the eighteenth and nineteenth centuries most direct protests against social injustice were reasoned arguments written in the belief that, given time, people would come to see reason, and that, finally, history was on the side of reason. Today this is by no means clear. The outcome is by no means guaranteed. The suffering of the present . . . is unlikely to be redeemed by a future of universal happiness. And evil is a constant, ineradicable reality.

In these terms, Howdendyke is the world in microcosm. All that is solid melts into air (Berman 1982).

Note

I thank all the officials of private corporations and public services, as well as Boothferry district politicians, who accorded me interviews. I gratefully acknowledge the interest, help and empathy of my friends and former neighbours in Howdendyke. When quoted in the text, their names, of course, have been changed. Both the Social Sciences and Humanities Research Council of Canada and the University of Victoria provided research funds for this investigation.

References

Abrams, C. (1971) *The language of cities*, Avon, New York.
Adams, D. (1979) *The hitch hikers guide to the galaxy*, Pan Books, London.

Adams, W. (1980) 'The dead community', in Gallagher, A. and Padfield, H. (eds), *The Dying Community*, University of New Mexico Press, Albuquerque, 23–54.

Berger, J. (1984) *And our faces, my heart, brief as photos*, Pantheon, New York.

Berman, M. (1982) *All that is solid melts into air*, Simon & Schuster, New York.

Brown, G. M. (1976) *Greenvoe*, Penguin Books, London.

Cybriwsky, R. (1978) 'Social aspects of neighborhood changes', *Annals of the Association of American Geographers* 68, 17–33.

Giddens, A. (1976) *New rules for sociological method*, Hutchinson, London.

Jackson, P. (1980) *Ethnic groups and boundaries*, Oxford University School of Geography Research Paper No. 26, Oxford.

Jones, S. (1985) 'Depth interviewing/The analysis of depth interviews', in R. Walker (ed.) *Applied qualitative research*, Gower, Aldershot, 45–70.

Porteous, J. D. (1971) 'Design with people: the quality of the urban environment', *Environment and Behavior* 3, 155–78.

Porteous, J. D. (1977) *Environment and behavior: planning and everyday urban life*, Addison-Wesley, Reading, Massachusetts.

Porteous, J. D. (1988) *Planned to death: the destruction of the village of Howdendyke by private enterprise, politicians, and planners*, Manchester University Press, Manchester.

Rowles, G. (1978) *Prisoners of space?*, Westview Press, Boulder, Colorado.

6

Decoding Docklands
Place Advertising and Decision-making Strategies of the Small Firm

Jacquelin Burgess and Peter Wood

Within formal economic location theory, and especially its 'behavioural' variants, many commentators have identified important subjective factors affecting the establishment and survival of firms. Preferences for certain locations combined with prejudices against others are thought to influence strongly the decision-making and location strategies of entrepreneurs. Thus, in the hunt for new investment to regenerate the economies of declining industrial areas, local authorities and development agencies have relied heavily upon area promotion in the hope that investment decisions will be influenced by the content of advertisements. Places have become commodities to be packaged, marketed and sold.

To establish convincingly whether place advertising is a significant influence on the process of location decision-making it is, however, necessary to move beyond the largely quantitative and behavioural analyses of economic geographers (Wood, 1987). We must also focus on the cultural dimensions of the problem. As Cosgrove and Jackson (1987) argue: 'culture is not a residual category, the surface variation left unaccounted for by more powerful economic analyses; it is the very medium through which social change is experienced, contested and constituted' (p. 95). Contemporary media, especially television, play a powerful ideological role in 'mapping' the social and cultural characteristics of different places (Burgess, 1985). To understand how place advertisements 'work' on decision-makers, we need to combine economic analysis with a cultural interpretation of media texts themselves. How do place advertisements create meanings for different localities? How do different audiences read and interpret these visual and linguistic texts? Whose purposes are best served by the commodification of people and place in area advertising?

In this chapter we shall attempt to demonstrate the value of a semiotic analysis for decoding area images, having first described the economic circumstances in which they are interpreted. We shall suggest that the transformation of an area's image through advertising can be significant for the promotion even of locally-based enterprise. While the analysis here is applied to area-development policies, it also has a much wider significance for the ways in which place meanings are constructed in the modern, media-dominated age. Myth is more important than reality in selling places; economic decision-makers are no more or less susceptible than anyone else.

Place advertising and small businesses

Whether shouting from a 30-foot hoarding on Westway, whispering seductively from the pages of *Penthouse*, or inserted stridently into the evening television news, advertisements are a major feature of contemporary culture. Studies of advertising cover the spectrum from technical handbooks, historical reviews, insights into the working practices of agencies, and studies of the supposed effects of product promotions (see Ogilvy, 1964; Dyer, 1982; Fox, 1984). There is also a growing critical literature, concentrating less on the 'transparent' content of messages and more on the forms through which advertisements produce meaning and the role they play in reinforcing particular ideologies (Langholtz 1975; Gauthier 1976; Williams 1980; Williamson 1982; Nye 1985).

By comparison, relatively little attention has so far been given to the forms, messages and impacts of place or area advertising (Burgess, 1982). Employing the analytical separation of 'place' put forward by Agnew (1987), into locale, location and sense of place, we find that all three components are directly implicated in the manifest content of place advertisements. The locale, the physical setting of everyday life, is marketed as an assemblage of environmental features contributing to quality of life and attractive settings for new commercial development. For example, personal and commercial prestige is acquired through the 'unique' possibilities of waterside or parkland landscapes. The location of places, in the sense of their interrelationship with others, becomes significant especially in terms of their 'centrality', their closeness to the heart of economic and political power. Finally, sense of place, which encompasses both the association of identity with place experienced by local communities and outsiders' images and myths about places, is a vital component of place advertising. The workforce of an area finds that it is being sold as friendly, docile, hardworking and cooperative, for example, while aspects of historical and cultural heritage are used to entice the new middle class into traditionally working-class localities.

Place advertising has been increasingly used over the last twenty years in attempts to attract firms from overseas and to capture a share of footloose investment by large UK companies. The era in which area-development policies could rely almost exclusively on such 'mobile' investment has, however, long since past (Damesick and Wood, 1987). As a consequence, greater emphasis has been placed upon encouraging locally-based regeneration, and especially upon a revival of small firms. This might suggest a diminishing role for advertising as part of any development policy (Young and Mason, 1983; Mason and Harrison, 1985). Most potential local entrepreneurs are likely to know their area already and be less easily influenced than outsiders by image promotion. The world of small firms is also supposedly dominated by more concrete issues such as identifying market opportunities and adapting to new patterns of competition and cost, serving the needs of dominant customers, dealing with problems of labour recruitment, capital availability or cash-flow, or making decisions to invest in critical pieces of equipment or suitable premises.

These 'objective' aspects of small firm formation and growth have been exhaustively surveyed as a result of the growing interest in their role in local economic regeneration. Markusen and Teitz (1985) nevertheless conclude that the small firm segment is 'enormous and richly complex' due, in large part, to the individualistic and localized nature of the foundation, growth and survival of small firms. Personal considerations therefore loom particularly large in their behaviour. While it may certainly be necessary for an area-development programme to provide the right economic conditions for small firm foundation and growth, including appropriate land, buildings, infrastructure and advisory services, the individual who operates a small firm is in fact as likely to be susceptible to the impacts of changing area imagery as any other citizen. On the one hand, therefore, small firms might be expected to operate beyond the reach of place advertising, and may certainly *say* they do, claiming to have to know their local area to survive. On the other hand, the very individuality of small firm existence leaves them open to the impacts of any campaign to change the image of an area such as Docklands. This aspect of area development policy cannot be explored through conventional methods of economic inquiry. Its impact cannot be 'objectively' measured, and may well not be overtly recognized by recipients. A theory and method of inquiry are needed that can identify the qualitative effects of changing area imagery, whether consciously induced or occurring accidentally, on the attitudes of small firm entrepreneurs and their behaviour.

The Docklands study

The London Docklands Development Corporation (LDDC) has become prominent in the United Kingdom since 1981 through its strategy of urban regeneration and economic development. Its success in attracting private capital to an area previously characterized by economic decline and environmental dereliction reflects wider policy changes, including the relaxing of controls on development in London, a marked national switch in emphasis from regional to urban aid since 1979 and very considerable public expenditure on making Docklands attractive to private investment. It also reflects one of the most aggressive, expensive and sophisticated public relations, marketing and advertising programmes ever mounted on behalf of a local area in Britain. Between 1982 and 1985, the LDDC spent £6,574,000 on publicity and promotional activities.

In 1984, we were asked by the LDDC and its advertising agency, Gold Greenlees Trott, to evaluate the impact of their 1982–3 poster, newspaper and television advertising campaign on the location decisions of small businesses that had moved into new industrial units in the Isle of Dogs Enterprise Zone. At this time these businesses were the main occupiers of the Enterprise Zone. The purpose of the survey was to judge the effectiveness of the campaign, and the lessons it offered for further promotion policies. We present below the results from semi-structured interviews with the directors of companies operating in the Enterprise Zone. We explore their location decisions and perceptions of the importance of advertising *vis-à-vis* other factors which influenced their decision to move to the Isle of Dogs. We then consider, through analysis of the encoding and decoding of the area, how in these cases advertisements created a new meaning for Docklands, principally through the use of imagery from popular television programmes.

A survey of all the companies operating within three industrial units of the Isle of Dogs was completed in June 1984. The Cannon Workshops, developed by the Port of London Authority (PLA) during the period of transition to LDDC control in 1978–81, contained 96 small units in refurbished military barracks at the entrance to the Millwall docks. Eighty-six were occupied at the time of the study. Indescon Court was one of the first 'high-tech' units to be built on the Island and six out of seven units were occupied. The third development, the Lanterns, built to a more conventional design, was being completed during the survey period. Thirteen companies were in occupation in June 1984. We visited all the occupied premises, having first written to the managing directors outlining the purposes of the survey. A total of 62 companies were interviewed. Most of the non-respondents were in businesses which used the premises for storage only, or who worked elsewhere, for example in the construction trade. Four directors declined the interview.

The aims of the survey were to chart the history of the company prior to its move to the Enterprise Zone, to discover the search procedures adopted by each company and to assess the impact of the 1982–3 advertising campaign on individual location decisions. Given this brief, we needed to devise a methodology that would enable us to explore some of the personal attitudes and values of the company directors, especially their interpretive strategies when 'reading' advertising texts, as well as collecting factual information about their companies' activities. For these reasons, we chose a semi-structured interview format in which we specified the key topic areas to be discussed but framed the questions in an open-ended fashion. The interviewer wrote down verbatim responses as far as possible and always encouraged the interviewees to expand and elaborate their views. Morton-Williams (1985) argues that 'a semi-structured questionnaire may be used when some of the flexibility and detail of qualitative research is required in conjunction with the opportunity to aggregate answers . . . for example when interviewing minority groups who are expensive to contact' (1985: 28). It has similar benefits when interviewing business people who are unwilling to give up the large amounts of time required for depth interviewing.

Trying to assess the impact of advertising on decisions that have already been made is also problematic and so we invited respondents to discuss their decision-making strategy before raising the issue of area advertising. The advertising agency prepared a series of large cards, depicting different aspects of the Docklands campaign. These consisted of:

a. Four boards showing black and white newspaper advertisements published during the year (see figure 6.1, p. 105). The contact points for these advertisements were the quality press such as the *Financial Times* and magazines oriented to the business community.
b. Three 'story-boards', with colour stills narrating the television commercials (see figures 6.2–6.4, pp. 106–7 and 109). These were screened by London Weekend Television which has the franchise for South-East England. They were shown in the commercial break of the 10 p.m. *News at Ten* during April–June 1982, and June 1983. Additionally, stills from the commercials were used for poster hoardings in sites around London.

Towards the middle of the interview, we showed the cards to the interviewees and encouraged them to talk freely about the content, presentation and impact of the campaign. The visual material generated an enormous amount of interest and critical comment.

The context of the 1982–3 campaign

The policy background for the regeneration of the dockland localities is complex and need not concern us directly here (see Ledgerwood, 1984; GLC, 1985). Government restrictions on advertising by the GLC and boroughs had undoubtedly hindered earlier attempts to regenerate the five boroughs of Newham, Tower Hamlets, Southwark, Lewisham and Greenwich within whose jurisdiction lay both the riverside and the enclosed docks of the Port of London. The Docklands Joint Committee (DJC 1974–9) was eventually permitted to launch a promotional campaign in 1978. Whether the DJC would have succeeded in regenerating the area is now conjecture for they were overtaken by the election of the Conservative government in 1979 which appointed the Urban Development Corporation to take over responsibility for regeneration. The prime requirement of the LDDC was to lever private capital into the dockland localities. Advertising, marketing and public relations were regarded as essential in creating an environment in which capital would be prepared to undertake the 'risk' of investing in East London.

A crucial feature of the context of Docklands advertising for any interpretation of the 1982–3 campaign concerns the physical, psychological and socio-cultural reality of 'Docklands' as a place. Prior to the closure of the upper docks (1967–70), 'Docklands' had no currency or meaning for local people. The docks themselves were part of the Port of London, administered by the PLA, while the communities around the individual dock complexes were tied intimately to their own localities in Bermondsey, Wapping, Millwall and North Woolwich, for example, but were quite distinct from one another. 'London Docklands' was 'created' by Peter Walker, Secretary of State for the Environment, who commissioned the Travers Morgan study (HMSO, 1973). The DJC took over the word and it has subsequently entered general currency through both the title and the activities of the LDDC. But local opposition groups still protest against the appropriation of their localities through this usage by political and commercial forces. By contrast, if 'Docklands' was a place concept without meaning, the location of the enclosed docks within East London is a very different matter. Strong, clear and deeply-rooted myths and images about the 'East End' circulate within contemporary popular culture (see Keating, 1973; Worpole, 1983) and were actively exploited in the GGT campaign.

The firms and their relocation decisions

At the time of the survey, small firms predominated in the Enterprise Zone, especially in the Cannon Workshops. In the sample, a little over one half employed fewer than five workers and only five firms employed more than ten. Thirty-eight firms were in service activities, including packaging, the storage and distribution of a wide range of mechanical and electrical spares, computer software and services, office stationery and supplies, and professional services related to architecture, design, advertising and legal activities. Twenty-four firms manufactured or processed materials on site, including printing and photography, clothing and textiles, construction-related activities, metal processing and food preparation.

One striking characteristic of the firms was that many of them were newly established, including half of those in the Cannon Workshops and most in Indescon Court. For the great majority, the Isle of Dogs was their main base of operations. Of the 34 established firms that moved in from outside, 24 had formerly operated in the East End, Central London or in adjacent areas of Inner London. The new Lanterns Court development, however, was especially attractive to branches of firms based in the City or West End. Essex was the principal origin for firms coming from outside London. The overwhelming impression in the survey of newly-established firms was also that they had originated in adjacent areas of London.

The search for premises which led to their choice of the Isle of Dogs had seldom lasted for more than six months, and was often of less than three months. The search procedures varied widely. About one in five of the firms looked only at the Enterprise Zone while the majority had reviewed a large number of sites in the East End, Inner London and the City. The choice of the Isle of Dogs was clearly influenced by existing knowledge of the area by the owner/managing director on the basis of business, residential or personal connections. Twenty-two firms, however, mentioned without prompting that various aspects of the publicity and advertising had attracted them to investigate the area. Only a small number mentioned direct contact with the LDDC or agents.

The general strategy adopted by the firms could therefore easily be understood. The search for sites were carried out mainly by owners/managing directors, evaluating the options within severe constraints of finance, their own time, and area of search in relation to existing patterns of commercial contacts. The main stimulus to move for established firms was the unsatisfactory nature of existing premises and the main attractions of the new location, as with new firms, was low initial costs and minimum financial risk. In the case of companies ambitious to succeed, scope for development and expansion was also desirable. The localization of the search and the significance of local knowledge was therefore to be expected.

In this context, the impact of area-promoting advertising came as something of a surprise. For reasons mentioned earlier, we had thought it unlikely that the campaign would have a major impact on these small firm decision-makers compared, for example, with its primary targets, the senior managements of large outside firms and the general public. A realistic expectation might have been that the campaign would have *no* effect on the location decisions of small, locally-based companies. Yet it was clear from the interviews that advertising had played a significant role in attracting small companies to the Enterprise Zone and further, that the promotional activities were having a cumulative impact upon the attitudes of local small businesses to the Docklands developments.

When asked formally to enumerate the factors that had influenced their choice of premises in the Enterprise Zone, most firms described a variety of interacting influences. Two-thirds of the firms felt that the rate relief offered in the Enterprise Zone was a significant factor. In other cases this incentive was regarded as a useful supplement to a more urgent need, such as a suitable building, the speed with which it could be occupied, or an appropriate location at a reasonable rent. The distinctive qualities of the buildings and the area, whether historic or high-tech, were mentioned by over 60 per cent of the firms; 60 per cent also cited the importance of business and market contacts in the East End or Central London. Most respondents had very positive expectations about the future potential of the area, sometimes bolstering their own somewhat risky decision.

Evaluations of the campaign content

The effect of the 1982–3 campaign within this decision-making process was to draw the attention of entrepreneurs to the opportunities available in Docklands. More generally, however, it seemed to fulfil two related functions for many of the small firms, reinforcing the more 'rational' calculations of benefit. First, it countered negative images of the East End/Isle of Dogs held by company personnel, customers and competitors. Second, it reduced perceptions of risk, reinforcing executives' decisions to locate in the area.

In response to the story-boards, it became clear that attitudes towards the advertisements were mixed. The majority were favourably disposed, some were ambivalent and a few highly critical of the messages and their style. A few executives denied that advertising had any effect on their location decisions: 'advertisements are purely coincidental. They don't influence you at all. It has to be right for economic reasons.' In the sample, a third of the companies had been stimulated to seek further advice or visit the area for themselves through exposure to an advert. The stimulus was most often based on chance. One executive described how he was driving round aimlessly 'just looking for somewhere' when he heard an ad. on LBC radio and drove down to take a look. Two directors passed posters on their way to work and phoned once they realized the need to relocate. As one director put it: 'The advertising was crucial – I wouldn't have started looking in the first place otherwise.' The ads were particularly effective with people who did not have detailed local knowledge or contacts, and often served to redress unfavourable images of East London long enough for the individual to make personal contact with LDDC or some other agency in the area.

The majority of interviewees felt that the advertising and promotional activities of the LDDC were important in supporting their own location decision. People said that they had become more aware of promotional material after their decision to move. 'You only really notice ads once you've made up your mind to go. It makes you feel good,' said one director; while another who had moved in from another part of the country said, 'I've noticed ads occurred more and more. Once you've made a conscious decision to move you become more aware. Each time an ad. came up on TV I sat up and took notice. I wanted to know more about what was happening.' Other companies told us that the advertising was having a marked spin-off in terms of publicity, influencing their customers as well as personal friends and business contacts. 'You know, looking back, it probably did influence me. It suggested a place. My customers now know where the Isle of Dogs is because of the ads. Previously they wouldn't have had a clue.' And a few of the smallest companies were using the advertising to help allay their anxieties. One manufacturer spent a considerable time reading the story-boards: 'I've not seen these but it's quite right, it's all truthful, isn't it? This island is definitely going to take off'.

One major benefit of the campaign for interviewees was to counteract negative images of the Isle of Dogs/East End. Twenty-seven companies referred specifically to the poor image of East London – either their own or those of clients, customers or competitors. The 'East End' image has two separate strands: an industrialized, run-down, poverty-stricken slum; or a remote, isolated area, miles from the City. The small businesses were receptive to the advertising campaign because they felt it effectively challenged both false images. As one local businessman said: 'The ads are very gimmicky. To an East Ender like me it doesn't really come over, but to outsiders who imagine the East End to be dirty, scruffy, kids with no shoes, no transport, people not working, then these ads really do something. It sets in their mind. It makes people think.' The newspaper advertisements, in particular, were seen as giving an idea of the future, a stark contrast with the nineteenth-century image. The claim to centrality came principally from the LDDC slogan – 'Why move to the middle of nowhere when you can move to the middle of London?' – and several interviewees referred specifically to that aspect of the campaign. 'Clients think it's miles away. They all think the docklands is in Frinton . . . large companies will follow us pioneers.' One computer company executive liked the slogan 'because people are worried about being in the middle of nowhere'. And the director of a major company in Indescon used it quite spontaneously. 'Let's face it, blind prejudice does come in to it. Why should I go and sit in the middle of nowhere? I would have left the company if we'd gone to the East Midlands.'

Signifying Docklands

The Gold Greenlees Trott (GGT) campaign

The 1982–3 campaign was concerned primarily with corporate image-making: raising levels of awareness of the LDDC, giving the Corporation a certain 'style', and signalling development and investment opportunities in Docklands. The target audiences of both the newspaper advertisements and the television commercials were professional people – the audiences delivered by quality newspapers and the *'News at Ten'*. Other strategies in the campaign included large outside hoardings, and a slot on commercial radio during journey-to-work times. As we have seen, the campaign in fact reached a far wider audience than anticipated and, in consequence, there was some confusion within the different segments of our sample about who specifically was being addressed by the ads. Several felt that the newspaper ads were not aimed at small businesses, while some executives were highly critical of the television commercials because they were directed 'at Joe Public'. It was 'low-intelligence advertising'.

The basic function of advertising, from the client/agency perspective, is to create a 'unique' product which is differentiated from all its potential competitors. In the late 1970s and early 1980s, advertising by the major competitors to LDDC had not been very successful in establishing place differentiation. Towns all over the United Kingdom relied on very similar propositions to sell themselves: claims to centrality, expanding business opportunities, successful migrant companies and an excellent quality of life.

How does the GGT/LDDC strategy compare? As with all place advertising, the copy addresses those tangible and intangible factors thought to influence perception and location decision-making. Like all its competitors, the major claim of the campaign is that of 'centrality'. The slogan, taking a popular cliché, *asks* receivers: 'Why move to the middle of nowhere, when you can move to the middle of London?' It connotes several meanings and works at several different levels. 'The middle of nowhere' differentiated from 'the middle of London' takes much of its force from a powerful cultural myth of the backwardness of 'provincial' places when compared with the dynamism of 'the City'. At the same time, it demonstrates the impact of appellation by constituting the individual reader as the subject – 'you' – of the advertisement and then playing on executives' anxieties that a location out of London will jeopardize their competitiveness through the loss of face-to-face contacts. An ultimate depersonalization is encapsulated in the surreal, Magritte-like representation (figure 6.1).

The crows in the television commercials provide another vehicle for conveying messages about Docklands. On the face of it, crows would seem to offer little for the corporate image but analysis of the three commercials reveals how an identity is being created. Each commercial has a narrative which deals with different areas of LDDC activity. The first introduces the Corporation, the second signals the Enterprise Zone in the Isle of Dogs, and the third flags the new private house-building programme. In the first (figure 6.2), the crows animate the slogan: 'as the crow flies' is a figure of speech meaning the shortest distance between two points. Whilst not mentioning its competitors by name, the dialogue firmly places Milton Keynes (the New Town) and the Welsh Development Agency (150 miles away) a long way from London. The text then makes the most of the grindingly obvious point that the London Docklands can be differentiated from every other place, because they are in London.

Following hard on the heels of this positional piece, the second commercial turned attention specifically to the Enterprise Zone (figure 6.3). In this story, the crows represent different television personalities. The message concerns business opportunities available in Docklands and introduces the novelty 'Enterprise Zone'. It makes no explicit reference to competitor locations, claiming simply to be 'the biggest business opportunity in Europe'. The commercial appeal is addressed to financial benefits – tax incentives in the Isle of Dogs, cheaper phone bills and those 'intangible' business contacts.

A year later, the third commercial was screened and reflects confidence by LDDC/GGT that the campaign had successfully established the LDDC in the public mind. The ad. uses the logo but no name (figure

How will you look to your clients if you move out of London?

If you move to a development area outside London, you'll leave a lot of important clients behind.

So you'll end up doing most of your business dial-to-dial instead of face-to-face.

But, if you move to London's Docklands, you'll be just a few hundred yards from the city.

And you'll also be part of the biggest city centre redevelopment scheme in Europe.

With an Enterprise Zone, which offers you auto-matic rate exemption for ten years, bigger and better capital allowances, exemption from development land tax, and a refreshing absence of red tape.

So you enjoy the advantages of a development area – without the hassle of cancelled trains, grounded planes, and a phone bill to leave you speechless.

Don't wring Buzby's neck... ring 01-200 0200 and ask about the London Docklands Development Corporation. **L.D.D.C.**
LONDON DOCKLANDS DEVELOPMENT CORPORATION

WHY MOVE TO THE MIDDLE OF NOWHERE, WHEN YOU CAN MOVE TO THE MIDDLE OF LONDON?

Figure 6.1 One of the newspaper advertisements

Figure 6.2   The first London Weekend television commercial (April 1982)

Figure 6.3   The second commercial (June 1982)

6.4). The overt message is that house-building opportunities exist within the Docklands area, and the voice-over comment is addressed, ambiguously, to builders and developers, and potential home-owners. The crows meanwhile have taken on another persona of small-time crooks. The ways in which these commercials create a meaning for Docklands is complex and requires analysis of both their content and form.

Decoding the commercials

Key ideas originating in the work of the Swiss linguist de Saussure (1916) provide the basis for the interpretation and analysis of a great variety of material cultural practices, including advertisements (see Blonsky, 1985). All kinds of text are composed of *signs* which are divided, for analytic purposes only, into two parts: the *signifier* is the material object or 'sound' in linguistic terms, the *signified* is the meaning or the 'referent concept'. Signs may be *iconic*: visual representations which bear a resemblance to the referent, as, for example, in sketches of landmarks. They may be *indexical*, having a direct causal relationship with the referent as, for example, in a fingerprint. Finally, signs may be *symbolic*, of which language itself is the major example. Words have an arbitrary and conventional relationship with their referent: not only can the same word mean different things but the meaning of words changes through time.

The interpretation of signs is dependent upon the shared understanding of the codes which structure the message, and studies of the 'encoding' and 'decoding' of messages constitute a major research focus in the dynamics of meaning. Hall (1982), for example, discusses the complexity of televisual messages in which the frameworks of knowledge, relations of production and technical infrastructure influence both the encoding and decoding of 'meaningful' discourse in television programmes. Codes provide a way of classifying cultures through their propensity to relate signs to their 'maps of social reality [which] have the whole range of social meanings, practices, and usages, power and interest "written into them"' (Hall, 1982: 34).

Judith Williamson (1982) describes these maps of meaning as *referent systems*, arguing that the receiver must share the cultural values and beliefs of the referent systems in order to decode an advertisement. It therefore follows that 'images, ideas or feelings, then, become attached to certain products, by being transferred from signs out of other systems (things or people with "images") *to* the products, rather than originating in them.' (1982: 30). Language is obviously the primary referent system, but Williamson shows how, for example, social myths referring to the distinctions between nature and culture structure the messages of many

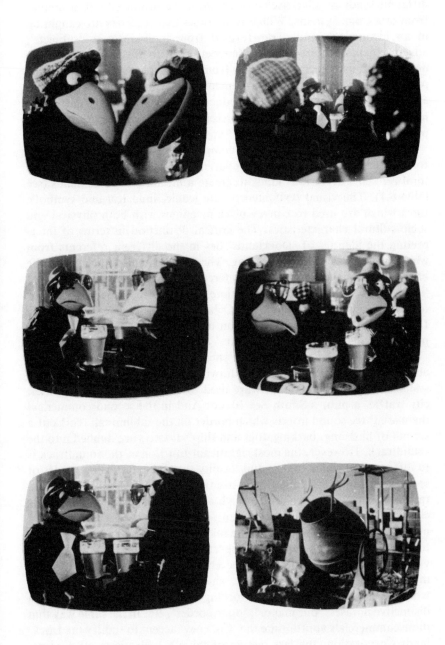

Figure 6.4   The final commercial in the 1982-3 campaign (June 1983)

different kinds of advertisement. By investing products with meanings from other sign systems, Williamson argues that receivers are caught up in an ideological bind. Transformed from individuals to 'subjects', advertisements require that we 'cooperate' with them in making the necessary transference of meaning from the referent sign system to the product. Simultaneously, advertisements offer us pictures of ourselves, as we might be if we consume the product. In the example of the telephone-heads (figure 6.1), individuals are presented with a very disturbing image of what they might be if they 'buy' any other location.

The television commercials are complex texts within which different forms of signs are structured by a variety of codes. These draw on cul-tural referents of various kinds to create a meaning for Docklands (see table 6.1). The visual texts incorporate iconic, indexical and symbolic signs which are used to convey place meanings with both physical and socio-cultural characteristics. The critical distinction in terms of inter-preting the identity of 'Docklands' lies in the different referents from which the signs draw their meaning. These we have distinguished on the basis of 'material' and 'mythical' referents. Thus, within the category of 'iconic signs', the commercials connote London through representations of material landmarks – Nelson's Column, Tower Bridge (taken as the LDDC logo), the Tower of London and the River Thames. Mythical place referents are the idealised 'City' and 'Docklands' signs.'

The indexical and symbolic signs encode both aural and visual associ-ations and function primarily by drawing on referents from other sign systems. Sounds, for example, are used to connote different localities: city traffic, a pub, a South Sea island. And in the second commercial there are three sound inserts which border on the subliminal: tenths of a second of birdsong, barking dogs and ship's hooters are dubbed into the soundtrack. However, the most significant function of the soundtrack is to differentiate class, culture and locality through contrasting modes of speech. Crucially, the (male) voice-over is not official, Standard English, rather the LDDC is signified through a subtle, but distinctive working-class 'Cockney' accent. The slogan – 'Why move to the middle of nowhere when you *can* move to the middle of *Lon*don?' – is impossible to convey in print but emphasizes the 'can' and 'London' in a unique and very distinctive way. The 'local' accent is evident in the second com-mercial with a Cockney Beefeater, and most pronounced in the third where every character uses a working-class, East End idiolect with distinctive phrases: 'our manor'; 'out of order', etc. In the same way that these commercials appropriate the 'Cockney' accent to signify the Dock-lands Corporation, the last section of table 6.1 identifies other visual elements which connote class and locality: bowler hats and briefcases signify 'middle-class businessmen'; fedora hats, dark glasses and wide ties signify 'working-class, East End criminals'.

Williamson argues that 'all signs depend for their signifying process on the existence of specific, concrete receivers, people *for* whom and in whose systems of belief they have a meaning' (1982: 40). The transference depends on our cooperating, and humour is used to make us 'work' to decipher the advertisement. These commercials are funny but they acquire their humour and coherence from another sign system, that of television itself. The first commercial refers to *The Fall and Rise of Reginald Perrin*, a BBC situation comedy about a redundant, rebellious businessman, which had large audiences during 1981. The actor Leonard Rossiter reads the lines for the New Town crow, while the 'boss crow' rehearses C.J.'s key phrase 'I didn't get where I am today . . . '. In the second commercial, direct associations are drawn with caricatures of Alan Whicker who makes documentaries in exotic places, and Jimmy Saville who is known nationally for his catch-phrases and jogging activities.

The third commercial exploits the current preoccupation of both television and film with representations of working-class localities in London, in series like *The Sweeney* (ITV), *Minder* (ITV), and feature films such as *The Long Good Friday*. A dominant theme in these portrayals is criminality in East End communities: small-time crooks, petty crime and drinking clubs. At the same time, the shadow of serious crime and gang warfare lurks beneath the surface. The Kray twins were imprisoned in the 1960s for a series of murders and violent crimes in the East End of London. The commercial draws on a myth of the East End as a criminal, working-class locality through its use of the *Minder* genre: a pub/club interior, a distinctive idiomatic dialogue, the voice of Glynn Edwards, one of the main actors in the series, and a direct reference to 'Arthur' – the principal character in *Minder*, who never quite manages to pull off his shady deals. It also puns the Kray/Crow connection and gangland murders.

To what extent did the business people we interviewed decode the commercials in these ways? The view of one director in Cannon summarized the majority view: 'The ads are making people aware of the docklands. They need to know how it is and the ads are helping to create an identity.' The identity emerged partly from the meanings given to the animations. Over 70 per cent of the sample recognized the TV ads and remembered the crows. Nelson's Column and Tower Bridge attracted most comments. Most interviewees were enthusiastic and amused by the ads, greeting the story-boards with a smile and spontaneous acknowledgements. 'That's the guy. I think that's good.' The association and

Table 6.1 The signification of Docklands

	Commercial 1 'Nelson's Column'	Commercial 2 'Tower of London'	Commercial 3 'East London pub'
A. *Iconic signs*			
i: with material place referents	Nelson's Column Tower Bridge The River Thames	Tower of London Tower Bridge The River	
ii: with mythical place referents		Warehouses = 'Docklands' Cranes PO Tower St Paul's = 'The City' Office blocks	
B. *Indexical and symbolic signs*			
i: aural:			
a) with environmental referents	Traffic	Cheering crowds Hawaiian guitars Bird song Barking dogs Ship's hooters	Pub conversation

B. Indexical and symbolic signs (cont.)

	Official English	'Pronounced' Official English / Welsh / 'Subtle' Cockney	'Pronounced' Cockney with East London idioms / 'Subtle' Cockney
b) dialect & idiomatic speech with mythical regional/socio-cultural referents			
ii: Visual:			
a) Calligraphic with material place referents	Logo	Tower of London - signboard; London Enterprize Zone - signboard; Logo; 'Pronounced' Cockney; 'Subtle' Cockney	
b) Props with mythical socio-cultural referents	Bowler hats / Briefcases / Financial Times / Pocket watch = 'middle-class business men'	Royal Coach / Livery/Beefeaters = Historic London; Stetsons / Glasses / Headscarves / Cameras = 'tourists'; Bowler hats / Financial Times / Briefcases = 'Middle-class business men'	Tweed caps / Pints of beer / Piano = 'Working-class East End'; Fedora hats / Dark glasses / White/striped kipper ties = 'Working-class East End criminal'

pleasure came primarily from the humour in the ads. 'I like these, always did. Terrific. Humour is very important in advertising places. It's something to liven it up.' Only one person – in advertising himself – raised the question of animation: 'Could be any animation: "friendly crows". Could be anything – crocodiles, if you like. Advertising is 90 per cent bullshit.' For others, the crows were appropriate and seemed 'to stick in your mind'. One woman read the connection between the idea of distance and the crow: 'I loved the crows. A silly symphony . . . as the crow flies appealed to me because I'd been telling people how close it was.' In terms of reading the codes beneath the surface of the commercials, only one respondent picked up the associations with television. 'I was very taken with the ads but they didn't put the EZ in mind. Heard Rossiter – "I didn't get where I am today . . ." I was so busy being amused that it didn't strike home.'

The clearest example of people bringing their own meanings to the advertisements is the extent to which the crows become part of a locality. A number of people read the commercials in terms of an identifiable place, but it was the East End rather than Docklands – 'The crows really go with the East End'; while one or two enjoyed the gangster commercial: 'A classic. Real East End characters. It really caught you knowing the character of the area. I like these, they are ads on our level. It wasn't the crow, could have been any bird, but it was just the way the crow put himself about. They appeal to people who know the area, like me.' It could be argued that the commercial, through its appropriation of *Minder*, is offering the respondent a mirror-image of himself, the way he would like 'to put himself about'.

The most critical reactions to the commercial came from two community-based organizations with offices in the Enterprise Zone. A member of the Docklands Community Posters project said that she 'was offended by the Kray association. The East End isn't criminal', and argued that 'the appropriation of the name of the area confuses the institution [i.e. the LDDC] with the local area. They always present Docklands as an area without a local population. The gangsters image is geared towards ignoring local people. It's geared towards outside entrepreneurs. The ads put us off. They created a sleazy image.' This view, as that expressed earlier about the animation, reflects the experience of individuals who have expertise in the field of visual image-making: the DCP produce photomontage posters critical of the LDDC. It is not the general view of the small locally-based businesses in the Enterprise Zone.

Conclusions

The conclusions to be drawn about the role of place advertising and its impact on small firms will depend on whether we take an economic or a critical stance towards the advertising system itself. From the economic standpoint, it is clear that the Docklands campaign had a significant impact on the small firms relocating in the Enterprise Zone. Some companies were directly stimulated to seek premises within the area through advertising material. Many others were influenced by the messages in more subtle ways. The essential problem facing small firms is the high risk of failure. These entrepreneurs need to boost their own self-confidence and to feel that their business is associated with a successful enterprise. They need to feel that the 'authorities' are giving them encouragement and support. Clearly, the promotional activities of the LDDC are providing psychological and commercial reinforcement for their location decisions. This was in sharp contrast to the generally critical view of the LDDC's attitude to small businesses in their formal dealings with them. Area advertising is significant for the development of local economic self-confidence, in communicating and pulling together in people's minds the effects of other forms of incentive.

From a critical perspective, the analysis reveals the complexity of commercials and the sophistication through which they create an amusingly 'transparent' message. The television commercials and associated posters had indeed succeeded in changing negative attitudes to Docklands in a way that seems to have been rare in other area promotions. They did so by manipulating the undoubted cultural power and significance of popular television programmes. It was not the *reality* of East London that was presented in dressed-up form to sceptical recipients, as so often happens in area advertising. Instead, the commercials 'invited' the audience to connote meaning to the changes taking place in Docklands through associations with popular television programmes and characters. The largely unintentional effect was that small local entrepreneurs had their confidence in the development prospects boosted by this creative strategy.

Raymond Williams has argued that advertising is a kind of 'organized fantasy' which pretends 'to a linkage of values between quite mundane products and the now generally unattached values of love, respect, significance or fulfilment' (1980: 193). With the development of area promotions, places have become products offering emotional and economic benefits to their 'consumers'. Thus, the richness and diversity of the specific localities within East London have been reduced to a commodity to be packaged and sold. And perhaps what is more important

about the GGT campaign, certainly when compared to other place promotions, is that the 'meaning' of Docklands is being created primarily
through the transference of fantasies and myths from television
programmes. Nothing in these commercials signifies geographical or
cultural realities.

Turning finally to conclusions about the qualitative methods employed
in this piece of research, we believe that the combination of semi-
structured interviews, story-boards and a semiotic analysis of the
structure of the television commercials has afforded insights into
subjective aspects of the process of location decision-making that cannot
be explored in other ways. Conventional questionnaire studies in
economic geography tend to take what people say at face value. But the
complexity of place images, the interpenetration of personal, economic
and cultural factors, requires an interpretive stance – one which
recognizes that language and meaning are not self-evident. The open-
ended comments, the readings of the story-boards and the deconstruction of the advertisements reveal the extent to which place meanings are
sedimented into people's everyday understanding and behaviour through
the activities of the mass media.

Note

We wish to thank the LDDC for permission to reproduce the commercials in this
chapter.

References

Agnew, J. (1987) *Place and politics*, Allen and Unwin, London.
Blonsky, M. (ed.) (1985) *On signs: a semiotics reader*, Basil Blackwell, Oxford.
Burgess, J. (1985) 'News from Nowhere: the press, the riots and the myth of the
    inner city', in J. Burgess and J. R. Gold (eds), *Geography, the media and
    popular culture*, Croom Helm, London, 192–228.
Burgess, J. (1982) 'Selling places: environmental images for the executive',
    Regional Studies, 16, 1–17.
Cosgrove, D. and Jackson, P. (1987) 'New directions in cultural geography',
    Area 19, 95–101.
Damesick, P. and Wood, P. (eds) (1987) *Regional problems, problem regions and
    public policy*, Oxford University Press, Oxford.
Dyer, G. (1982) *Advertising as communication*, Methuen, London.
Fox, S. (1984) *The mirror makers – a history of American advertising and its
    creators*, Morrow, New York.
Gauthier, G. (1976) *The semiology of the image*, British Film Institute, London.

Greater London Council (1985) *Four year review of the LDDC*, Docklands Consultative Committee.

Hall, S. (1982) 'Encoding/decoding', in S. Hall, D. Hobson, A. Lowe and P. Willis (eds), *Culture, media, language*, Hutchinson, London, 128–38.

HMSO (1973) *London Docklands*, Travers Morgan, London.

Keating, P. J. (1973) 'Fact and fiction in the East End', in H. J. Dyos and M. Wolff (eds), *The Victorian city: images and realities*, vol. 2, Routledge and Kegan Paul, London, 585–602.

Langholtz, L. V. (1975) *The hidden myth*, Heinemann, London.

Ledgerwood, G. (1984) *Urban innovation: strategic planning in London Docklands, 1968–1978*, Gower, London.

Markusen, A. R. and Teitz, M. B. (1985) 'The world of small business: turbulence and survival', in D. J. Storey (ed.), *Small firms in regional economic development*, Cambridge University Press, Cambridge, 193–218.

Mason, C. M. and Harrison, R. T. (1985) 'The geography of small firms in the UK: towards a research agenda', *Progress in Human Geography*, 9, 1–37.

Morton-Williams, J. (1985) 'Making qualitative research work – aspects of administration', in R. Walker, (ed.), *Applied qualitative research*, Gower, Aldershot, 27–44.

Nye, D. E. (1985) *Image worlds: corporate identities at General Electric, 1890–1930*, MIT Press, London.

Ogilvy, D. (1964) *Confessions of an advertising man*, Longmans, London.

Saussure, F. de (1916, 1979) *A course in general linguistics*, Fontana, London.

Williams, R. (1980) 'Advertising: magic system', in R. Williams, *Problems in materialism and culture*, Verso, London, 170–95.

Williamson, J. (1982) *Decoding advertisements: ideology and meaning in advertising*, Marion Boyars, London.

Wood, P. A. (1987) 'Behavioural approaches to industrial location studies', in W. F. Lever, (ed.), *Industrial change in the United Kingdom*, Longman, London, 38–55.

Worpole, K. (1983) *Dockers and detectives*, Verso, London.

Young, K. and Mason, C. (eds) (1983) *Urban economic development: new roles and relationships*, Macmillan, London.

7

Social Interaction and Conflict over Residential Growth
A Structuration Perspective

David Evans

Introduction

With the increase of theoretical discourse in social geography in recent years discussion of interaction has been relatively eclipsed. It is the primary purpose of this chapter to correct what I view as an imbalance in this respect. In the first part of the chapter this theme is developed in terms of the long-standing, but often neglected, tradition of qualitative research which has undergone revival and extension with the increase in theoretical discourse. These claims are then demonstrated both by reference to examples in the literature which have come some of the way to accepting this perspective and through a detailed case-study undertaken by the author in Canada, which links the study of social interaction to conflict generated over residential growth on the urban fringe.

It is noteworthy in this respect that relatively few recent reviews of social geography refer directly to interaction as a discrete topic. One clear exception to this, however, is Jackson and Smith (1984) in which interaction and community identity are touched on in a consideration of the legacy of the Chicago school and the reinterpretation of its contribution in a non-positivist light. That the development of the subject should owe so much to yet another revival of a one-time discredited area of study is perhaps paradoxical, but nevertheless the tradition stemming not so much from the ecological aspects of Park's work but rather his pragmatism or 'moral order' (Park, 1926) and subsequently social interactionism (Mead, 1934) is viewed here as forming one part of an understanding of qualitative research. The other one stems from Giddens' exposition of structuration in the explanation of social phenomena (Giddens, 1979; 1982). These two threads will be brought together in this chapter, and the utility of so doing pursued in a case-study.

Social interaction and social thought

The importance of distinguishing two distinct aspects to the work of the Chicago school is now better recognized and need not be reviewed further (Ley, 1983; Jackson and Smith, 1984, chapter 4). Park's pragmatism, which included recognizing the importance of everyday experience in the formulation of interaction and group relations, has been much more clearly carried forward in sociological as opposed to geographical research. Perhaps best known in social geography in Suttles' work on inner city territoriality (Suttles, 1968), although as the subject has widened other work in this strongly anthropological bent is being appreciated (see Duncan, 1978, for a detailed example; and Ley, 1983, for general discussion). These illustrations are more than intersubjective reconstructions of the life-worlds of particular social groups and the interaction that bonds them, however. The hermeneutical importance of such studies has never been lost on the Chicago school, even if only implicitly, in the sense that all action has a particular context or frame of reference in which it takes place. The content of this is much more problematical, however, in the work of Chicago sociologists. Park's original studies were undertaken in an atmosphere of humanism and qualified optimism for the future of capitalism – this indeed was the main facet of pragmatism, although Ley (1983) does not accept this interpretation. It is not surprising, therefore, that recent radical geography has dismissed their contribution as naive and even justifying the status quo. Symbolic interactionism, on the other hand, includes a perspective which views reality as socially produced through the meanings given to objects by individual and group action – inherently then dealing with communication. It has, however, been criticized as falling uneasily between individual and society, even though this should be its strength in overcoming the antinomy between the two (Duncan, 1980).

In an environment where structuralist thought derived primarily from Marxism has tended to straightjacket social groups into rigid and generally unproblematical divisions along class lines, it might seem that there can be no meeting of interactionist theory and questions thought of as belonging to 'society in general'. I want to suggest that this is a flawed assumption, for whilst a too narrowly defined radicalism cannot accommodate status as opposed to class, there is no reason why interactionist theory cannot make a substantial contribution to radical debate. Indeed this makes strong sense since problems have occurred within Marxism over translating structural categories to actual active class actions (Jackson and Smith, 1984: 63).

Central to this assertion is the view that the theory of structuration epistemologically links questions of the objective basis of society with the ways in which its members construct and then reproduce their everyday reality within this. The crucial link between these two lines of thought is meaning and its hermeneutical basis. As outlined above, symbolic interactionism posits that all objects carry meaning which is socially constructed through group reference – these meanings may be shared within a small or large group but set definite parameters within which norms operate therein. Within social geography these constructs have been used to examine landscape identity. Duncan (1976; 1983) in particular has investigated different social landscapes to see how these are maintained and frequently threatened by other symbols of identity. Stable groups require these symbols less overtly because other rules are utilized, through peer group action for example. From these analyses whole social group divisions can be examined and their landscape identities explained.

Change is not easily dealt with in this framework, as readily admitted by symbolic interactionists, and therefore some other theoretical approach is required to supplement this. Structuration can tackle this difficulty because hermeneutically its framework of reference is wider. Giddens (1982) shows that post-positivist social theory became too subjectivist in its search to stress human construction of reality because it feared relapsing into structural thought which was itself too deterministic of action. Much 1970s social geography examining the life-world can be faulted for this over-reaction. Ley (1978) offers a good overview of the problem but concludes by rejecting a balanced perspective. As a result no explanation of human action is forwarded. On the other hand, structuralist theories of community have simply viewed them as 'bearers' of the wishes of finance capital, for example in creating suburbs, reducing them to the level of contingent relations only (Walker, 1981).

In structuration, however, 'structure is not a constraint or a barrier to action but is instead essentially involved in its reproduction' (Giddens, 1979: 10) and 'neither human agent nor society or social institutions should be regarded as having primacy. Each is constituted in and through recurrent practices' (Giddens, 1982: 8). By this Giddens means that actors as 'agents', in drawing on the norms and interpretative schemes provided by previously defined rules ('structure'), must reproduce this same set of governing guidelines to action. But in doing so they display an understanding of the practicality of everyday life revealed in those 'structures' which essentially removes from them the element of constraint or barrier. These rules are communicated through a common body of knowledge. Hence action and structure in the sense defined are

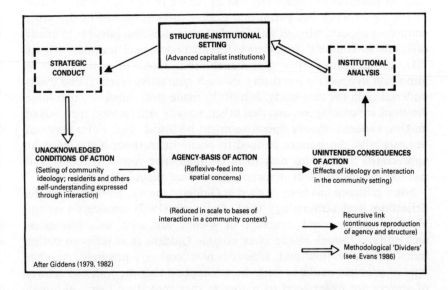

Figure 7.1   The theory of structuration and social interaction

recursive – each constitutes and guides the other. This does not make for a static social structure (recurrent practices), however, because all action involves both unanticipated or unacknowledged conditions and unintended consequences. The former deals largely with the ideology or taken-for-granted assumptions behind action, the latter the unforeseen outcomes of it, which may of course challenge the nature of recurrent practices and modify them. This schema is illustrated in figure 7.1 in terms of social interaction in a community-based study, such as will be outlined later, and more discussion of the complete framework is provided in Evans (1987).

As Giddens (1982) points out, there is actually a double hermeneutic within this approach – the meaning given by the social actor (observed) and that of the researcher. Cultural anthropologists would no doubt claim that this has long been accepted within their research, but this reflexiveness is somewhat more novel in qualitative research in sociology and geography.

Macro-theory as posited by Giddens needs to be made more specific when examining social interaction. There is no logical difficulty in reducing the scale to particular cultures and groups provided that the reference is both meaningful to actor and researcher alike (see figure 7.1). In practical examples this will be shown to be equivalent to much interactionist work but permitting change to be examined in the wider context of society, without reifying that term. It is also possible to create divisions in Giddens' framework for methodological purposes (figure 7.1), distinguishing structural issues from those of action; this is important in applying the theory through qualitative research and this is undertaken in the case-study. It must be made clear, however, that these divisions are contingent, and that other, equally satisfactory, methods of making Giddens' theory operative might be found. This claim may rest uneasily with those more attuned to positivist method, but it must be appreciated that in this new form of qualitative research, theory and method cannot be easily divorced, nor indeed should they be.

Some criticism has been levelled at Giddens' theory, particularly in the definitions and terminology used. Dallmayr (1982) considers that the ideas of systems and structure of society are used with too much ambiguity, although in the same volume Giddens is at pains to define terms such as 'action' and 'recurrent practices' very precisely. Another type of problem could lie with the assumption that the wider structures of society are understood by actors as they reproduce them, although again Giddens is aware of this and notes that unconscious action is being considered as well. However the original impetus for the theory of structuration does owe much to studies of relatively closed cultures (Bourdieu, 1977) where change is slow.

Probably the most serious criticism yet brought against Giddens is that structuration is too abstract to be translated to empirical research (see Gregson, 1987 in particular). For Gregson, structuration is a second-order theory and no way can be found to use rational abstraction to translate its constructs to meaningful empirical contexts. Now all this is fine in the world of realist philosophy where very specific and limiting rules are followed to judge theory, but it seems to be rather bad sociology and anthropology. Why should theory be constrained to these narrow bases of judgement in a reality where irrationality is present, where some practices appear to be ahistorical whereas others are extremely specific to time and place? Gregson appears to fear relativism, but this is necessary to understand the historically specific. After all, to take a simple example, the Trobriand Islander might use a table as a shelter whereas we write papers on it, but this does not mean that cultures switch arbitrarily from one meaning of the object to the other. These diverse meanings do come together relationally in a structured way within a society, however, and it is one of the primary aims of this chapter to demonstrate this.

In the final analysis Gregson wants more of structuration than it can offer: it can never directly generate substantive issues, for it is a theory of action and its consequences. Even though Giddens has further refined the detail of the theory, this basic aspect has not changed. Although I agree with Gregson that structuration offers an ontology of society, fundamentally it is epistemological, dealing with communication and ways of knowing ground rules of action. A more balanced interpretation is offered by Duncan (1985), who explores the social-psychological link between action and structure through Giddens, bringing to bear the importance of ideology and unequal power of actors – an aspect of structuration which is weak in Giddens, even though he is acutely aware of power relations in his writings generally. There have, of course, been a number of other attempts to use structuration as an empirical referent, but most of these fail to return to the core of Giddens' argument after paying initial lip-service (see Thrift, 1986).

Social interaction and localism: A review and case-study

In the previous section I have tried to demonstrate that the study of social interaction has not been closely allied to radical developments in the subject itself, and that structuration can aid in filling in this missing link. The reasons for this hitherto unappreciated link have been reinforced by the tendency for studies of social interaction to take an extremely localist interpretation, at least in social geography. By this I mean that the structure of groups and the extent of interaction are usually seen as spatially very limited (community and neighbourhood identities, suburban 'enclaves', inner city ghettoes, for example). This is not surprising given that positivist social geography has assumed that proximity is in and of itself a means to measure and define social groups (Fischer, 1976). Loose ideas of localism have also been defined by surrogate measures of neighbourliness and the spatial extent of networks (Fischer and Jackson, 1976).

More recently there has been an attempt to link ideas of localism or locale with the wider structures of society and this ·has become most evident in the work which is being actively pursued in the United Kingdom through the ESRC urban and regional systems study. This has led to differences in interpretation of localities research (Smith, 1987; and reply in Cooke, 1987). Smith is wary of 'the empirical turn', fearing a relapse to ideographic place studies with an abstracted theory bearing little relevance to this. Notwithstanding the taunts of realism (a perspective to which I do not subscribe) that a meeting of abstract theory of necessary relations and empirical reality founded on contingent relations is impossible, I think that Cooke's answer is essentially correct. Research involves fundamentally (still!) exploration and the discovery of new knowledge in the field; this is as true now by becoming a consultant at the sharp end of economic restructuring as it was when Engels ran his cotton factory. This is part of the 'clinical inference' to which Cooke alludes. Structuration is not simply 'dynamic structuralism' (Smith, 1987), nor a theory to be tested in some positivistic way. It must find empirical referents, and a single case-study will not throw up all aspects of the substantive research issue under investigation. My own study below is no exception and I would not claim an all-embracing explanation of advanced capitalist society from it.

Within social geography more specifically there have been some studies examining locale which have not simply used the term as an organizing or typological tool but have sought to explain social interaction and identity through it; that is, the content of the group and its coherence is defined. General definitions of localism are outlined, some examples detailed, and a wider interpretation of the term given which can be applied to the case-study. Not all aspects of the term are explored as this would require a separate chapter in its own right.

Localism has often assumed that there are 'limited horizons', a belief that in terms of identity no interest in or commitment to places far from one's own is held. More crucially the social, economic and political issues that dominate those spaces are also viewed as irrelevant, a most crucial point, since it can be seen that in reality this is unlikely to be the case and the strategic conduct of capitalist institutions will affect these locales. Localism as a generic term has been used widely in political studies and associated with metropolitan fragmentation (see Evans, 1984 for a short review). In more fundamental terms it is also essential to the definition of property. More specific links again to the development of capitalist institutions have been made by Bell and Newby (1978) who see localism as a guide to social control itself. The local spheres of influence found in pre-capitalist society were broken down by the expanding market. Locally-oriented interests subsequently reappeared, however, through an ideology of community, particularly neighbourhood units which were to guide local loyalties and social control. Inter-war planned neighbourhood units are given as one example of these; others could be added from unplanned suburban 'defensive' spaces to inner-city enclaves, depending on the identity so defined.

This approach is rather too functional without further clarification, which can be found in the social interactionist perspective outlined in the first part of the chapter. Landscape identity is used to communicate cues as to the socially-shared meaning of tastes and identities, which both define the extent and content of social interaction. Duncan (1981) has sought to expand this idea further in an intriguing set of papers which examine the meaning of the objects within the home in market society. This aims to balance earlier work which has shown that to middle-class social groups the local landscape matters more than it does to other groups, hence a symbolic defence of the community results particularly when unacceptable symbols threaten to intrude. Duncan and Duncan (1984) have also compared upper-class group landscapes in North American cities, arguing that their control derives from the social status invested into these, itself part of market society norms. There is, however, a far less clearly stated theoretical position in this later work which may devalue its contribution to a better appreciation of social interactionism.

The concept of localism can in fact be taken further (Evans, 1984; 1987). With particular reference to 'turf' defence, protecting our own or 'defensive' space, social group identity is very much linked to fear of symbolic presence. This symbolic avoidance behavior, so-called because money can be used temporarily as wealth to buy the desired exclusion of undesirable objects and persons, can be outlined as follows. Social groups who maintain a certain consensus of status identity through shared landscape cues will aim to preserve that identity via landscape control, and exclude objects threatening to their esteem. These same objects mediate between the social group, other status groups and institutions representing the wider external world, so that particular symbols are associated with them. For example, cluster homes may be associated with lower-income groups and the developers and planners who have given institutional backing to their intrusion. Wider societal change is important, since the landscape identity can seemingly be preserved by the apparent substitution of space for time. For example, as long as locales are available in which to implement ideologies, then other communities can resist change, but only up to a point, as will be seen in the case study. These aspects of identity construction both define and are in part created through social interaction in locales.

The foregoing review and explanation of localism is now developed further by reference to a case-study (Evans, 1987). Primary emphasis is placed on a community within the Greater Vancouver Regional District of Canada where no-growth policies and sentiment impinged considerably on local groups and their interaction. The nature of qualitative research undertaken is discussed both in terms of Giddens' framework – the grounding of structuration in an empirical context – and in demonstrating its general value in the study of social interaction.

The selected municipality, the District of West Vancouver, is a well-established community of over 36,000, lying in the north-west corner of the Greater Vancouver Region under the range of mountains which form a backcloth to Vancouver itself. Figure 7.2 shows the setting of West Vancouver and details of the sites referred to below. Research was conducted during a six-month period during 1977, and then selectively until 1984 on the response of the community to growth pressures, in particular for new tracts of middle and upper-market housing on the mountain slopes. A mixture of conventional and more novel qualitative methods were employed including semi-structured interviews with planning officers, newspaper content analysis and absorption into the community through contacts and attendance at key meetings, involving some participant observation. Such analyses were not, however, aimed solely at describing or classifying actions, but involved searching for wider consequences. The process of synthesis could not be undertaken at the time of research investigation – indeed, the large majority of the work was completed before Giddens' theory was published. I make no apology for this timetable, nor is it critical, for the application of structuration depends on a detailed 'taking-apart' of findings and their reconstruction into the wider context in which these actions have taken place. In an earlier paper (Evans, 1984) this was referred to as descending the ladder to the least chaotic conceptions (those based on suburbanites' sentiments, for example) and then reclimbing it to build in the implications of those localist actions. From this 'suburb' could be seen to take on a wide set of meanings, but neither arbitrary nor based on a subjective typology as had been apparent in much previous research.

It was during this research that an awareness grew of the locality as a 'defensible space', both in the more commonly known sense of exclusionary social practices aimed at ethnic and lower-income groups (e.g. Danielson, 1976; and Johnston, 1984), and in a newer sense of anti-growth sentiment opposing the entry of *any* social group into new housing landscapes. This led to a definite view of localism in the sense discussed generally in the previous section, which as a force in social interaction (see Evans, 1984) can be interpreted in terms of the structuration thesis.

The municipality developed as a series of largely disconnected villages, always hemmed between mountain and water, which over time became linked through urbanization. The District Council had a reputation for excluding industrial development from these early days and until the 1960s large-scale commercial activity as well (Walden, 1947). The general residential development since the Second World War had at the start of the research resulted in the community being viewed as middle- to upper-

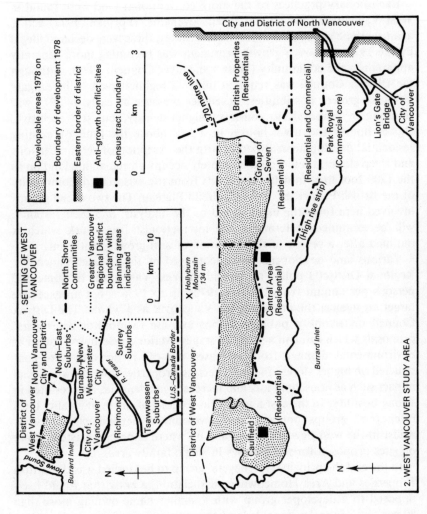

Figure 7.2   Setting of West Vancouver and the study area

class, popular with in-migrants of the *nouveaux riches*, which earned it the label of 'Martini Mountain', an image in keeping with an exclusive suburb. Excluding the commercial core and contiguous blocks along the waterfront, where high-rise development is dominant, virtually all residential areas are single-family with densities as low as one to the acre.

Exclusionary practices of the more conventional kind were found in West Vancouver through 'restricted covenants' (Forman, 1971) acting against ethnic groups. As in the United States, these were declared illegal by the 1970s, but zero-growth sentiment was becoming more generally apparent in the community (West Vancouver Council, 1975). Although the District Council was required under a regional plan to investigate seriously growth possibilities, developer pressure as early as 1975 was resulting in proposals to construct higher-density, but still exclusive, cluster homes and town houses in a belt above the limit of existing residential development. Broadly, with the exception of certain canyons and steep slopes, these would ultimately occupy all remaining land up to the 1200 foot line, moving westwards from the existing sub-community of the British Properties to the Caulfeild Plateau. The two social groups involved here form the main strand of the analysis, and their response will be examined in terms of the interactionist framework which is outlined after a review of the evolution of anti-growth sentiment.

Various land developers were encouraged by the Greater Vancouver Regional District's policy to expand in West Vancouver by some 500 persons per annum from the late 1970s up to 1986 – not an excessive target set against the proposals for Vancouver as a whole. The District Council undertook a public relations exercise to monitor developers' proposals which came in a series of stages. Major concern was voiced at environmental damage from increased run-off if housing were constructed on higher slopes, in turn affecting properties lower down. Social impact such as household mix and increased net densities also resulted in strong hostility. In the east and central sections of the municipality local ratepayers' groups opposed any development beyond existing sites, whilst in the west new groups sprang up where none had existed before on sites proposed for townhouses in single-family areas.

In the east the principal ratepayers' group to be studied was the British Properties and Area Homeowners Association, a body that found itself opposed to a developer group with a similar name owning more than 80 per cent of the developable land above the existing limit. In Canadian terms the British Pacific Properties formed a very striking landscape with a 'gate' entrance and curvilinear structure. Referring to Giddens' framework the unacknowledged conditions of action of the group mirrored those of the community as a whole and were based on an assumption, rarely stated, that West Vancouver was in some way 'outside' the norms of advanced capitalist society and hence not subject to speculative development or indeed any kind of overt business ethic. Nevertheless links could not be denied – the chief director of the Association was a vice-president of a major industrial group, and its policy and planning officer the former editor of one of the city's newspapers. The views of the Association were largely expressed through an annual news-sheet, insidiously titled *Tally Ho!*, which acted as a medium for uniting this group in its attempts to prevent new housing development.

Socially the homeowners of British Pacific Properties were largely seen as *nouveaux riches* by the other groups in West Vancouver. Furthermore no established resident of the sub-community would ever publicly accept that he or she resided there – only those at the very bottom of the social ladder, and of recent arrival, made public expression of their status. This view was ratified during a public meeting at which a resident opposing new growth was later reported in the local press as a 'newcomer' to British Pacific Properties. Other investigations through council officials (West Vancouver Council, 1977) suggested that the external stereotype of British Properties was that it had the only strong Homeowners' Association in the municipality. This was backed up by an exaggeration of the *nouveaux riches* image in the city-wide press, with typifications of avid status expression. Examples included the ownership of large single-family homes, but no income to furnish them whilst keeping garden meticulously in order. In practice, however, the Association was viewed as politically weak by older established elite groups in the west of the community such as the Caulfeild Property Owners Association. This and other central area social groups took the attitude that the British Properties should be given 'first chance' to oppose new housing and having failed would let the established groups take over. This was a paradoxical development given that the Caulfeild sub-community only formed any sort of a claim to represent community feeling when conflict over landscape control became rampant throughout West Vancouver. Clearly, elite groups were supposed to be sufficiently well known that they did not normally require expression through ratepayers' groups!

Differences between the two main social groups in the community were most evident in the question of landscape control and identity. This became a central issue in opposition to new housing since population growth as such was something of a red-herring. From 1971 to 1976 West Vancouver experienced zero population growth but considerable house-hold formation, the total remaining close to 36,400 (Census of Canada, 1976). This was connected to most of the opposition to new growth which focused on provision for smaller families including younger professionals and executives in up-market townhouses and condominiums often fetching higher prices than existing single-family properties. At public meetings it was generally argued, however, that these types of home would lead to the in-migration of lower-income families and it was here that symbolic contamination as defined in the previous section of the chapter emerged.

This reaction was not quite the same in the two main social groups, however. In the case of the British Properties and Homeowners' Association great play was made on overt features of the landscape itself. A letter stated: 'Why should we be subjected to a 3000 townhouse development in a fine residential area such as this . . . [the road] should be untouched and a 600 foot greenbelt retained at the end of [it]' (*North Shore News*, 4 May 1977). This type of comment was backed up by a small pressure group which acted independently of the main Association at public meetings. In keeping with the image of the British Properties it called itself 'The Group of Seven' after a famous set of Canadian artists of the same name, and which included landscape painting in its work. Social degeneration of the area was associated with higher densities than previously agreed under zoning ordinances which the Association believed were going to be imposed on them by the municipal council.

Central ratepayers' groups, who did not have to sustain the *nouveaux riches* image, tended to focus closely on environmental damage caused by increased run-off on the higher slopes. This more considered opposition was also evident in the Caulfeild part of the community. One petition from the Association here well represents the use of symbolic landscape stereotyping, in addition to the other tactics used that were similar to the British Properties Association, such as zoning alterations. This accepted that some new housing development was inevitable to satisfy the Greater Vancouver Regional District's demands and to spread the burden of costs associated with drainage improvements on the mountain side. All in all this was a more realistic attitude than that expressed by the British Properties Association. The petition then suggested adding only one new access road with the town house development, which it was claimed 'would not pass a single existing home'. More closely questioned on the explanation for this view one petitioner responded: 'Well, townhouses and access roads go together, don't they? If these people will be living in townhouses then they should put up with busy roads.' This is an excellent example of symbolic typification, illustrating the (unacknowledged) reification of a group who are deemed to be of a different status. It is argued that there is a type of household right for a townhouse and which must 'suffer' access roads with that identity. In this way the social group was able to preserve some of its own identity whilst controlling access to the landscape.

Of course, the overall group representation within West Vancouver as a whole was considerably more unified in the face of growth proposals. Previous positivist research on social interaction has tended to throw up red herrings here by attempting to measure linkages and structures in the context of a defined network. Yet the real distinction is between the subtle but real differences across a social group and what Suttles (1972; 1984) calls the 'representative image' or 'average differences' that are used to give identity to one group or landscape over another. Even if there are variations in perspective individuals will nevertheless attempt to live up to these representative images and often let them guide their social and political norms. These are part of the recursive agency-structure link which has become imbued in the group.

So far little mention has been made of the unintended consequences of action, which themselves can aid in building a wider perspective than might at first appear. These can be seen to have effects both on the locale itself and in the wider structural setting: as suggested above these should not be seen as epistemological distinctions – they serve methodologically to demonstrate how the use of a structuration thesis adds to previous approaches. Both affect the form and the content of the social inter-action examined.

In the case of West Vancouver the internal consequences of the anti-growth sentiment defined by political localism were largely expressed through socio-demographic changes. As a result of higher house prices the possibility of an increasingly ageing population arose, due to the reduction of in-migration of younger families with children, a position directly contradictory to the 'average image' held up of the community. In turn this was viewed as having undesirable consequences on community life, making it 'unbalanced' with falling school enrolment and reduced use of facilities.

Such a conclusion is fairly consistent with findings in more con-ventional community studies. But the wider consequences of such senti-ment, if successful, could be seen to lead to a major contradiction for the social groups of West Vancouver, in that ultimately anti-growth would challenge the very foundations of the business ethic upon which these groups claimed their lifestyles and source of employment, even though this was denied as applicable to 'their' community. Several developers and many businessmen were living in the community and active in rate-payers' groups, as has been seen; on these contradictions they were remarkably quiet. Their former belief that West Vancouver could some-how exist 'outside' capitalism only survived whilst the land development industry had elsewhere to go; when this ended due to city policies of growth restriction, the myth was shattered. This is consistent with structuration as suggested above – spatial expansion is used in an attempt to avoid in situ temporal change. Referring to figure 7.1, through the institutional procedures that in turn affected the unacknowledged conditions of action the reality of the local groups was seen to be untenable without major disruption. The attempt by residents to develop in their own eyes a post-industrial ethic was not realizable without conse- quences and contradictions. The avoidance of change through spatial expansion which had worked so well in the development of the com- munity image long before stronger preservationist attitudes grew up could not continue when other groups in the metropolitan region began to achieve their own slow-growth aims, described by Ley (1980) as the creation of a 'Liveable Region'. The response of particular social groups in West Vancouver was varied. Those in Caulfeild tended to accept reluctantly the inevitable loss of open space, which was completely developed by 1984, but considered leaving the sub-community. In the British Properties and Central Area the groups did not see much actual development until after 1984 due to an unexpected rise in house values throughout the Province which for several years virtually ended all market exchanges (although not private swaps) and new starts. The nature of this development appeared, however, to be consistent with many expressed views of 'a post-industrial landscape', there being a plethora of varied house types, most at one plot to the acre, and reminiscent of Californian coastal estates.

Summary and conclusions

In this brief review and research case-study I have tried to demonstrate that the approach to understanding the nature and impact of social interaction can benefit from absorption into the wider issues that are now being tackled in social geography. This potential has been shown to have existed for a considerable time in the subject through qualitative research but not to have been furthered until recently. It has been suggested that the theory of structuration is most useful in fulfilling this aim, although the framework Giddens has offered is not taken up totally uncritically. In particular it is accepted that certain social group formations may be better understood than others through this epis- temology, most commonly where there is pressure of change to identity occurring. It is also important to realize that basic qualitative investi- gations made in locales have no specific claim to 'belong' to a structur- ation thesis: this link depends on the satisfactory incorporation of the findings into a wider structural context as outlined in this chapter. In this contribution the link between intersubjective reconstructions of community interaction and issues concerning suburbanization in late capitalist society have been combined in a different way from previous writings.

A major aim of this contribution has nevertheless been to demonstrate that the theory of structuration is *not* solely a macro-concept which lacks the power to find applicability in individual examples. Such a view, if upheld, would leave societal theory wavering in thin air and give credence to highly atomistic interpretations. Yet it is widely accepted now I think that empirical observations are 'theory-laden'. Following from this there cannot be different theories for macro and micro – the two must be brought together satisfactorily.

Although some slight reservations may be seen to detract from the power of Giddens' concept, I nevertheless do not deviate from defending, like Jackson and Smith (1984) the basic value of structuration in the explanation of social phenomena, when seen in the wider context in which it has developed. I would also urge qualitative researchers in social geography to beware of becoming diverted into philosophical debates espoused by theories such as realism (Sayer, 1984) which are difficult to apply empirically. From these sources comes much of the criticism of structuration. Equally, they should not be afraid of developing theory as their empirical enquiries throw up new issues – again too much criticism of Giddens is *in situ* and not based on experimenting with practical results of utilizing the theory. In the emerging research frameworks of social geography structuration can form a strong building-block for qualitative studies.

Note

I would like to thank Peter Jackson and Denis Cosgrove for commenting on earlier drafts of this chapter.

References

Bell, C. and Newby, H. (1978) 'Community, communion, class and community action: the social sources of the new urban politics', in D. T. Herbert and R. J. Johnston (eds), *Social areas in cities*, John Wiley and Sons, Chichester.

Bourdieu, P. (1977) *Outline of a theory of practice*, Cambridge University Press, Cambridge.

Caulfeild Property Owners Association (1978) *Submissions and petitions to West Vancouver Council*, West Vancouver, B.C.

Census of Canada (1976) *Tables for the Vancouver Region*, Ottawa.

Cooke, P. (1987) 'Clinical inference and geographic theory', *Antipode* 19, 69–78.

Dallmayr, F. (1982) 'The theory of structuration: a critique', in A Giddens, *Profiles and critiques in social theory*, Macmillan, London.

Danielson, M. N. (1976) *The politics of exclusion*, Columbia University Press, New York.

Duncan, J. S. (1976) 'Landscape and the communication of social identity', in A. Rapoport (ed.), *The mutual interaction of people and the built environment*, Mouton Press, The Hague.

Duncan, J. S. (1978) 'The social construction of unreality: an interactionist approach to the tourist's cognition of environment', in D. Ley and M. Samuels (eds), *Humanistic geography – prospects and problems*, Maaroufa Press, Chicago.

Duncan, J. S. (1980) 'The superorganic in American cultural geography', *Annals, Association of American Geographers* 70, 181–98.

Duncan. J. S. (ed.) (1981) *Housing and identity*, Croom Helm, London.

Duncan, J. S. (1985) 'Individual action and political power: a structuration perspective', in R. J. Johnston (ed.), *The future of geography*, Methuen, London.

Duncan, J. S. and Duncan, N. G. (1984) 'A cultural analysis of urban residential landscapes in North America: the case of the anglophile elite', in J. Agnew et al., *The city in cultural context*, Allen and Unwin, Boston.

Evans, D. M. (1984) 'Demystifying suburban landscapes', in D. T. Herbert and R. J. Johnston (eds), *Geography and the Urban Environment* Vol 6, John Wiley and Sons, Chichester.

Evans, D. M. (1987) *Anti-growth movements on the urban fringe: a cross-national perspective*, unpublished MS, Loughborough University, Loughborough.

Fischer, C. S. (1976) *The urban experience*, Harcourt Brace, New York.

Fischer, C. S. and Jackson, R. M. (1976) 'Suburbs, networks and attitudes', in B. Schwartz (ed.), *The changing face of the suburbs*, University of Chicago Press, Chicago.

Forman, R. (1971) *Black ghettos, white ghettos and slums*, Prentice-Hall, Englewood Cliffs, N.J.

Giddens, A. (1979) *Central problems in social theory*, Macmillan, London.

Giddens, A. (1982) *Profiles and critiques in social theory*, Macmillan, London.

Gregson, N. (1987) 'Structuration theory: some thoughts on the possibilities for empirical research', *Environment and Planning* D 5, 73–91.

Jackson, P. and Smith, S. J. (1984) *Exploring social geography*, George Allen and Unwin, London.

Johnston, R. J. (1984) *Residential segregation, the state and constitutional conflict in American urban areas*, Academic Press, New York.

Ley, D. (1978) 'Social geography and social action', in D. Ley and M. Samuels, (eds), *Humanistic geography – prospects and problems*, Maaroufa Press, Chicago.

Ley, D. (1980) 'Liberal ideology and the post-industrial city', *Annals, Association of American Geographers* 70, 238–58.

Ley, D. (1983) *A social geography of the city*, Harper and Row, New York.

Mead, G. H. (1934) *Mind, self and society* (ed. C. W. Morris), University of Chicago Press, Chicago.

Park, R. E. (1926) 'The urban community as a spatial pattern and a moral order', in E. Burgess (ed.), *The urban community*, University of Chicago Press, Chicago.

Sayer, A. (1984) *Method in social science – a realist approach*, Hutchinson, London.

Smith, N. (1987) 'Dangers of the empirical turn: some comments on the CURS initiative', *Antipode* 19, 59–68.

Suttles, G. D. (1968) *The social order of the slum*, University of Chicago Press, Chicago.

Suttles, G. D. (1972) *The social construction of communities*, University of Chicago Press, Chicago.

Suttles, G. D. (1984) 'The cumulative texture of local urban culture', *American Journal of Sociology* 90, 283–304.

Thrift, N. (1986) 'Personality, practice and politics', in K. Hoggart and E. Kofman (eds), *Politics, geography and social stratification*, Croom Helm, London.

Walden, P. S. (1947) 'A history of West Vancouver', MA Thesis in History, University of British Columbia, B.C.

Walker, R. (1981) 'A theory of suburbanization: capitalism and the construction of urban space in the United States', in M. Dear and A. J. Scott (eds) *Urbanization and urban planning in capitalist society*, Methuen, London.

West Vancouver Council (1975) *Draft report of the Task Force appointed by Mayor Peter Jones to examine the implications of policies limiting growth in West Vancouver*, Chairman C. R. Day, Mimeo, West Vancouver Council, B.C.

West Vancouver Council (1977) *Communication with director of planning/officers*, West Vancouver Council, B.C.

8

The Geography of Popular Memory in Post-Colonial South Africa
A Study of Afrikaans Cinema

Keyan G. Tomaselli

Spatial relations are increasingly being studied within texts (e.g. Butler-Adam, 1975; 1981). Little work though has been done on relating texts to contexts. Only one book by geographers attempts this, but does not provide specifically geographical insights on language, culture or ideology (Burgess and Gold, 1985).

Different classes interpret urban and/or rural 'spaces' in terms of their divergent experiences within and between them. Meanings are not only to be found in the topographical forms perceptible to the senses. 'Space' consists of a layered and collective memory, of residual, dominant and emergent cultures, each incorporating the historical scars of class, ideology and economics. Examining human habitats through semiotics, as signs and codes which express the status of class struggle at any moment, it is possible to manifest the content of mental texts (ideas, perceptions and interpretations) of classes or groups in relation to the hidden material processes of history, economics and politics. While geographical outcomes of struggle are easily visible, causation is obscured by language and ideology.

This study offers a Marxist reading of South African history and its symbolic representation in Afrikaans cinema. Geographical analysis is largely implicit, but elements of a spatial imagination will be teased out. Not only are cinematic signs cultural indicators of the wider society, but their forms are shaped by productive forces of specific historical conjunctures. Together, these create popular memory of space, spatial trajectories and environment.

Myths: Moulding reality

The study addresses three myths: Eden, the urban trek and the outsider or *uitlander*. Myth is defined as recurring themes, icons and stereotypes which claim common recognition within a cultural group with a shared ideology (Tomaselli et al., 1987: 18). Even in their original form, these myths were idealized fictions of the historical experiences of the Afrikaner petty bourgeoisie. By the early 1940s, when they were set out as the proper content of Afrikaans-language films (Rompel, 1942), they bore little resemblance to actuality. It is over these myths that the film-makers of the 1960s and 1970s encoded the traumas experienced by the Afrikaner working class, those facing proletarianization or embourgeoise-ment, as well as ruralites who witnessed the break-up of their families as their progeny migrated to the cities.

Representations of cultural space

Particular attention is given to the distinction between outsider and insider. The insider/outsider genre was repeated and reinterpreted by the same 'authors' (and actors) during its cinematic cycle between 1965 and 1980. It is this repetitive reaffirmation of ideas which makes them the 'ruling ideas' of the 'new class' (Marx and Engels, 1970: 66). The ideas of the emergent urban petty bourgeoisie and bourgeoisie were represented in cinema as the interests of all Afrikanerdom.[1] Directors (and the earlier novelists who initiated the genre) were sympathetic to these 'new classes', notwithstanding the trauma such relocation (both social and geo-graphical) caused Afrikanerdom as a whole.

Every text is part of a dynamic process which is continually re-evaluating and reconstructing history. The past is reproduced through historiography, as well as popular genres which draw on networks of public memory. One of the main functions of genre is the containment and regulation of meaning such that it 'can be considered as a single continuous text' (Leutrat, 1980: 51). The conflict/love genre, a specific instance of the general insider/outsider category, is a belated legitimation of the restructuring of class alliances which occurred earlier in the century. The encoding of the 'ruling ideas' was facilitated by Afrikaner ownership of the film industry during the genre's life, with the discursive incentive of a state subsidy paid out on the film's ability to reaffirm the hegemonic ideas.

Until the discovery of diamonds and gold after 1886, the Boer republics had been subsistence agrarian economies. With the concen-tration of foreign capital into mining, the emerging urban centres became the locus of black and white migration. Ruralities had been close to the means of production; in the towns they were oppressed wage labourers jostling with blacks for social and economic space. The cultural trauma that followed this spatial and economic fracture formed the crucible for the development of Afrikaner hegemony based on cultural identity and the idea of a separate Afrikaner 'nation'.

The radio and film coverage of the symbolic re-enactment of the Great Trek in 1938 gave a considerable boost to the recapture of a popular pastoral memory. Four broadcasts a week over four months amplified this historic moment. It united agricultural capitalists, the urban working class and the petty bourgeoisie, by locating both English and blacks as outsiders. The original trek was an attempt to escape from British colonial rule. Splitting the symbolic trek into two, one proceeding to the Voortrekker Monument site in Pretoria, and the other to the site of the Battle of Blood River in Natal, represented Afrikaner triumphs over both English and blacks respectively – two kinds of outsider.

Reconstructing the 'national' past

Central to the turn-of-the-century Afrikaans writing is a Babylonian image of Johannesburg whose most accessible monument is an hotel (Hofmeyer, 1981). In contrast, the most important building in rural towns is the church. The spatial and economic relations which linked town and country were first, mine and cash-crop production for export into which European investments went, and secondly, larger areas which produced little for export. Though they received no investment, they were indispensable because they supplied the zones of extractable profit with cheap labour and food (Davidson, 1978: 148). The massive inflow of international capital invested in Johannesburg after the Boer War had an indelible effect on the connections within the space economy and the structure of the region's political economy. Given that the cogs of town and country impelled the colonial economy, these two areas informed the world-views of different social groups. Town and country stood as two important beacons from which people, and the classes to which they belonged located their sense of history, identity and reality (Hofmeyer, 1981).

The Eden film: the never-never land of pastoral harmony

The Eden film stems from the myth recurrent in Western art, that of the Fall from the Garden of Eden. The myth represents a peaceful integration with the environment. It offers an explanation of urban dis-content and the hope of a remedy in return. Two versions of history coexist in the Eden film. The first suggests that:

once upon a time, the Afrikaner was the independent master of his own pastoral destiny. He lived, as is common in myths, in amity with nature and his surround-ings. These included his Coloured servants. Neither Blacks nor the English disturbed the idyll. (Greig, 1980: 16)

No reference is made to the Great Trek or the wars out of which Afrikaners matured. The Eden myth is timeless, filtered of social origins, causation, conflict or cultural destination. The Eden film centres on a couple who, with the help and guidance of a matriarch, have the problem of partners resolved for them. The son of the soil, the *boereseun*, marries the daughter of the earth, the *boeredogter*. They live happily ever after.

The second dimension of history admits to the Fall, and the idyll is shattered with the intrusion of the urban Afrikaner or outsider antagon-istic to the natural pastoral harmony. This version accepts the fact of the Great Trek, the dispossession by the British of Afrikaners and the sub-sequent Anglicization, the migration from the farm to the town, and what, at first, seems as alien, but later, natural way of life.

The genesis of the outsider in the film, *Debbie* (1965), symbolically encodes most of the signs pertaining to both versions of history. Paradoxically, *Dit Was Aand en dit Was Môre* (*It was Evening, It was Morning*), made thirteen years later, denies the Fall and acts out its drama in the pastoral simplicity of the dominant memory. This unpol-luted form of refracted history which oscillates to a greater or lesser degree during the genre is superimposed on the second version symbol-ized in the move to the city.

An Eden-like nostalgia facilitates an identification of the genre cycle and allows a certain dynamism whereby the signs signifying the myth fade in and out of different treatments. The linkages are intertextual: the genre was adapted into radio soap operas; from there it became the content of films and photocomics. After 1976, the genre was encoded in television serials. There are backward linkages too, from film and television to radio and literature. The film periodization of the genre is thus not an anomaly but the apex of an ongoing text which has spanned different media and popular memory since the turn of the century.

A decreasing emphasis occurs during the genre's life on a simple, rurally-based religious lifestyle. Audiences increasingly failed to identify with Eden mythology or the reconstructed pastoral values of the 'national' past as evidenced in *Aand/Môre*. Emergent material values indicated the Afrikaner's ambivalent relationship with capital.

The insider/outsider conflict: the traumatic love affair with capital

Whereas the Eden film reaffirms mythical values, the tensions between the insider, whose origins derive from Eden, and the outsider, who represents the Fall, are resolved by the affirmation and inevitability of a material urban lifestyle. The *nouveau riche* urban Afrikaner as outsider is characterized by conspicuous consumption and signs which the insider attributes to an alien way of life. The outsider is socially remote, selfish and arrogant. As visitor to the farm, the outsider is destructive to its harmony. Like urban capitalist culture which the outsider represents, he sexually attracts and ultimately co-opts the insider, transforming him or her into a restless urban animal who forsakes the farm, family and the rural community. The social practices associated with individualistic urban living initially bring with them an uneasy cultural in-betweenness.

Genesis of the uitlander

The relationships in the genre involve a threesome, two vying for the love of a third. One of these is the outsider. The variation in roles and genders, the plot and locales provide the essential differences between films. The range of difference in repetition varies markedly within the genre. Difference usually involves the insertion of a new locale, the city for the farm, for example, or a new site of cultural struggle, the Border, for the city.

The year 1903 crystallized circumstances resulting in the rural urban value clash between insiders and outsiders. The Anglo-Boer War had created a large number of Afrikaner refugees ousted from their farms and forced to work in the towns. Anti-British Afrikaner hostility had been intensified through a change in mining methods. Whereas previous to the 1880s, a single prospector aided by a few 'natives' was able to pan for gold, deep-level mining required large capital commitments and centralized rights in the hands of a few, usually British, entrepreneurs. Gold and the wealthy individuals associated with it were identified as the enemy. High unemployment caused a drop in remittances, migrant workers returned to their families who had remained on the farms, and this in turn stimulated further urban migration. These conditions gave rise to the formation of the northern-dominated Afrikaner *Broederbond* which created the conditions for capital accumulation independent of mining. Newspapers and the big insurance companies were financed by the rural bourgeoisie, run by the urban petty bourgeoisie and grew through the mobilization of the full spectrum of rural support (O'Meara, 1977: 160).

Prior to 1934, Afrikaner nationalism in the Transvaal saw the solution to 'poor whitism' requiring a return to the land or 'the farm' as it was referred to colloquially. Thereafter, however, the *Broederbond*:

saw the problem . . . as an urban rather than rural phenomenon. Its solutions were never to be sought simply at the level of politics, but in the ownership structure of the *industrial* economy, by challenging the nature of South African capitalism itself. (O'Meara, 1977: 160)

The capture of the alien economy, initially relying on agricultural capital, was later consolidated with urban capital generated by the now large financial houses, supported by an increasingly powerful Afrikaans-language press. These are the symbolic themes of the conflict/love genre. Given the conditions of its genesis, and the growth of Afrikaner capital through companies like SANLAM, it is not surprising that film directors were sympathetic to the outsider who metonymically represents the urban Afrikaner. The interpretation was, furthermore, aided by the capture by Afrikaner-dominated capital in 1969 of the film industry itself.

Given their poverty and a cultural anathema to urban living, it was not surprising that Afrikaners preferred life on the *veld* where the dominant popular memory spoke them as the masters of their own economic destiny. In *Dit Was Aand en Dit Was Môre* Afrikaners live in that 'never-never land before gold was discovered, *uitlanders* intruded and agitators invented the race problem' (Greig, 1977). The Eden film, however, in which rural values – 'no sex, no violence, no cities' – were paramount, was replaced by that strain which admits the fact of the move to the city, even if it sometimes denied the permanency of urban life. A nostalgic longing for a return to the ancestral farm articulated the aim of migrant workers to accumulate sufficient capital to enable them to return. 'The farm', its soil – a timeless state of being – is a memory of recent origin. Thematically, 'the farm' functions as a cultural memory and represents the 'traditions' on which the Afrikaner 'nation' tries to maintain group cohesiveness.

The uitlander: the shifting enemy of Afrikanerdom

The *uitlander* stands for a two-tiered social role. The first is the outsider in the widest sense. The *uitlander* is identified with British imperialism, and latterly, with English-speaking South Africa. The *uitlander* rarely spoke English. This was partly due to the warping effect of the state subsidy which demands language purity, rewarding purely Afrikaans films at a higher rate than English-language versions. At the termination of the genre in April 1980, however, the *uitlander* was English-speaking. The role is symbolic of capital's attraction for the 'new classes' of Afrikaner.

The second tier refers to urbanities who have cut their ties with the 'solid inherited *boerekarakter*' (farmer character) (Rompel, 1942). They are portrayed as traitors to Afrikaner values and ideals. This is a consequence, not of the fact that Afrikaners are essentially rural in character, but because they were historically thwarted in their attempts to wrest economic power from the British.

The Boeredogter

The *boeredogter* is pivotal in determining the relationship between insiders and outsiders. She stands for the ideological connection between capital and culture. The *boeredogter* sets the pace for social adaptation as she is constantly exposed to and interpellates new social practices thrust upon her by adjustments occurring in the political economy. At the start of the genre she is a *maimed heroine*, a status she maintains for nearly three-quarters of the genre cycle. Iconically, the *boeredogter* stands for the idea of a young girl; indexically, she represents severe cultural trauma; and as a symbol she stands for first alienated, but later repurified, Afrikaner capital. The *boereseun* and *boeredogter* signify the unity/disunity of the group as well as the popular Afrikaner response to the penetration of English capital from the early days of the mining industry.

The *boeredogter* is marked as the proper companion for the *boereseun*, equally enshrined in the mythical values of the Eden-farm. However, the *boeredogter* only gains her full significance when she spurns her pre-ordained partner and attempts to escape from her culturally inherited and spatially restricted way of life.

Typically, the *boeredogter* matures into her ideologically designated role as *boerevrou* (farmer's wife). Her link with the *uitlander* is sexual and violent and exposes her to the culturally alienating influences of imperial and international capital. She forsakes the cultural purity of the Garden of Eden and adopts a way of life which acknowledges the Fall. Her shift from one ecological[2] setting to another symbolizes a disintegration of pastoral values. The *uitlander* is seen as a force which threatens group cohesion and identity. Her association with the *uitlander*, even if a member of the 'new classes', creates an alliance which threatens the integrity of pastoral culture. To maintain cultural cohesion, the group has to remain closed; the *uitlander* is rejected and the wandering *boeredogter* is excommunicated.

The *boeredogter* must be punished for her betrayal: she is the communion wine which cleanses the body of the group. The methods by which she is purged include unnatural death, often at the hand of, or because of, the jilted party; alternatively, she may be blind, pregnant out of wedlock, commit suicide, be raped, traded in for cash, rejected because of her colour, or even a leper!

Symbolically, insider/outsider films show the demands being made by an industrial economy locked into the global function of capital. These imperialist impulses can neither be rejected nor captured. The only course remaining was adopted by the *Broederbond* which accepted that the establishment of a *volkskapitalisme* would require massive urbanization. The *boeredogter* represented both the trauma of this change as well as the determining capitalist influences of it.

During the Anglo-Boer War (1899–1902), it was the women who tilled the soil, raised the children, and supplied food and shelter to the commandos in the area. A strongly matriarchal society emerged. As wife of the Boer soldier, often sole parent of the children, and as behind-the-lines supplier, she became mythified as a *volksmoeder* (mother of the people). The *volksmoeder* provides spiritual and moral guidance, is unwavering in her ideals but flexible in her actions, pure and determined as she watches over the *volk* and its efforts to cope with external threats. The myth of the *volksmoeder* was enhanced as she stoically endured the terrible conditions in the British concentration camps into which she and her children were herded during the latter part of the war. These women took on the status of martyrs and symbolized the continuing flame of cultural purity in the midst of a genocidal assault by British imperialism against Afrikaners. Even after the British victory, she remained on 'the farm', now impoverished and laid waste, while her husband and older children laboured for the enemy in the cities.

The *boeredogter* is the progeny of the *volksmoeder*. It is she who is destined to carry on the task of mothering as many babies as possible, as well as the Afrikaner 'nation'. Where the *volksmoeder* resisted the imperialist onslaught, the *boeredogter* is more expedient as seen in her collaboration with English and, by implication, international capital. She is the sell-out, the traitor, however inevitable her actions in terms of the destiny of the *volk*. In *'n Beeld vir Jeannie* (*A Statue for Jeannie*, 1976), the conflict is manifested through the antagonism between the 'new class' of enlightened urban Afrikaner and the old unyielding self-righteous stalwarts. The setting is the *dorp* (country town) which stands for South Africa. The town councillors decide to erect a statue in memory of 2000 women who died in a concentration camp near the present-day town during the Anglo-Boer War. The long-haired Pretoria artist engaged by the Council questions their motives. He is opposed by the town's lawyer and town clerk who demand to know the sculptor's attitude towards Afrikaner sentiment. The sculptor gets a sympathetic though initially uncommitted hearing from the *dominee* (minister of religion). Having questioned the cultural suitability of the sculptor, the Council is enraged at his choice of model, school student Jeannie Moolman, for she is an unmarried mother censured by the church, unfit to epitomize Afrikaner womanhood. The *boeredogter* is drawn to the sculptor. Jeannie despairs of winning the sculptor *uitlander* and commits suicide. His grief is, however, balanced by his moral victory over the *verkrampte* (reactionary) councillors.

　'n Beeld vir Jeannie identifies adaptability as a crucial element of the *boeredogter*. Though reviled by the 'older Afrikaner' she is symbolically tied to the spatial trajectory of Afrikaner economic power. The direction was inexorably towards the cities for they were the site of economic struggle where imperial capital engaged with national capital. The *boeredogter* was prepared to die for her dream and legitimized the striving for an urban-based *volkskapitalisme* just as the *volksmoeder* supported it in agricultural form. The resulting urbanization offered an escape from the social restrictions of rural communities, and above all, the opportunity to interpellate different social practices. It is to this urban interpellation that we now turn.

　The recurring cinematic sign of the *boeredogter* first appeared in 1965. Its transference was direct: *Debbie* was adapted from a bestseller published in 1948. Comments producer Tommie Meyer;

> it was a book that had authenticity and which dealt with something that every family experienced . . . that at one or another time there is a girl in the family who is experiencing a baby out of marriage . . . (that *platteland* [country] parents) send their sons and daughters to university and then they remain in the city. (Interview, April 1981)

The setting is the fun of an Afrikaans university campus versus the diligence, austerity and hard work of 'the farm'; fast cars versus the tractor; individuality versus the group/family/community; urban claustrophobia versus the unspoiled spaciousness of the countryside. Debbie's humiliated parents disown her, while the cynical, social-climbing parents of the city-reared boyfriend suggest an abortion. Tear-jerkingly melodramatic, the film constantly stresses the social, cultural and psychological dangers of 'deviance'.

　Reaction to *Debbie* included a 4–21 age restriction. The extent and influence of the film's supporters had the result of conferring the quality of 'authorization' to its makers and the restriction was lifted. Not only was the sign of the *boeredogter* legitimized within the ecological setting of cinema (it was already accepted in literature), but even the most conservative of Afrikaners acknowledged the social problems of urban living. Though the *boeredogter* had been 'lost', her experience was argued to be of didactic significance to those who were not yet lost.

The sign of the *boeredogter* works on various levels. First is the idea of a young girl; purity, group ties and respect for traditional values. She attains a relatively autonomous identity in the face of others, the villainess for example. Her identity does not result from the opposition *per se* but is manifested in the opposition. At this second level the icon intercepts cultural meanings not derived from the sign itself, but from the way Afrikaner society uses and values both the signifier and signified. The *boeredogter* stands for 'maimed heroine', indicating trauma about her social status. This trauma, a consequence of capital, is manifested in her individuality and her attraction to the *uitlander*. Since she is the vehicle for social and cultural procreation her perceived betrayal of the *volk* means that she must be maimed or defiled. She cannot, therefore, carry the torch of cultural purity handed to her by the *volksmoeder*. In *Debbie*, she has become a threat to 'the farm' with its discourse of 'authority', 'tradition' and the 'fine and noble'. Despite this ostracism, her assimilation into the 'new class' is often equally traumatic. She becomes estranged from her lover and friends by the end of the movie. The *boeredogter* nevertheless survives, if not in body then in spirit. Whether blind, maimed or a leper, she will never return to 'the farm'. Her prodigal tendencies (symbolizing the quest for industrial/ financial capital) traumatized Afrikanerdom and, while 'the farm' existed as a guarantor of cultural integrity within the confines of Eden, this national trauma would only build up during the unfolding of the plot with the maiming, degradation, self-imposed isolation or death of the *boeredogter* occurring at the end of the film. By 1979 she was dead before the film even started. In *Herfsland* (*Land of Autumn*), the opening scene starts with her funeral. Whereas Debbie and Jeannie were but country-born unmarried mothers, in *Herfsland* the *boeredogter* not only committed suicide, but was also a drug addict, neurotic, 'mixed up with hippies' and separated from her husband. Her early death indicated an intensified trauma needing resolution in the films to follow. This occurred through the intervention of the *dominee* (pastor), who was the main character through which the director advocated a change in social attitudes.

The dominee: *tension management*

The *dominee* is cast as the purveyor of traditional values. He is one of the *volk*, indexical of social stability. As affirmative symbol he has the trust of his flock who turn to him in times of uncertainty. Drawn into the conflict between the insider and the outsider, he is, at first, noncommittal; he is torn between the hypocritical reactions of the *volk* and his sympathy for the *boeredogter*, her problems and the positive aspects she signifies as Afrikaner of the future. In *'n Beeld vir Jeannie*, the *dominee* initially sides with the town councillors, but is immediately sympathetic to the ideas of the *uitlander*.

The full significance of the *dominee* is seen in *Ter Wille van Christine* (*For the Sake of Christine*, 1975). Here the church itself is the site of conflict. Symbolic of the state, it witnesses conflict between the church council and its two ministers. The *boereseun* is *dominee*, Paul. His father is a *dominee* in the same church. Paul has fallen in love with the outsider, a Catholic nurse, Christine. The antagonistic elder wants his daughter to marry Paul. The choice presented by Paul's love for Christine are, according to his father, between following the letter or the spirit of Christ's teachings, and between adapting to change and ossifying. Christine, who escapes back to the city, is fetched by Paul. Following a tirade from the hostile elder on how Christine had caused a split in the community, Paul takes up a calling in another congregation.

Forced to make his choice, the *dominee* usually defends the *boeredogter* (or *boereseun*) against the hypocrisy of the group. Sometimes his actions are overt, often they are implied. Ultimately, through his defence of the *boeredogter*, the *dominee* comes to reassess his own values. He becomes, as in *Ter Wille van Christine*, the moderator between the old and the new. The *dominee* is both leader and follower; leader because he commands inherent respect as a man of God who represents the chosen people (*volk*), follower because he has been awakened to a new set of social relations separate to and away from 'the farm'.

The *dominee*, however, is sceptical of the *nouveau riche* urban Afrikaner. If his presence is synonymous with Eden and those films located on the farm or in the *dorp*, in films acting out their conflicts in the city, he is much less visible. Where he does appear as in *Eensame Vlug* (*Lonely Flight*) and *Herfsland*, he is subdued, ineffectual though understanding.

Development and ideological reorientation of the Boeredogter

With the economic and political stabilization of the early 1970s the *boeredogter* was found more in the cities and less on 'the farm' or in the *dorp*. The second trek (or urban trek) is taken for granted. The conflict, no longer caused by urbanization, is now located mainly within the characters themselves in their representations of social roles. The rural urban conflict becomes the struggle between the 'good' and 'bad' Afrikaners within the city itself. This shift accepts the Rompel stereotype that city Afrikaners are not all that different from their rural counterparts. They have merely relocated themselves to a new farm, the peri-urban smallholding.

Insiders now live in ostentatious mansions staffed by a citified *bywoner*.[3] The tractor has been replaced by a Mercedes 350SE, the farmyard with an office tower, and the *voorkamer* (sitting room) with a snooker table. In *Rienie* (1980), the farmer is dominant, the *bywoner* a drunkard and sole parent of Rienie. The *bywoner* sells his daughter to a childless wealthy urban couple. This *boeredogter* is underage, forced into the urban trek against her will and unaware as to why she is spending her 'holiday' with surrogate parents. Spared the traumas of maturation undergone by the older, wiser *boeredogter*, she is a naive pawn traded for financial gain by the *bywoner* who is embarrassed by his identity.

Rienie develops the role of the *boeredogter* and provides a unique example not only of the rural-urban transition, but also a parallel evocation of family groups, one part of the rural bourgeoisie located on 'the farm', and the other located on the surrogate farm. In the former, the farmer is a successful and dominant personality who is not ungenerous to his *bywoner*. Having sold his daughter, however, the *bywoner* undergoes a metamorphosis and the best traditional Afrikaans values come to the fore. The urban 'farmer', in contrast, is ruthless and avaricious. He also has a *bywoner*. This city *bywoner* is old and wise, kind and gentle, an avuncular figure who dispenses good sense and sympathy. He is the one who keeps this urban family together, whereas it is the farmer himself who holds the rural unit together.

Rienie's stepmother buys and shields her from the knowledge of her father's terminal illness. She weans the *boeredogter* from the farm and protects her from the ruthless methods of wealth accumulation represented by her foster-father. *Rienie* encapsulates both sides of the rural–urban trek and bridges the two spatially distinct (rural/urban) sets of farms in the genre and shows that they are not separate, but parallel.

Symbolically, *Rienie* shows the interpenetration of urban and rural capitals. Although 'the farm' is not depicted as an impoverished area, the fact of the migration by the *boeredogter* or *boereseun* suggests that it is outshone by the material attractions of the city. It will be remembered that the Afrikaner attack on the foreign-dominated capitalist system was financed by rural capital but fought in the cities. It would have been surprising if some of the benefits of the victory did not rub off on the rural bourgeoisie itself. *Rienie* alludes to such effect; the well-to-do, socially remote farmer who lives in his modern urban-style house. Unlike his city counterpart, however, he retains a measure of compassion. In *Rienie* the *boeredogter* is an unwitting, but total slave of capital. Being blonde, however, she remains pure. Although a victim of social degradation, she is no longer a maimed heroine.

Rienie resolves many of the issues raised in earlier films and suggested the genre's future. The genre, however, stagnated because of the truncating effect of television, where it recovered a more complex historical path (see Tomaselli and Van Zyl, 1985).

Capital's ultimate defilement of Afrikaner cultural space

At its most introspective, the urban conflict/love story which is critical of mindless wealth and destructive individualism is found in *Plekkie in die Son* (*Place in the Sun*, 1979) where insiders have retreated into a leper colony. Those inside talk about the *uitlanders*, those outside the asylum. The urban-born *boeredogter*, married to a Trust Bank whizz-kid is gradually rejected by her family. The metaphor of being a leper suggests that the maimed heroine has undergone a degrading contact. Her touch is defiled, affecting not only the present generation, but the next as well. This sense of pollution, of isolation, is reinforced when the elderly cured couple are rejected by their children and are again forced to seek sanctuary in the asylum. Dark-haired and naive, not only has the *boeredogter* lost the innocence of rural purity, but she is rejected at her destination. The mirrors of the genre have turned inward with a terrible vengeance suggesting something seriously wrong with the social structure. The conventional patterns are disintegrating and new destructive material practices are replacing them. Group cohesion is being ruthlessly superseded by anonymous and selfish capitalist values.

With the location of plot in the urban milieu alone, the conflict, often seen in generational terms, has added a new dimension, the embarrassment of classes.

Class fractions: the embarrassment of culture

Ideological tendencies and cultural differences between the elite of Waterkloof Afrikanerdom, and the raunchy lower middle class who live in Krugersdorp is seen in *'n Seder Val in Waterkloof* (*A Cedar Falls in Waterkloof*, 1978). The two groups are not displayed as discrete classes; 'they were branches of the same Baobab which had grown in different directions and were now coming at each other' (Greig, 1979). The 'differences' were: BMW's versus a hotted-up Ford Cortina with an orange on the aerial, gracious living versus *plaasjapie* (country bumpkin) behaviour, decorum versus mayhem, sexual restraint versus lust, and so on. These oppositions are not found in different classes for that would suggest that the Afrikaner group is not a group, but within the same family. The cedar or pillar of Afrikanerdom, Professor van Vuuren, wants to be the chairman of a prestigious Academy. Success depends on the support of two professors who are invited to sojourn at his mansion in Waterkloof. Into this rustic environment arrive van Vuuren's undignified and loquacious family from Krugersdorp. Peeved at their unfriendly welcome, they employ a 'sex-bomb masseuse' to discredit the professor before his superiors and then blackmail the eminent visitors.

Where *Plekkie in die Son* shows distinct group disintegration, *'n Seder Val in Waterkloof* suggests that that disintegration is merely the result of the pretension of the 'new classes'. The group may have divided in terms of ways of life and residential location, but self-examination can result in the *rapprochement* between the two branches, as when van Vuuren discards his hypocritical lifestyle and absconds with one of the masseuses. The integration of different social and sexual mores which no longer separate the group heralded the redefinition of the outsider or enemy. The enemy is no longer 'imperial capital' represented in the sinful city. Capitalism and its corresponding social practices, sexual permissivity under certain circumstances and looser social ties are now accepted. The enemy has shifted location and now represents the external threat beyond South Africa.

The war film

The *uitlander*'s new position is the result of a new war, a new set of traumas bent on the destruction, not so much of Afrikaner culture, but of the South African way of life. The oppositions are capitalism versus communism, or more specifically, *volkskapitalisme* versus communism, and within that, black versus white. This conflict is manifested in a new mental state, typified by 'the Border'. 'The Border' stands for the world onslaught (articulated as the 'total onslaught') which, like the British war on the Boers, seeks to appropriate the wealth and God-given privileges of Afrikanerdom. Causation is taken for granted, no explanation to account for this state being necessary.

The sign of the *uitlander* becomes more complex in the transition from 'the farm' to 'the Border'. It is now three-tiered. First, though now less important, remains the image of the liberal English-speaking South African. Second, is a new kind of villain, defined by his urban location, and the fact that he wants to flee the country. The third element is a revolutionary one, contingent upon intensified racial conflict generated out of the smoke, killing and rhetoric of 'the Border War'. No longer limited to English speakers and the urban petty bourgeois Afrikaner, the outsider has become a mortal enemy characterized by his blackness (and communism) and his AK47 rifle.

The rationale by Tommie Meyer for *Die Winter van 14 Julie* (*The Winter of 14 July*, 1976) is reminiscent of his reasons for making *Debbie* twelve years earlier; 'Every parent in South Africa . . . has at least a family member or a child or nephew or a friend who is at the Border, or who will go to the Border' (interview, April 1981). The conventional plot unfolds. A soldier meets a girl. They fall in love, sleep together; she falls pregnant. An orphan, he is considered unsuitable for the *boeredogter* by her interfering mother. The girl breaks off the relationship telling the boyfriend in a letter to be given to him by her brother, a fellow conscript, once they have reached South-West Africa. The boyfriend goes absent without leave (AWOL) and persuades the *boeredogter* to marry him. The parents take steps to have the marriage annulled. Her brother, also AWOL, opposes this and the mother eventually condones the marriage for the sake of family unity.

The outsider is now an insider though he degraded the *boeredogter* and brought shame to the group. Originally a symbol of alienated Afrikaner capital represented in her move to the city, in the city itself the *boeredogter* stands for miscreation as she marries this capital with international capital. Out of this integration flows a repurified capital, seen most clearly in *April '80*. Whereas the treatment of the *boeredogter* remained constant during the first thirteen years of her cinematic life, between 1978 and 1980 she underwent a rapid modification, responding to adjustments in the South African economy as Afrikaner and English capitals began to merge in their collaborative efforts to thwart the 'total onslaught'.

The war film created the opportunity for a new kind of white male hero. The men pair up as twins, one tough and hard, the other sensitive and soft (Greig, 1980: 21). In *Die Winter van 14 Julie*, the impulsive love-stricken orphan is balanced by the *boeredogter's* stable and pragmatic brother. The drama is symbolic of a man divided and having to lose that side of himself that might threaten group membership. These films deal with civil war – war within the body politic and within the individual.

The thematic oppositions reveal a society which confronts reality by a simplistic reduction to binary opposites; good versus bad; war versus peace; black versus white; communism versus capitalism; Marxism versus Christianity; and so on. More specifically, the themes found in the subtexts exhibit the following oppositions; terrorist (black) = bad;

soldier/policeman (white) = good; and loyal black (especially those fighting on the side of whites) = good + bad (a sort of reformed black).

In *Grensbasis 13* (*Border Base* 13, 1979) the love triangle involves a police lieutenant, a female doctor and a stay-at-home girlfriend. The doctor on 'the Border' is Aryan; she is the city *boeredogter*-gone-north. The outsider is a smooth, hip Afrikaner who wants to flee the country. The girlfriend's mother wants her to marry this new villain rather than the policeman. The daughter is torn between the outsider and her mortally wounded ex-fiancé who was shot by the black enemy when rescuing his girlfriend's brother.

Having lost her virginity in the city, the *boeredogter* is again blonde. She has regained her purity and moved to the bush (*not* 'the farm'). The bush on 'the Border' is the site of battle. Just as capital-in-general supports the war so the *boeredogter* supports the policeman who is fighting the war. He is rewarded for his bravery with a sexual intimacy outside marriage. Where Debbie was ostracized for her sexual conduct, the doctor in *Grensbasis 13* is venerated. Since the *uitlander* is now shown to be the personification of influences originating from the outside South Africa, the *boeredogter* cannot be degraded anymore. The outsider who remains within the country is no longer a threat. The *boeredogter's* new status and affirmation of her sexual conduct is endorsed when she accepts a medal at a ceremony on behalf of her dead lover. In *Grensbasis 13* she performs some of the functions of the *volksmoeder*: she is behind the lines dispensing not food and shelter, but healing and sexual support. Like Rienie, she suffers no cultural trauma, just a personal loss. She is unaware of the influences guiding her actions. No longer an outcast, like the *volksmoeder*, she is an intrinsic element in the battle for the security of Afrikanerdom. She has re-established her mythical status under the conditions determined by a new conflict, a new set of social relations and an enemy which can only be defeated militarily.

Social disorganization is countered by absorbing the outsider-within into the group while identifying a clearly discernible *uitlander* in terms of skin colour. From maimed heroine in earlier films, the *boeredogter* has been elevated to a new, repurified though passionless status within Afrikanerdom. The structures of authority and values of 'the farm' have been modified and transplanted to 'the Border'. Group cohesion has given way to a more abstract institutionalism managed not by the *dominee* but by the police and defence forces.

April '80: *the case of the reclaimed* boeredogter
April '80 closes the conflict/love story. the *boeredogter* is not only born in the city but is *English-speaking* (i.e. bilingual) as well. She is dark-

haired, defensive and naive. In losing her Aryan status, Carol has gained capital as an ally. Her home life, however, remains difficult, for the clash of cultures has yet to be resolved. Her mother, of Afrikaans origin, is a civil rights lawyer who now speaks English. Her father, a professor of English, is accused by his ex-wife of acting liberally but 'votes Prog and says thank God for the Nats'.

The *boereseun*'s father belonged to the anti-British *Ossewabrandwag* (OB – Oxwagon Sentinel, sympathetic to Nazi Germany) during the Second World War. She, he and her brother, Alex (the outsider), are university students. In igniting some pamphlet bombs, Alex inadvertently kills two innocent bystanders (who just happen to be Opposition Progressive Federal Party (PFP) voters). The *boereseun* is persuaded by the security police to spy on Alex through Carol. He falls in love with her and refuses. In a discontinuity, the *boereseun* does inform on Alex. Alex lures the *boereseun* into a deserted building. In the meantime Alex's father, who has disowned him, his sister, who will no longer protect him, and the police arrive on the scene, Alex shoots the *boereseun* and is killed by the police. Carol runs to the *boereseun*. The last shot is of the couple strolling along a beach at sunset. They live happily ever after.

Afrikaner-hater Alex is the stereotypical 'terrorist'. His political motivations are reduced to an unhappy childhood, while the treatment is reminiscent of the late 1960s when students perceived apartheid as an irrational racial ideology. Though set in 1980, the film is unaware that activists now see the clash as one between capital and labour where apartheid discourse mobilizes racial and cultural differences to legitimize exploitative class and spatial structures. Where students once identified Afrikaners as the source of apartheid, by the mid-1970s, it was realized that the perpetrator was capital itself. Whether that capital was of English or Afrikaner origin was irrelevant.

The continuity lapse is not only a function of the *boereseun*'s ties with the *volk*, but also of the genre which calls for a socially reassuring movie, not one that classes the terrorist acts of the OB and student activism in the same category. The outsider must be punished and dies, as do the two PFP supporters, killed by their own kind.

Unlike earlier films, criticism is not levelled at the self-righteous *volk*. Following her liberated role in the war movie, the *boeredogter* becomes the heroine: she is marked for *and marries* the *boereseun*. Thus, *April '80* brings the *boereseun* and *boeredogter* together. Blacks will accept what is deemed good for them and insiders, both Afrikaans *and* English-speaking, will coalesce into the new group which will remain closed to outsiders.

Where earlier films criticized Afrikaner ideology unresponsive to changes in the political economy, *April '80* reassures the viewer that the consequences of that ideology – terrorism and subversion – can be reduced to non-structural elements such as the immaturity of dissidents. By shifting causation onto the biographical-psychological, the script-writer isolates Alex from his family, the world, and his black allies.

The essential difference in *April '80* is the switching of roles: the terrorist outsider, Alex, not the *boeredogter* (or *boereseun*) dies. The trauma originally experienced by the *boeredogter* as she adjusted from rural to urban life has been replaced with a conflict rooted in cultural differences between English and Afrikaner which is resolved in a happy marriage. The sign of the *boeredogter* now stands for cultural attainment and social self-confidence through resolution of the politico-economic causes of her trauma. Having asserted her individuality in *Debbie*, she lost her relative autonomy, becoming a stock albino whose identity is no longer manifested in the opposition. She returned to a relocated fold amidst a new enemy.

April '80 deployed the *boereseun* to reclaim the second-generation English-fathered *boeredogter*. Although an English speaker, she always spoke Afrikaans to the *boereseun*. The pairing of these two characters symbolizes the *rapprochement* of English- and Afrikaner-dominated capitals – both rural and urban – united in the face of an external foe, despite continuing language and cultural differences.

Earlier conflict/love movies examined relations between insiders and outsider, all of whom were white. In the war film the (predominantly black-skinned) *uitlander* too, has switched allegiances. No longer representing British imperialism, he now represents communist expansionism. Unlike the earlier *uitlander* who was white and whose character was developed, the black outsider is a 'dark inscrutable inhuman enemy: to portray the outsider would entail humanising him and this would imply at least a partial denial of the category of enemy' (Greig, 1980: 19).

Where the *dominee* once mediated in a receding Eden, the security police now tread; where 'the farm' enshrined tradition, 'the Border' condones sexual liberation; where the *boeredogter* was once degraded she is now heralded; where the *boereseun* was drawn to the villainess he is now matched with the *boeredogter*. The state of Eden has been replaced by a state of materialism, militarism and the security police.

Conclusion

This chapter has examined spatial imagination within film texts in relation to contextual processes of political economy and history. It revealed the contradictions and tensions between social, spatial and environmental images of rural versus urban life. Location, area of residence and 'where people belong' are shown to be major themes. The foregrounding of destination – and the consequences of arrival – have a unique cultural and emotional impact in South African spatial mythology. The trauma caused by the move to the city is shown to be of a cultural, historically inevitable nature. The memory and unattainability of a receding Eden diminished as the conflict/love genre ran its course.

The Afrikaans language and its representation has an intrinsic penchant for spatial connotation. Not only do words like *dorp*, 'the farm' and 'the Border' evoke a symbolic sense of place, but also a sense of relationships (particularly ethnic and race) in struggle. While struggle may be presented in ahistorical terms, Afrikaans words often encode a geographical content which connote race/space correlations. Language is mobilized to *hide* the geographical implications, but they remain in the subtexts of political discourse as when, for example, National Party politicians talk of 'orderly urbanization', which is a de-racified way of saying that racist influx control remains. Similarly, the concept of 'culture' is irrevocably tied to the idea of 'nation', which itself denotes a specific geographical area. As argued above, geography in words and images is part of the hidden subtext of the Afrikaans language and cinematic depictions. To understand Afrikaner history, one has to be aware of the symbolic subtexts in language and imagery which contain geographical assumptions.

Notes

This chapter is derived from the author's PhD Thesis, 'Ideology and cultural production in South African cinema', University of Witwatersrand (1983). Thanks are due to the Institute for Social and Economic Research, University of Durban-Westville, for permitting a shorter version of this chapter first published in Haines and Buijs (1985) to be published here.

1   'Afrikanerdom' refers to the patriotic spirit of the Afrikaner 'nation'.
2   The term is Therborn's (1980) and refers to the restrictive reception of discourse. Used here, it takes on a spatial connotation as well.
3   A *bywoner* is a sub-tenant who lives on a farm. The term usually has the connotation of a 'poor white' who has been displaced from his property and forced to subsist on the charity of another.

References

Adam, J. (1975) 'Human spaces and the landscape of heart of darkness,' *Isizwe* 2, 1–16.
Burgess, J. and Gold, J. R. (1985) *Geography, the media and popular culture*, Croom Helm, New York.

Butler-Adam, J. (1981) 'Literature and the night-time geography of cities', *South African Geographical Journal* 63, 47–59.

Davidson, B. (1978) *Africa in modern history*, Allen Lane, London.

Greig, R. (1975) *'Ter Wille van Christine'*, *The Star*, 7 October.

Greig, R. (1977) 'Before the *uitlanders*, a dream of utopia. Review of *Dit Was Aand en Dit Was Môre'*, *The Star*, 4 August.

Greig, R. (1980) 'An approach to Afrikaans film', *Critical Arts: a Journal for Media Studies* 1, 14–24.

Hofmeyer, I. (1981) 'The Political Dimension of South African Literature: An Analysis of Images of Town and Country in Turn of the Century Writing', paper presented at the History Workshop, University of Witwatersrand.

Leutrat, quoted in Neale, S. (1980) *Genre*, British Film Institute, London.

Marx, K. and Engels, F. (1970) *The German Ideology*, Lawrence and Wisehart, London.

O'Meara, D. (1977) 'The Afrikaner Broederbond 1927–1948: Class vanguard of Afrikaner nationalism', *Journal of Southern Studies* 3, 161–181.

Rompel, H. (1942) *Die Bioskoop in Diens Van die Volk. Deel II*, Nasionale, Kaapstad.

Therborn, G. (1980) *The Ideology of Power and the Power of Ideology*, Verso, London.

Tomaselli, K. G., Tomaselli, R. E. and Steenveld, L. (1987) 'Myth, Media and Apartheid', *Media Development* 34, 18–20.

Tomaselli, K. G. and Van Zyl, M. (1985) 'The structuring of popular memory in South African cinema and television texts', in Haines, R. and Buijs, G. (eds) *Urbanization in Twentieth Century South Africa: The Struggle for Social and Economic Space*, ISER, University of Durban-Westville, 191–269.

9

The Concept of Reach and the Anglophone Minority in Quebec

Courtice Rose

The Anglophone minority in Quebec, numbering about 700,000 people in 1981, are rapidly approaching a situation where their presence within a Francophone majority of some 5½ million is becoming less and less secure. The effects of a relatively low rate of net natural increase and a high rate of out-migration among both Anglophones born in Quebec and arriving immigrants who have gravitated toward the Anglophone minority coupled with the effects of recent language legislation (notably Bill 101, the Charter of the French Language), have decreased the general use of English, restricted access to English schools for some portions of the Anglophone population and has, in many instances, changed the language of work to French. Taken together, these conditions produce the very real possibility of the rapid disappearance of the Anglophone population and its culture from Quebec. The 1981 Census has revealed that the Anglophone minority is now declining in both absolute terms and in relative strength when compared to the Francophone majority.[1] In all probability this majority will, through a slow process of net natural increase and increased assimilation of immigrants from outside the province, gradually build in strength, thus further polarizing the two official language groups in the province (Joy, 1978). Given this situation, it becomes pertinent to ask: What are the chances of survival of the Anglophone minority in Quebec? And further, how can we understand the process of cultural degradation which appears to be taking place within the Anglophone minority? It will be suggested that a qualitative, phenomenological approach to this process of cultural conflict can be shown to generate an adequate description of the cultural dynamic in question and perhaps even a description which advances along several dimensions previously absent in more demographic and historical treatments of the Anglophone minority in Quebec.[2]

Specifically, the concept of 'reach' as developed by Schutz[3] can provide an alternative framework for the analysis of lived worlds and as such offer some access to the qualitative changes which individuals experience during periods of change in their lives. Such a framework is ideally suited to the description of changes presently confronting the Anglophone population of Quebec. Briefly, Schutz postulates that in the commonsense world of everyday living, people are, above all, interested in what lies within their reach, that is, within 'this sector of the world of perceived and perceptible objects, at whose center I am' (Schutz, 1962: 307).[4]

Not only does what is included in a person's reach consist of what is within present tactile, auditory and visual ranges, but it also includes what has been or potentially could be in those ranges. Since it includes other people, the world within reach has social and cultural dimensions to it and an equally important symbolic dimension. Of particular interest is the spatial arrangement of the worlds within a person's reach; these are described by Schutz as 'zones of operation' and they are differentiated by personal intentions, personal actions and meanings, as well as by the technological and geographical limits to movements in a particular society. The world within reach is also temporally differentiated into three types: the world within *actual* reach corresponding to the present time period, the world within *restorable* reach is identified with past time periods and the world within *attainable* reach delineates expectations for the future life-world.[5] The first section of this chapter examines the concept of reach as it developed in the writings of Alfred Schutz and the second is an attempt to apply this concept to the situation of the Anglophone minority in Quebec. Formulated in Schutz's terms our question becomes: is the world within reach for Anglophones in Quebec an adequate one?[6]

Alfred Schutz and the concept of reach

In his attempt to connect Weber's *verstehende sociologie* with Husserl's transcendental phenomenology, Alfred Schutz was effectively engaged in developing a new epistemology for the social sciences (see also Donovan's discussion in chapter 10). This epistemology was based on a phenomenological account of knowledge as derivative of experience (as opposed to reason) and as basically social in origin. For Schutz, reality was undeniably and self-evidently intersubjective. Not only was knowledge a social product and all action fundamentally socially conditioned but also the spatial and temporal relations that structure the world of everyday life were social in nature. Further, the very style of lived experience *and* cognition in the everyday world was also social and hence his epistemology was grounded in the concept of social action and not in perception.

The everyday life-world

Edmund Husserl's general thesis of the natural standpoint provided Schutz with his starting-point for the description of the natural attitude of daily life. In the natural attitude, the world and its contents are real for me and taken for granted. These contents are coherent and ordered into a spatial, temporal and social framework which is accepted on faith – the objects in this grounding framework are well defined, have definite properties and present themselves to us at face value. Most importantly, the world includes other people who are assumed to have experiences 'just like ours' such that the world of natural objects (e.g. trees, streets and houses), appears to those other people just as it appears to us. The thesis of the natural standpoint also states that the world of everyday living is also a social world: there exist other people with whom I can communicate and for whom I can assume that the meanings of common words, gestures and acts are understood.

For Schutz, one begins the study of the everyday life-world by starting with one's own biographically-determined situation. This includes my position in

space, time and society, but also my experience that some of the elements of the world taken for granted are imposed upon me, while others are either within my control or capable of being brought within my control. (Schutz, 1962: 76)

In this biographically-determined situation each person becomes the spatio-temporal centre of a world; everything is organized around a 'here' as the zero-point of a system of spatial and temporal coordinates which determines the dimensions of the surrounding field. All things are therefore arranged in front of or behind the zero-point, to the right of it, above it or below it.

Part of the reason why the biographically-determined situation is basically 'given' is that, by moving from my 'here' to another person's 'there', I do not lose the perspective already gained at my previous 'here', rather I assume the interchangeability of standpoints: while moving will alter what is within reach in a physical sense, it will not cast doubt on the fact that if another person were to make the same move, that similar things would be within reach for him as well. For Schutz, this feature of experience was called the *reciprocity of perspectives* and he claims that it would apply to the socio-cultural world as well. There would be enough typical constructs shared between two people (e.g. words, symbols, concepts, traditions) so that they could go beyond their individual biographically-determined situations and talk meaningfully about a common world.

Another fundamental feature of the life-world for Schutz was that every object appears to us in a certain pre-acquaintanceship or familiarity. Consequently, all objects were seen as partaking of some portions of a typical object and hence: 'The individual's common-sense knowledge is a system of constructs of its typicality' (Schutz, 1962: 7). Objects in the world are thus not taken as completely unique things but as events and things of some kind or sort. Typification was a general feature of all experience for Schutz and was a major determinant of our knowledge of the life-world.

Typifications are also plans of actions for Schutz; 'recipe' or type knowledge therefore implies ways of acting and reacting in common social situations. For example, riding on a bus we display the typical actions expected of a bus-rider, that is, producing the correct change or a ticket upon boarding the bus, leaving the bus by the rear door, and so forth. These courses of action are followed because they are *socially* sanctioned but also useful in obtaining our immediate goal, that of arriving at our destination without infuriating the bus driver or the other passengers. As long as the recipes we use for such actions obtain the desired results, they are applied without question (Gurwitsch, 1974). Thus the stock of knowledge built up in the life-world is not dependent on any particularly logical structure (although it may be logical in character), but rather is built up by the sedimentation of certain 'recipes' or typifications, some of which are individually apprehended but all of which are *socially* transmitted (Schutz, 1973: 14).

Besides its biographical, spatial and temporal characteristics, the stock of knowledge is also, of course, social in origin. Only a very small portion of our stock of knowledge could be labelled 'my knowledge', most of it arises from the *social* character of past experience, reports of which are handed down to us as rules, concepts, symbols or theories. In a sense, no individual's knowledge acquisition process can be isolated from its social origin if one considers this process to take place in a linguistic or symbolic medium (Gurwitsch, 1974). Most of this social knowledge defines what has previously been problematic in societal settings but has now been accorded the status of a recipe which is 'natural', 'correct', 'appropriate', 'useful' or 'this is the way one does things'. As such, the broader and more inclusive the stock of knowledge is, the more anonymous and objective it becomes, in the sense that it can be made to subsume large numbers of problematic social situations. The stock of knowledge at this scale ceases to be merely 'my stock of knowledge' or 'your stock of knowledge' but is rather 'everyone's knowledge'. That others possess some of this stock of knowledge as routine and taken for granted is evident to me when I observe that other people utilize 'solutions' or recipes similar to mine to solve their problematic situations: for example, whom to consult about a medical problem, where to find a plumber, where to find an income tax form, and so forth. This social character of the stock of knowledge also assures us that the typifications built up in our own stock of knowledge have a general application to the world at large.

The social world

The study of the social world for Schutz meant principally the study of what he termed 'we-relationships', 'thou-orientations', and 'they-relations' (Schutz, 1973: 59–92, 243–331; Schutz, 1967: 139–207). In the world of the natural attitude one accepts the existence of other people as taken for granted and also that their experiences of the objects in the life-world are similar to our own. Following Scheler, Schutz held that the problem of intersubjectivity in human relationships was mundane rather than transcendental in nature. This was the case since knowledge of the social aspects of the life-world is derivative of either face-to-face relationships (we-relations), thou-orientations or typifications (they-relations). In all cases, the subjective meanings taken are from signs and symbols in a social context: words, gestures, facial expressions, sighs and individual actions. The least mediated of these expressions and therefore the least anonymous, are those belonging to the we-relation and thou-orientation. Specifically, the thou-orientation occurs when

I experience a fellow man directly if and when he shares with me a common sector of time and space. The sharing of a common sector of time implies a genuine simultaneity of our two streams of consciousness, my fellow man and I grow older together. (Schutz, 1964: 23)

If the thou-orientation is reciprocal, rather than one-sided, a we-relation is formed. By means of words, gestures and expressions, all of which have a direct social root, the partners in a pure we-relation grasp easily the meaning of the other, reveal their interests, opinions, goals and personal stocks of knowledge. As long as this pure we-relation lasts, Schutz says, one lives in the vivid present, in which both inner and outer time dimensions are fused.

However the majority of social relationships are made not by means of we-relations but are made with contemporaries and occur in they-relations. In a they-relation, the other is experienced only by inference. These types of relationships are simply the result of typifications. The experiences of they-relations are thus much more indirect and depend heavily on the personal stock of knowledge concerning types of people. Most social interaction depends on the continuation of these typical they-relations and the knowledge of contemporaries as derived from they-relations is never determined in a first hand sense (as it is in a pure we-relation) but only in a *post-hoc* fashion.

The world within reach

Given the existence of persons whose style of lived experience resembles what Schutz has described as the 'wide-awake person in the natural attitude', the dominant form of living in the natural attitude consists of meaningful action, action which 'gears into' the external world. For Schutz, this action always takes place in the world within reach:

This sector of the world of perceived and perceptible objects at whose center I am shall be called the world within my actual reach which includes, thus, the objects within the scope of my view and the range of my hearing. Inside this field within my reach there is a region of things which I manipulate. (Schutz, 1962: 307).

The world(s) within reach formed a basic spatial and temporal arrangement for everyday experience. Their characteristics were that they were always centred on the individual, they were changeable at will by the person involved, they always contained a temporal dimension and lastly they consisted of both thematic and horizonal components. This latter characteristic enabled Schutz to postulate four descriptions of the world within reach.

The world within actual reach

The world within actual reach refers to that most central of all worlds, the private world. Here, now, at the centre of my private world, certain things and acts are well within my world within actual reach: I can read, write, talk on the telephone, or with other people in this office, rearrange my files, or perform any number of other tasks. This world within reach provides me with my starting-point for all activities; I can manipulate some things within this immediate world within reach quite easily: this pen, this book, that calculator; other things are manipulated with less ease, for example, in order to close the door I must push back the chair and walk over to the door. As the horizon of my actual world within reach extends to its physical limits I am not disturbed by the distorted appearances of objects some distance away. This problem is immediately overcome since all notions of distance include within them a tacit anticipation of some physical act made to overcome that distance thereby rendering the distant object back to its standard size. For example, people on the other side of the street appear to be only half an inch high to my eye, but a walk over to the location of those people would hastily restore my notion of the 'natural' size of such people. When I turn back to my writing these people remain in my world within reach (at the horizon) in the sense that they are still within my field of vision and I could probably talk to them if I raised my voice and shouted, but they are not part of my manipulatory area. This constant definition and redefinition of theme and horizon is, for Schutz, a basic characteristic of the world within reach. All of these personal activities taking place in the world within reach are quite habitual – they create no problem for me nor do they necessitate any modification of my personal stock of knowledge.

The world within restorable reach

Although the spatial dimension is the most immediate aspect of the world within reach which concerns us, its temporal component renders the concept much more extendable. The world within restorable reach refers to what was formerly in the world within actual reach and the assumption is made that the world within restorable reach can be brought back into the world within actual reach. (Schutz, 1962: 224–5). This restorability characteristic of the world within reach does not refer to any *absolute* reproduction of circumstances 'exactly-as-they-were-then' but rather to the fact that, in principle, I can always find again the same world which I had previously experienced when it was within my actual reach. I can, in some relative sense then, restore whole portions of my private world given the desire to do so. Obviously, since 'outer' time for all men is irreversible, no absolute restorability is possible, rather it is the features of a general repeatability of experiences and the constancy of known and familiar portions of the world within restorable reach which allow Schutz to make such claims about the temporal succession between the worlds within restorable reach and actual reach. Whereas the content of the world within actual reach is constantly changing, the content of the world within restorable reach is fixed to a certain degree. Once an act has been completed, it resides, for the actor, in the 'perfect tense' and it is the memory of these acts *as ongoing actions* that enters into the personal stock of knowledge. Thus the world within actual reach, while in no way necessarily connected to the world within restorable reach is definitely derivative of it. There is no suggestion (now) that the world within restorable reach could be *transferred* into my world within actual reach but there are elements of sameness and familiarity, and linkages of experience which connect the two for me.

The world within attainable reach

Corresponding to the world within restorable reach is the world within attainable reach (Schutz, 1973: 39ff). The world within attainable reach is based on potential acts to be taken in the future: the basic expectation is that, given certain physical activities and the existence of an amicable social world, there is a zone of potential working acts in which one can participate in the future. Apart from the physical limits set to this world within attainable reach by purely technological constraints, such as the range of airplanes and outer space vehicles, the most important feature of this world is that it is entirely changeable, depending only on the world within actual reach as a jumping-off point. Since the world within attainable reach is never an existing world, that is, it has not yet come to exist, there are certain degrees of probability attached to actions to be taken in the world within attainable reach. The greater the distance (both in the spatial and temporal senses as well as in a social sense) of the world within attainable reach from the world within actual reach, the less chance that world has of attainment.

The world within common reach

What has been stated to hold for the individual, the system of worlds within actual, restorable and attainable reach, can also be said to hold for any other person in the world of the natural attitude. The implication is that there must exist some overlap or coincidence of my world within reach and that of someone else, or a world within common reach.

The social lifeworld within our reach will be called the domain of direct social experience and the subjects encountered in it, our fellow men. In this domain, we share with our fellow man a common span of time, moreover, a sector of the spatial world is within our common reach. (Schutz, 1966: 119)

The world within common reach can extend from intimate we-relationships to the most anonymous they-relationships. In the pure we-relationship, a large portion of each partner's world within reach would be found within the world within common reach – there is almost complete access to the other's body, speech, mannerisms, actions and expressions. Such coincidence of worlds within reach can of course be found in marriages, lifelong friendships, and so forth, but in other types of face-to-face relationships which are less familiar, the segment of the world within common reach is less complete, for example, with a neighbour, a social acquaintance, a relative or a colleague. In even less familiar they-relationships the shared portions of the world within common reach are minimal, for example, with the postman, the caretaker, or the sales assistant.

The gradation of worlds within actual, restorable, attainable and common reach point ultimately, for Schutz, to a system of spatial arrangements extending over the whole social world and in a certain sense, they can be generalized as the structures of 'everyone's world'. The interdependence of the two systems, the spatial and the social is evident: the spatial arrangement of the everyday world into various zones of reach enters directly into the differentiation of ideas such as intimacy versus anonymity, strangeness versus familiarity and social proximity versus social distance. In sum, Schutz's definition of the world within reach consisted of well-stratified, temporally-differentiated, portable action zones dependent not only on the visual, auditory and manipulative capabilities of the subject but also on certain other basic characteristics of the life-world: its consistency, its repeatability, its universality, its predictability and its genuine social character.

The Anglophone minority in Quebec

Traditional analyses of the Anglophone minority in Quebec generally accept the fact that there have been significant changes in the socio-economic conditions and the general cultural climate now present for Anglophones in Quebec (McLeod-Arnopoulous, 1980; Caldwell and Waddell, 1982). However, the question of whether the *lived-world* for Anglophones has also undergone significant changes has not been addressed to date.

It is possible to see the question of there being an adequate world within reach for the Anglophone inhabitants of Quebec as one part of a larger (and more severe) question concerning the maintenance of a primary internalized stock of knowledge, those things obtained in childhood and still held as part of one's everyday world, in the face of a situation where that knowledge is being rendered increasingly marginal or irrelevant. This type of reality maintenance is accomplished for some sociologists through the day-to-day routines and ongoing individual interaction which one finds as a regular, taken-for-granted feature of the world within reach (Berger and Luckmann, 1967). In Quebec, so long as these routines continue and so long as the larger Anglophone community continues to provide a plausible structure for the *belief* in an Anglophone way of life, then the individual's existence within a larger world is confirmed. If, however, some of the features of the world within reach are 'broken up' either by the wholescale incursion of other individuals or by the slower erosion of the familiar routines found in the world within reach, then presumably some type of crisis in reality maintenance could be precipitated as the former plausibility structures break down and subjective worlds are gradually or abruptly transformed. There is now evidence that, at least with respect to the world within reach for Anglophones, some type of crisis in routine reality-maintenance is approaching.

The world within restorable reach

The need to express one's pride in a cultural heritage derives from the most basic types of experience shared by all people with that cultural background. If one accepts this notion, then it would appear that the existing Anglophone minority of Quebec is becoming quite isolated from its authentic beginnings. On all sides, the world within restorable reach is receding, and receding at a rate which threatens to leave this minority completely severed from its heritage within certain regions of Quebec in the next generation or two. As this world within restorable reach contains the thematic and symbolic features absolutely necessary for the preservation of a cultural heritage as well as the memories of a multitude of shared experiences for members of that cultural group, the changes now taking place in the perception of this world within restorable reach are fundamental to the understanding of the process of Anglophone cultural maintenance and cultural transfer between generations.

The first change, that of the truncation of the world within restorable reach, relates to both the constancy and repeatability features of the world taken in the natural attitude. With the closing of more and more Anglophone schools, the loss of social and community services formerly available in English, the continued out-migration of large firms and corporate headquarters symbolic of Anglophone involvement in the business world, there is simply no easily *accessible and desirable* world within restorable reach for much of the Anglophone population. In a simplistic geographical sense, it may still be possible for many Anglophones to return to their birthplace in Quebec, but with over one half of the working male population stating 'outside Quebec' as their birthplace, this is obviously not the case for a large portion of the Anglophone population. Moreover, there is a very great symbolic distance being built up between the elements of the world within restorable reach and the world within actual reach. What is problematic about this trend is that the more that the world within restorable reach is set at a distance from the world within actual reach, the greater the chances of there being no taken-for-granted character to those elements in the world within restorable reach and consequently, a loss in authenticity with respect to the meaning of these elements. Schutz was very clear that meaning, for the individual, is built up by a series of 'backward glances' over the 'relief' of the world within restorable reach; this is a process in which we are constantly engaged and a process which we probably, unconsciously, refer to in order to position or make sense of new developments within our present world. If, however, at a symbolic level, one can no longer easily return to the world within restorable reach and further, if there is no sense of consistency to the symbols appearing in that world, then there is every possibility that the world within restorable reach will be permanently cast adrift from our present concerns and the preservation of a cultural heritage at the grass-roots level simply evaporates.[7]

The sequence of events beginning with the St Leonard school crisis (1968–9)[8] and ending with the adoption of Bill 101 in 1977 now indicates a rather abrupt truncation of the world within restorable reach for a large portion of the Anglophone minority. One simply cannot return to the era before 1967 when the two cultural groups dominated different sectors of the economy and society, an era in which they were geographically separated and in which great gaps appeared in the income, occupation and education scales.[9] The consequence of this fact is that the world within restorable reach before 1967 is for most Anglophones very much a creature of history, a receding world for which there can be no hope of a repeatability of experiences. Hence its universal character, a quality Schutz thought was present for all individuals who shared a world within restorable reach, is now almost obliterated; it is no longer even 'restorable in principle'.

Another factor probably responsible for the loss of familiarity with the world within restorable reach for the Anglophone population is that, in a general sense, the mediation of experiences within the world within restorable reach through common symbolic vehicles is now less present for many Anglophones and where present, less effective. Besides the obvious examples of an Anglophone press largely controlled by foreign-born Anglophones and the question of this press acting as if it were the spokesperson for the whole Anglophone minority (AEMJQ, 1972), there are more basic examples such as the lack of celebration of historical English holidays such as Victoria Day and Dominion Day. While there is certainly a demographic factor at work here, the loss of familiar mediation vehicles which were embedded in the world within restorable reach is probably indicated as well.[10]

Finally, there is the problem of unrestorable we-relations among the Anglophone population. As out-migration continues, there are not as many opportunities to meet on a face-to-face basis with large numbers of people in one's own linguistic group and within one's own occupational and educational background. As personal friends, colleagues and family relations move away or die, this increases the probability that the world within restorable reach will become more personally distant from the world within actual reach. The restorable we-relation, Schutz noted, was at the basis of our ability to acquire an adequate stock of knowledge concerning other persons. Conversation with others, particularly those of one's own culture, is fundamental to the routine maintenance of reality features for individual persons. Even though this type of reality maintenance through conversation is rarely made explicit, the mere exchange of pleasantries with its reference to commonly known people, places, events and other taken-for-granted paraphernalia confirms the existence of a subjective world – a subjective world *within which* these casual day-to-day conversations take place. Without conversation and without the possibility of reaffirming this we-relationship, our confidence in that stock of knowledge is increasingly suspect and for our understanding of others we must begin to rely on our knowledge of they-relations or type knowledge. All of the signs, expressions, gestures and actions so easily identified in the restorable we-relation are lost, and the process of groping about for some commonly held meaning structures must begin all over again. It can be argued that the existence and continuation of restorable we-relations is vital, if not crucial to the continuation of a healthy cultural tradition. If there is a decline in the frequency, the quality and the dependability of such restorable we-relations, there can be little doubt that, at the experiential level at least, the elements of 'sameness', 'familiarity' and 'nearness' which help drive along any cultural heritage, will gradually fade away.

The world within actual reach

In the world within actual reach, or the 'arena' in which one engages the world at large, here also there are several changes affecting the continuation of the Anglophone cultural tradition. In its spatial, temporal and social dimensions the world within actual reach is of course derivative of the world within restorable reach, but unlike the latter which has a primarily fixed character, the world within actual reach is conceived as an open-ended situation, one that can enlarge or contract depending on the intentions and desires of the subjects themselves. The principal observation here is that, for the Anglophone minority of Quebec, the world within actual reach appears to be shrinking both in its absolute dimensions, that is, the number and distribution of the Anglophone minority, and in its relative dimensions, that is, in its social and political strength *vis-à-vis* the Francophone majority.

One feature of the world within actual reach which appears to be undergoing rapid change is the world of work. In spatio-temporal terms, the world within actual reach is not only contracting but at the same time changing in a qualitative sense. The increasing use of French as the language of work, the greater numbers of Francophones found at the management and corporate ownership levels of the Quebec business world, the failure of the federal government's bilingualism campaign and the lack of access for Anglophones to the Quebec civil service – all of these conditions have contributed to building more social distance into the world within actual reach for most working Anglophones. With these changes has come the realization that while the world of business is still an Anglophone concern, that is, it is still very much one of the areas where Anglophones gear into the world, the horizons of this world are gradually shrinking as more and more Francophones make their presence felt in this working world. As a result, the world within actual reach for many Anglophones has become qualitatively different: hours of working are often changed, procedures during meetings, conferences and seminars are handled differently and in almost every corner of the business world there seems to be a greater and greater involvement with the provincial government, a change which has become particularly evident since the election of 1976.[11]

If the world within actual reach for Anglophone Quebec can be characterized as shrinking, there have been several responses to this situation which are worthy of note. Earlier it was suggested that the non-existence of restorable we-relationships in the world within restorable reach was a major factor in the severing of that world from the present world; but conversely, among the Anglophones who are left, it would appear that concrete we-relationships between them are becoming more intense. Part of the reason for this may arise from the desire (perhaps unconscious) to continue the world within actual reach along a trajectory with as close a resemblance as possible to the years before 1967. But, more probably, it could be seen as a normal process of coming together for the discussion of mutual concerns. Hence, over the past three or four years, several Anglophone 'rights' groups have been formed (e.g. the Eastern Townshippers Association, the Council of Quebec Minorities, Positive Action, Freedom of Choice, Participation – Quebec, the Committee for Anglophone Social Action in the Gaspé, the Pontiac–Ontario Movement, the Voice of English Quebec). More recently, all of these groups have agreed to form one large pressure group, Alliance

Quebec. Here one does have the possibility of seeing the concrete we-relationships among Anglophones at work – and perhaps because of this renewed interest in the plight of Anglo-Quebec, there will result a determination to re-establish some of the genuinely English character to the Anglo-Quebec heritage.

There seems general agreement that the control over Anglophone school boards, social services and other institutions such as English hospitals and museums must remain within the manipulatory area of the Anglophone minority. These can be described as 'must do' areas where the Anglophone minority feels the very real threat of a loss of control, either through direct government intervention or by the slow attrition of Anglophone clients who leave the province, relocate within the province or die. For example, the amalgamation of several chronic-care hospitals in the Sherbrooke area would result in the closing of several wards of the only English hospital. On other concerns such as the protection of linguistic rights in the provincial legislature, the courts of law and on public signs, there is of course almost unilateral agreement by the various pressure groups that these items *must* be kept within the manipulatory area and any proposal to remove them will be widely resisted (Le Cavalier, 1982).

In some sense the picture which emerged of the world within actual reach for many Anglophones is one in which the thematic and social horizons of the world within actual reach are contracting and contracting quickly enough that many feel that the manipulatory area itself (the direct field of an individual's action) may in fact be threatened in the near future. This amounts to a situation in which many Anglophones can be expected to react in any way possible in order to insulate themselves from this perceived threat to their world within reach. To keep the world within reach as large and as variegated as possible is at least to maintain one's identity within a thriving culture, but as the world within actual reach shrinks in its dimensions – spatial, temporal, social and symbolic – this project becomes more and more problematic. It remains to be seen whether Alliance Quebec or some other pressure group is able to provide this insulation adequately or whether they will merely collapse thus allowing further incursions from the Francophone majority.

The world within common reach

Of all the areas concerning the relationships between the Anglophone minority and the Francophone majority in Quebec, one would expect that the characteristics of the world within common reach would be the best known of all the social worlds. Certainly there probably has been an increase in the spatio-temporal extent of the world within common reach between individual Anglophones and individual Francophones. With a greater necessity to encounter and deal with Francophones in almost all areas of the economic world, with the increasing use of French throughout the working world and a greater mixture of Anglophones and Francophones in the public and para-public sectors, there is an almost inevitable juxtaposition of the Anglophone's world within reach with that of the Francophone. In many cases this juxtaposition may result in a greater degree of overlap between the worlds within reach and as a result some Anglophones in the workforce have become not only fluently bilingual but probably very close to being bicultural as well. However much this reach coincidence may be desirable (because it promotes the occasion for concrete we-relationships), it still remains the case that at the social and symbolic levels, the worlds within common reach between larger groups of Anglophones and Francophones are not all that coexistent. Even though there is evidence that both French Canadians and English Canadians regard each other favourably on basic attitudinal scales and that this situation has not changed appreciably over the last fifteen years (SRG, 1965; Berry et al., 1977), there also appears to be some residual feelings of resentment of French Canadians among English Canadians (Kwavnick, 1965; Lambert, 1967; Milner, 1973). This is particularly true for the social class ranking of French Canadians and this may point to an intentional distancing off or setting out of view of the worlds within actual reach between the two linguistic groups. At the social level, even though Anglophones are gradually becoming more bilingual and there is a greater degree of general reach coincidence, this may have taken place for purely instrumental or circumstantial reasons and there remains the genuine question as to whether, when such reach coincidence is present, the individuals actually engage in changing former they-relations into concrete we-relations. At least one research group has concluded that:

In Canada there are few elements of culture (other than U.S. culture) and few, if any, symbols that are generative of solidarity between francophones and anglophones. . . . Most of the institutions for the creation and diffusion of culture are linguistically segregated. . . . There is some translation but by and large there exist two more or less independent systems of mass communication and cultural expression. (Breton et al., 1980: 302)

This conclusion would seem to support the notion that at the social and symbolic levels at least, the world within common reach extends over a very small area indeed.

Several reasons could be advanced for the persistent occurrence of this reach separation. At many levels of the individual Anglophone's day-to-day existence, minority status simply precludes large degrees of reach coincidence with a great number of Francophones. Normally there are established we-relations, mostly with fellow Anglophones which allow one to earn a living, provide oneself with food, clothing and shelter and the basic necessities of social life. Schools, hospitals, media and educational and cultural establishments are available for use in the English language. In short, there are vast unused portions of the world within common reach between most Anglophones and Francophones simply because of the institutional framework already in place for Anglophones and there is simply no need to search outside the world within reach (or zones of typical operation), or to turn one's interest at hand as Schutz would say, from one portion of the world within common reach to another portion. Hence there are diminutive amounts of a common stock of knowledge built up between the two linguistic groups, a fact which the parallel systems of media and cultural events will probably maintain, and there arise few situations in which the Anglophone's taken-for-granted knowledge of his world within reach becomes problematic or inadequate in any way.

There may, however, be some changes in the world within common reach which emanate from the changing socio-demographic conditions in Quebec. During the post-war period and continuing well into the 1960s, there existed well-defined spheres of influence for Anglophones and Francophones: Anglophones dominated the business and commercial sectors and Francophones were to be found in the government, the clergy, and in the educational and professional sectors. But as this world within common reach began to change, with the Francophone portion enlarging and the Anglophone portion shrinking, the limits of this common zone have become quite nebulous. Moreover, at the social level, with a Francophone population which is in the process of acquiring more wealth and power, the horizons of the world within common reach are quite unarticulated. Hence it would appear that simply the existence of an enlarged world within common reach between the two linguistic groups in no way guarantees that a large number of solid we-relationships will be formed between individuals nor that this will result in the creation of some genuine bicultural world. For Anglophones, at least, it would further appear that until some closure, constancy and repeatability can be brought to the world within common reach and until some mutual themes emerge from this world, no meaningful projects will be advanced in a world which, for them is increasingly not their own.

Conclusion

It can be suggested then, that while the concept of reach does not *explain* or account for the changes taking place in the lived-world of Quebec's

Anglophone population, the concept does portray some features of that lived-world which are vital to its continued existence. If one accepts the notion that it is the routine features of subjective worlds which through their very existence and institutionalization provide the 'contours of reality' on which we depend in our day-to-day living and if, furthermore, one accepts the idea that these subjective realities must stand in some relation to a larger objective reality, that is, the 700,000 Anglophones of Quebec who still call the province their home, then at least one conclusion is that it is *not* the Parti Québécois, *nor* Bill 101 *nor* the referendum of 1980 which has precipitated the crisis in routine reality maintenance for the Anglophones, but rather the slow erosion of the *socially defined* features of the life-world and the consequent non-realization of those taken-for-granted features and expectations which are now beginning to disconfirm the place of the Anglophone in Quebec. In short, their world within reach has become inadequate.

A note on method

This study is an attempt to apply some of the conceptual insights of Alfred Schutz to the social world of the Anglophone population of Quebec. In retrospect I would not term the account 'hermeneutic' or 'text-interpretative' in the narrower sense of being a *formal* analysis of texts but it would appear to fit into the broader category of an *informal* analysis of texts, whereby one understands that 'text' may mean any aspect of the lived-world for Anglophones of Quebec that is spoken, written or acted out in everyday events. The chapter starts from the premise that it is at least possible to build up some descriptions of the changes taking place in this lived-world and that the key to rendering such an account is basically interpretative in character. There has been at least some recognition of the viability of such an approach both within geography (Olsson, 1982; 1983; Gould, 1982; 1983) and outside it (Ricoeur, 1974; 1976; Gadamer, 1975; Schrag, 1980; Hekman, 1984).

The basic thesis is that the Schutzian concept of the world within reach can provide an experiential framework for portraying the interdependence thought to exist between 'social' knowing and the spatial and temporal referents for that knowledge in the daily life of the Anglophone population. One of the clear methodological antecedents for this way of proceeding is found in the *Geisteswissenschaften/Naturwissenschaften* distinction as made by Wilhelm Dilthey (Makkreel, 1969; Gadamer, 1976; Rickman, 1976). *Erlebnis*, or lived experience, was 'that unit of experience which is immediately recognizable or manifests a meaningful relation to human life' (Dilthey, *GS* VI: 314). In contrast to some of our perceptions of 'outer life', *Erlebnis*, because it arises from the interaction of an inner life with outward manifestations, has a quality of certainty and sameness attached to it which we do not always find in 'outer', more objective knowledge. For Dilthey, *Erlebnis* was the real subject matter of the life-world and knowledge of it was obtained only in a reflective attitude. One understands oneself and other events in the world in exactly the same manner; thus 'historical' consciousness is seen as a type of self-understanding. One assumes that the object to be understood, the person or event in question is a text that is to be deciphered and that once set apart from oneself in some given context, every encounter with a text can result in a correct interpretation. To understand another person is to decipher the text of that person's 'life-expressions': words, gestures, signs and so forth; the person is 'objectified' in the same way that one objectifies one's own action – by reflective thought after the fact. As long as the interpreter is able to grasp the tradition embedded in the text, a condition which is assured by the fact that the interpreter is just as much a resident of the life-world as is the 'subject', then a perfectly adequate comprehension of the other's world would be possible. The text is seen as a set of external signs which are intimately linked to the inner processes of the other and everything in the other is thus understood since everything in the other resembles a text. On this account, an interpreter who states that the existence of 'unrestorable we-relations' is one of the reasons why the Anglophone population lives in a shrinking social world, makes such a statement in the belief that there really is access to the actual psychic processes of typical Anglophones in Quebec. 'Reading other's minds' would perhaps be too strong a phrase here, but surely reading the external signs which are linked to internal processes would be a reasonable description of the interpretative leap that is necessary.

A major problem with such a strict Diltheyan approach is that the 'life-expressions' (words, signs, gestures, actions) are, of course, only historical in the sense of being the 'outer' sides of those events. Inferring that 'inner' events take place and that they somehow correspond to these outer events and to what the interpreter thinks is the case, is a difficult if not implausible step to take. Caught in this problem of inner states, outward manifestations and texts which are always at a distance from the interpreter, Dilthey ultimately wants an autonomous subject, one who is not affected by his own historicity, a perfect interpreter who can set aside his own prejudices, values and beliefs and simply read the text as it is. The real problem for such a 'romantic hermeneutic' (to use Gadamer's term), is that he or she believes that there really *is* a correct interpretation for every text and that it is available to any interpreter as long as the rules of textual exegesis are followed. The problem of method only becomes a problem whenever expectations about the outcome of this project are constantly being reviewed and changed by the interpreter in the search to return to the 'method' as a way of 'fixing' the interpretation, that is, making it the correct interpretation.

Another methodological problem has recently been posed with the adoption of the 'conversational' model of hermeneutical inquiry (Ricoeur, 1973; 1976; Gadamer, 1975; 1976). Dilthey's hermeneutics took the signs of the text to be indicative of what lay *behind* the signs but modern hermeneutics urges that we look *with* the text at what it says to successive generations of interpreters thereby involving the text, the interpreter and the interpretation in an on-going text-event. In the conversational model of text interpretation the text is constituted as a 'thou' for the interpreter – a 'thou' which one attempts to understand through successive approximations of the meaning of the text. Here the meanings of the text are not simply deciphered, they are 'prescenced' or 'mediated' through both the past formulations of other interpreters and the present formulations of still more interpreters. This is a dialectical process in which the text acquires certain horizons (past/present, their/mine, distant/near), and it is the fusion of these horizons which discloses the original correlation between being and meaning (Gadamer, 1975: 267f). Hence the text, *qua* text, is not the object of study, the 'object' arises out of the 'linguisticality' of the event of interpretation. We are apprised of some aspect of 'being-in-the-other' because we ourselves (as interpreters, and as actors) have contributed to it and as we continue to interpret other texts we encounter *ourselves* as 'authors' of the text event. To continue this self-encounter while at the same time being concerned with the understanding of other people's actions is the aim of the modern hermeneutical endeavour. In this sense, hermeneutics is not so much a method as it is a clarification for the conditions of being under which meaning can be understood. Gadamer lables this clarifying element 'effective historical consciousness' and the process of coming to understand in this way he calls 'effective history' (Gadamer, 1975: 305).

Despite his lengthy and profound treatment of the modern hermeneutical problem, Gadamer's emphasis on effective historical consciousness tends to eliminate many of the more solidified 'moments of the tradition' and leave us in a dilemma where what grounds our knowledge of others (and ourselves) can never be fully examined. Either we affirm the scientific conditions of objectification at the risk of seeing the amalgam of being and meaning evaporate *or* we affirm this original correlation and eliminate the scientific conditions necessary for any objectivity in the human sciences (Kirkland, 1977: 34).

Not wishing to grasp either horn of the dilemma, the descriptions offered in the case-study of the Anglophone minority in Quebec are in part 'scientific', in part 'hermeneutical' and in part autobiographical. I see no way to separate these strands in terms of their differences in method. The account proceeds by utilizing some conventional sources such as demographic and linguistic surveys as well as historical accounts, anecdotes, and so forth, but it does not proceed in any 'conversational' or fully dialectical manner. What seemed important was that the account should be coherent and recognized by Anglophones as consistent with the rest of their generally held beliefs as to their minority status. The 'amalgam of being and meaning' to which such an account might aspire seems (now) quite a distant objective when compared to the more mundane results achieved. But the problem here was that there appeared to be *no basis on which to express any difference* between 'the tradition-as-lived' (i.e. being English in Quebec) and 'a framework-as-an-analysis-of-that-tradition-as-lived', that is to say, the concept of reach. Again, if the account proves to be satisfactory, coherent and perhaps to some degree provocative for the Anglophone minority, then presumably it will be judged as acceptable or unacceptable. If the answer to this question is positive then this does not mean it is the correct account, it means only that it fits the situation at hand reasonably well. In this sense then the 'method' is not a set of techniques nor a set of rules or guidelines; the method is acculturation within the tradition itself. On this account, being 'interpretative' or 'hermeneutic' about how to proceed may mean not having any special method at all but rather casting around for some descriptions which help get the job done.[12]

Notes

This is a revised version of a paper originally published in *Canadian Ethnic Studies* 17(3), (1985), 1–16, and is reproduced here by permission.

1   The 1981 Census of Canada indicates that in 1971 the English mother-tongue population of Quebec was 789,185 or 13.1 per cent of the total Quebec population but that in 1981 these figures had declined to 706,110 or 10.9 per cent respectively. The English 'mother-tongue' population denotes those whose first language learned and still retained is English. If the 'language-in-use' definition is employed, then the decline has been even more precipitous: in 1971 those who declared English as their language in use numbered 887,875 but in 1981 this figure was only 601,160. The 'Quiet Revolution' of the 1960s saw the gradual fading away of the Catholic Church as a rallying point for Quebec national identity along with the increasing urbanization and secularization of institutions in the education, health and welfare sectors. Coupled with a drastic drop in the Francophone birthrate during this same period, it became apparent the French language itself might be the only remaining expression of a different cultural identity left in Canada.

2   There have been several recent works on the Anglophone situation in Quebec: (i) Sheila McLeod-Arnopoulos and Dominique Clift, *The English Fact in Quebec*, Montreal: McGill-Queens University Press (1980); (ii) Gary Caldwell and Eric Waddell (eds.), *The English of Quebec: From Majority to Minority Status*, Quebec: Institut québécois de recherche sur la culture (1982); and (iii) Susan Schachter (ed.), *Working papers on English language institutions in Quebec*, Montreal: Alliance Quebec (1982). Of these, perhaps Waddell's article 'Place and People', comes closest to the approach envisaged here, that is, attempting to grasp some of the experiential dimensions of being among the Anglophone minority in Quebec. (Waddell, in Caldwell and Waddell, 1982.)

3   A sociologist whose phenomenoclogical approach has found favour in human geography; see May 1960; Berger and Luckmann (1967); Bruyn (1966); Maslow (1968); Buttimer (1976); Ley (1977); Relph (1976); Seamon (1979) and Robinson (1982).

4   The concept of reach is considered part of the 'philosophy of the natural attitude' held by both Edmund Husserl and Alfred Schutz; see Schutz (1944; 1951; 1967; 1973).

5   It should be noted that the concept of reach is similar to other formulations postulated as structures of the life-world. Among its predecessors were G. H. Mead's 'manipulatory area' (Mead, 1932; 1938); Kurt Lewin's notion of psychological 'life-space' (Lewin, 1933; 1936); and among its successors are the 'patent zone' and 'latent zone' ideas of Ortega y Gassett (1957) and Erwin Straus' 'presentic space' (Straus, 1966).

6   'Adequate', here used in the Schutzian sense, would mean that enough of the features of one's everyday life-world were intact thereby preventing any sort of crisis in one's 'reality maintenance'. Such features might include the biographically determined situation, the personal stock of knowledge, typicality and relevance structures with respect to other people and of course the spatial, temporal and social structures of the worlds within reach (see Schutz, 1962; 1967; 1973).

7   That such a loss is now being experienced by Quebec Anglophones is evident in many quarters, e.g. (i) graduates from the Lake of Two Mountains High School returning to a recent reunion found that more than half of their number no long had any connection with Quebec and that they had *no intention* of returning to Quebec within the foreseeable future (*Gazette*, 5 June, 1982); (ii) a recent poll (CROP, April 1983) indicates that one of every five Anglophones now living in the province intends to leave within the next five years (*Record*, 5 May, 1983).

8   In 1968 there were riots in the Montreal suburbs of St Leonard after a local Catholic school board voted to eliminate English as the language of instruction at the elementary and secondary schools.

9   Evidence is mounting that the gaps in the income, education and occupation scales are now rapidly disappearing, e.g. while *average* Anglophone income levels are still higher than average Francophone incomes, after controlling for the education and age factors, the mean Francophone income has been higher than the mean Anglophone income since 1977 and in the Montreal region, unilingual Anglophones now earn less than Francophones (Vaillancourt, 1980; Veltman and Boulet, 1980).

10   It may very well be that with the loss of a well mediated Anglophone tradition, some younger Anglophones are now assuming the character traits of the Francophone majority while at the same time remaining largely within the Anglophone educational system. Schutz might explain this paradoxical situation by referring to the breaking down of our stock of knowledge of the types of 'common others' thought to populate the other cultural group and the subsequent need to reassess the accuracy of our 'they-relations'. Some objective evidence that this type of assimilation may be occurring has been reported in the 1981 census: the number of English Quebecers speaking French at home now stands at over 82,000, an increase of some 33,000 since 1971 (*Gazette*, 27 April, 1983).

11   Perhaps the most intractable problem for Anglophones dealing with the Quebec civil service has been that this type of (often bilingual) functionary tends to remain quite inaccessible as a compatriot in the world of provincial government, e.g.:

> . . . the traditional way of doing things, with its pragmatism and its informality, could no longer be applied to the management of community institutions, the bureaucrats had to be propitiated with an endless stream of papers and reports. The kind of personality which only a few years before had made for a successful community representative and negotiator suddenly became incapable of dealing effectively with provincial authorities. Painful tensions resulted from the need to replace many of these people with others who could better understand the new administrative procedures. (McLeon-Arnopoulos and Clift, 1980: 104).

12 Some readers will no doubt recognize my debt to the work of Richard Rorty, (1979; 1982; 1984). Rorty thinks that so far as the human sciences are concerned, there will not be much quarrel about method as long as we do not think that texts are something special from which only 'holistic' accounts emerge nor that they can be 'decoded' in some way so as to unlock some essential feature of the observer–observed relationship. Rather, different vocabularies are simply deemed adequate or inadequate, useful or useless, helpful or misleading but not 'more objective' or 'less objective', not 'more scientific' or 'less scientific' (see especially Rorty, 1982, chapter 11).

References

Association of English Media Journalists of Quebec (1972) 'The English media in Quebec: a distorting mirror of reality?', Reporter Publications, Montreal.

Berger, P. L. and T. Luckmann (1967) *The social construction of reality*, Doubleday, New York.

Bergson, H. (1910; 1960) *La pensée et la mouvant*, trans. F. L. Pogson, *Time and Free Will*, Harper and Row, New York.

Berry, J. W., R. Kalin and D. M. Taylor (1977) *Multiculturalism and ethnic attitudes in Canada*, Ministry of State for Multiculturalism, Ottawa.

Breton, R., J. Reit and V. Valentine (1980) *Cultural boundaries and the cohesion of Canada*, Institute for Research on Public Policy, Montreal.

Bruyn, S. (1966) *The human perspective in sociology*, Prentice-Hall, Englewood Cliffs, N.J.

Buttimer, A. (1976) 'Grasping the dynamism of life-world', *Annals of the Association of American Geographers*, vol. 66, no. 2, 277–92.

Caldwell, G. and E. Waddell (eds) (1982) *The English of Quebec: from majority to minority status*, Institut québécois de recherche sur la culture, Quebec.

Dilthey, W. (1958) *Gesammelte Schriften* 17 volumes, 1914–1974, volume IV, ed. G. Misch. B. G. Teubner, Stuttgart (first published 1924).

Gadamer, H. G. (1975) *Truth and method*, trans. G. Barden and J. Cumming, Seabury Press, New York.

Gadamer, H. G. (1976) 'The problem of historical consciousness', *Graduate Faculty Philosophy Journal*, 1–52.

Gould, P. (1982) 'Is it necessary to choose: Some technical, hermeneutic and emancipatory thoughts on enquiry', in P. Gould and G. Olsson, *A Search for Common Ground*, Pion, London, 71–104.

Gould, P. (1983) 'On the road to Colonos: Or theory and perversity in the social sciences', *Geographical Analysis*, vol. 15, no. 1, 35–40.

Gurwitsch, A. (1974) *Phenomenology and the theory of science*. ed. L. Embree, Northwestern University Press, Chicago.

Harrison, R. J. and D. N. Livingstone (1982) 'Understanding in geography: structuring the subjective', in D. T. Herbert and R. J. Johnston, *Geography and the Urban Environment*, vol. 5, John Wiley & Sons, London, 1–39.

Hekman, S. (1984) 'Action as text: Gadamer's hermeneutics and the social scientific analysis of action', *Journal for the Theory of Social Behavior*, vol. 14, no. 3, 333–54.

James, W. (1980) *Principles of psychology*, Henry, New York.

Joy, R. J. (1978) *Accent Quebec: Canada's official language minorities*, C. D. Howe Research Institute, Montreal.

Kirkland, F. (1977) 'Gadamer and Ricoeur: the paradigm of the text', *Graduate Faculty Philosophy Journal*, vol. 6, no. 1, 131–44.

Kwavnick, D. (1965) 'The roots of French-Canadian Discontent', *Canadian Journal of Economics and Political Science*, vol. 31, 509–23.

Lambert, W. E. (1967) 'A social psychology of bilingualism', *Journal of Social Issues*, vol. 23, no. 2, 91–109.

Le Cavalier, G., P. Fitzsimmons-Le Cavalier and D. Hewitt (1982) 'The view of Quebec's non-Francophone leaders on the linguistic situation', *Mimeograph Research Paper no. 2*, Concordia University, Montreal.

Lewin, K. (1933) 'Vectors, cognitive processes and Mr. Tolman's criticism', *Journal of General Psychology*, vol. 8, 318–45.

Lewin, K. (1936) *Principles of topological psychology*, McGraw-Hill, New York.

Ley, D. (1977) 'Social geography and the taken-for-granted world', *Transactions, Institute of British Geographers*, vol. 2, no. 4, 498–512.

Makkreel, R. (1969) 'Wilhelm Dilthey and the neo-Kantians: the distinction of the *Geisteswissenschaften* and the *Kulturwissenschaften*', *Journal of the History of Philosophy*, vol. 7, no. 4, 423–40.

Maslow, A. (1968) *Towards a psychology of being*, Van Nostrand Reinhold, New York.

May, R. (1960) *Existential psychology*, Random House, New York.

McLeod-Arnopoulos, S. and D. Clift (1980) *The English fact in Quebec*, McGill-Queen's University Press, Montreal.

Mead, G. H. (1932) *Philosophy of the present*, Open Court, Chicago.

Mead, G. H. (1938) *Philosophy of the act*, Open Court, Chicago.

Milner, H. and S. H. Milner (1973) *The decolonization of Quebec: an analysis of left-wing nationalism*, McClelland and Stewart, Toronto.

Milner, H. and S. H. Milner (1978) *Politics in the new Quebec*, McClelland and Stewart, Toronto.

Olsson, G. (1982) in P. Gould and G. Olsson, *A search for common ground*, Pion, London, 223–31.

Olsson, G. (1983) 'Expressed impressions of impressed expressions', *Geographical Analysis*, vol. 15, no. 1, 60–4.

Ortega y Gassett, J. (1957) *Man and people*, W. W. Norton, New York.

Relph, E. (1976) *Place and placelessness*, Pion, London.

Rickman, H. P. (1976) *Wilhelm Dilthey: selected writings*, Cambridge University Press, London.

Ricoeur, P. (1973) 'The model of the text: meaningful action considered as text', in *New Literary History*, vol. 5, no. 1, 91–177.

Ricoeur, P. (1974) *Conflict of interpretations* ed. D. Ihde, Northwestern University Press, Chicago.

Ricoeur, P. (1976) *Interpretation theory: discourse and the surplus of meaning*, Texas Christian University Press, Fort Worth.

Robinson, J. B. (1982) 'The quagmire of phenomena', in J. D. Wood (ed.),

Rethinking geographical inquiry, Toronto: Geographical Monographs, no. 11, York University.

Rorty, R. (1979) *Philosophy and the mirror of nature*, Princeton University Press, Princeton, N.J.

Rorty, R. (1982) *Consequences of pragmatism*, University of Minnesota Press, Minneapolis.

Rorty, R. (1984) 'Deconstruction and circumvention', *Critical Inquiry*, vol. 11, no. 1, 1–23.

Santayana, G. (1951) *Dominations and powers*, Scribners, New York.

Schachter, S. (ed.) *Working papers on English language institutions in Quebec*, Alliance Quebec, Montreal.

Schrag, C. (1980) *Radical reflection on the origin of the human sciences*, Purdue University Press, Lafayette, Indiana.

Schutz, A. (1944) 'The stranger', *American Journal of Sociology*, vol. 49, 499–507.

Schutz, A. (1951) 'Choosing among projects of action', *Philosophy and Phenomenological Research*, vol. 12, 161–84.

Schutz, A. (1953) 'Common sense and the scientific interpretation of human action', *Philosophy and Phenomenological Research*, vol. 14, 1–37.

Schutz, A. (1962) *Collected papers, vol. I: The problem of social reality*, ed. M. Natanson, Martinus Nijhoff, The Hague.

Schutz, A. (1964) *Collected Papers, vol. II: Studies in social theory*, ed. A. Brodersen, Martinus Nijhoff, The Hague.

Schutz, A. (1966) *Collected papers, vol. III: Studies in phenomenological philosophy*, ed. I. Schutz, Martinus Nijhoff, The Hague.

Schutz, A. (1967) *Phenomenology of the social world*, trans. G. Walsh and E. Lehnert, Northwestern University Press, Chicago.

Schutz, A. and T. Luckmann (1973) *The Structures of the Life-World*, trans. R. Zaner and T. Engelhart, Northwestern University Press, Chicago.

Seamon, D. (1979) *A Geography of the lifeworld*, St Martin's Press, New York.

Social Research Group (1965) 'A study of interethnic relations in Canada', SRG, unpublished mimeograph, Montreal.

Straus, E. (1966) *Phenomenological psychology*, Basic Books, New York.

Vaillancourt, F. and R. Lacroix (1980) *Attributs linguistiques et disparités de revenu au sein de la main d'oeuvre hautement qualifie de Québéc*, Université de Montréal, Centre de recherche en developpement economique, Montreal.

Veltman, C. and J. A. Boulet, (1980) *L'incidence de la mobilité linguistique sur la situation économique et le rang social des travailleurs montréalais en 1971*, Office de la langue française, Montreal.

Zeitlin, I. (1973) *Rethinking sociology: a critique of contemporary theory*, Appelton-Century-Crofts, New York.

10

'When you're ill, you've gotta carry it'

Health and Illness in the Lives of Black People in London

Jenny Donovan

Introduction

It is the aim of this chapter to report on and explain the methodology used in a study of the perceptions and experiences of health, illness and health care of black[1] people in London. The study grew out of an awareness of the racist[2] nature of much of British society and a concern with issues about health and health care. The racism endemic in Britain is easily discernible, but has also been exposed in scholarly works (e.g. Smith, 1977; Centre for Contemporary Cultural Studies, 1982; Sivanandan, 1982; and Brown, 1984). The report on the Black Committee's findings *Inequalities in Health* (DHSS, 1980) indicated that the poorest in Britain, particularly those in manual occupations, tend to have the lowest states of health. Ironically (considering the name of the committee) the report had very little to say about the health of Britain's black population, admitting that the evidence was scanty and of poor quality. A closer inspection of this medical literature (see Donovan, 1984) reveals that it concentrates on unusual complaints that are of interest to particular medical researchers, such as sickle-cell anaemia, rickets and low birthweights, typically attempting to explain non-genetic conditions by implicating people's cultural or traditional practices. Such 'explanations' have generally been insensitive and sometimes unfounded.[3] Very little research has considered the views of the black people or the black community about their health or modes of coping with illness (see Brent Community Health Council, 1981, for an exception).

This interest in people's opinions about their health led to a larger body of sociological and anthropological literature concerned with the

differences between lay and professional views of medicine, health and
health care (see, for example, Freidson, 1970; Dingwall, 1976; Kohn and
White, 1976; Mechanic, 1978; Eisenberg and Kleinman, 1981). Basically,
this research shows that people do not arrive in the doctor's waiting-
room without ideas, awaiting the doctor's judgement which they will
obey uncritically. Instead, people bring to the consultation a wide range
of opinions and theories about the cause of illness and possible treatment
options. They may have utilized home remedies, discussed matters with
friends and relatives (the lay referral network), or tried 'alternative'
practitioners such as herbalists or chiropractors. If the doctor's attitude
is not sufficiently sympathetic or the treatment suggested is impossible
given personal circumstances or of an unexpected nature, patients may
discount the doctor's advice, criticize the doctor and maintain their own
theories.

Lay ideas and theories are seen to be the product of the individual's
experiences and cultural inheritance or identity. Past episodes of medical
treatment will obviously affect an individual's willingness to obey the
doctor's orders. Culture affects perceptions in a much more subtle
fashion. Culture is, after all, the beliefs and customs a group of people
develop in attempting to manage the environment in, and resources with,
which it lives. Culture orders priorities, values and social norms (Fabrega
and Tyma, 1976). It is the historical development of a group of people,
being able to be transmitted through the generations (Mechanic, 1978)
and, consequently, can sustain the persistence of some behaviours that
appear today to be anachronistic. Culture is an implicit and complex
factor in people's lives, and as such, merges with other features such as
society and economic and political development. It does, however, lie
behind many types of behaviour including responses to ill-health. As
such, it provides people with 'recipes' for living in the world (see below
and also Schutz, 1972). These recipes are not static, although parts of
them may remain constant, but on the whole can be changed by personal
or group experiences over time and with the emergence of any new circumstances. Lay beliefs, then, are at least as important as professional
views (Freidson, 1970).

There has been much written about 'culture' in the literature on race
and ethnic minorities (see, for example, Hall, 1978; Barker, 1981; CCCS,
1982; Pearson, 1986). Culture has been used by some writers and politicians to define a 'British way of life' which is associated with respectability, decency and discipline (Hall et al., 1978). Other cultures, such as
those from Asia and the Caribbean have thus been defined as 'alien' and
'unwanted':

If we went on as we are now, then by the end of the century, there would be four
million people of the New Commonwealth or Pakistan here. Now that is an awful

lot and I think it means that people are really rather afraid that this country might be swamped by people with a different culture. And, you know, the British character has done so much for democracy, for law, and done so much throughout the world, that if there is a fear that it might be swamped, people are going to react, and be rather hostile to those coming in. (Margaret Thatcher, reported in the *Daily Mail*, 1978)

Culture has not only been used by right-wing politicians to espouse racist views (see also speeches by Enoch Powell, Alfred Sherman, National Front propaganda), but has also been invoked by academics to explain the different behaviours of cultural groups. They have extended such explanations to suggest that it is only a misunderstanding of and insensitivity to black people's cultures that has led to unintentional racism and that investigating their culture and educating service providers will eliminate any difficulties (see, for example, Kahn, 1977; Ballard, 1982). In education, this theory is reflected in the Department of Education and Science's policy of multi-cultural education. But there is a fatal flaw in such policies: they assume that all cultures are equal in power. This is obviously not the case in Britain, where the ideology of the white middle classes dominates. Cultural studies also underestimate the importance of racism which is an incontestable fact in the lives of many black people.

It is postulated here, then, that the lives of black people depend upon the interplay of culture and larger social processes which include racism. Culture provides people with their way of life and strategies of response to routine and unique events (such as illness). It may also include a set of tried-and-tested home remedies for illnesses or a network of individuals to whom a person can turn in times of trouble (including ill-health). Cultural practices and beliefs are not always negative: they provide choices people can employ depending on the circumstances, the context, of events. Larger social processes such as politics, the economy and the influence of race and racism, on the other hand, are seen to be out of individual control. For black people, the colour of their skin palpably affects their life chances in terms of getting jobs and houses (Brown, 1984) and may impinge upon their treatment in all aspects of life, including health and health care.

The study and its methodology

The basic aim of the research is to understand health and illness in the context of black people's lives. It demands, therefore, a methodology that is sensitive and flexible, and which embraces the views and opinions of ordinary people in their own terms. It also requires that the context of people's lives be incorporated, so that their views do not become divorced from the meanings in which they were originally situated. It was particularly important, being a white researcher asking questions of black people, that my perspective was not imposed on their ways of life. These demands are very strong ones, and there is no single school of thought that is able to provide a suitable pre-packaged methodology. The aims of the study produced its own methods, then, by drawing on material from several different areas and so the methodology may be termed eclectic. The methodology is drawn, essentially, from phenomenology, ethnomethodology and ethnography.

There is not the space here to provide a thorough critique of positivistic methods. Suffice it to say that they were not considered suitable for this project.[4] Positivistic methodology offers a well-established and widely accepted but taken-for-granted methodology, but such a methodology is usually imposed without a sensitive concern for the subject-matter, and it does not necessarily reflect the experiences of the people under study. Structural-functional theory, which postulates society as a self-balancing system based on consensus, is also inappropriate for a study looking at an oppressed group in society, whose position can be clearly seen to be the result of conflict and inequality dating from the imperial era to the present (see Sivanandan, 1982; Brown, 1984). Positivistic social surveys can offer tested questionnaires, but they may be ethnocentric and, as Cicourel (1964) points out, interviewers tend to reduce the complexity of respondents' accounts by placing them into arbitrary classification systems based upon the researcher's own implicit assumptions.

An alternative to positivism is phenomenology which is derived largely from the philosophy of Husserl. It is important both for its critique of positivism and production of more relevant theories. Unlike structural functionalism, it declares that the individual (not the system) is the fundamental unit of social research (Weber, in Parkin, 1982). The phenomenological critique alleges that methods adopted from the natural sciences miss the 'sense' of phenomena by using methods which detach them from their specific contexts (Phillipson, 1972b). The relevance of phenomenology to this study is that it aims to study phenomena in their own terms so that their integrity is not lost (Douglas, 1971); and to seek an understanding of the ways in which people make sense of their lives and the (social) worlds they live in. For specific behaviour such as an individual's response to an illness to be understandable, the phenomenologists claim, the meanings that people attach to their actions and the processes by which people act out their everyday lives must be investigated.

The way in which the social world becomes available and constituted is the subject of phenomenological sociology (Walsh, 1972a). Social facts are not seen 'as if they were things' (Durkheim's view), but as the practical accomplishment of the routine practices and experiences of people in their ordinary lives. These social facts are sustained and reaffirmed in the course of social interaction (conversations, etc.). Some of them are commonly held and have the same meanings for groups of people; others have meanings which are negotiated during conversation or experience. The phenomenologists stress the importance of the negotiable nature of the social world and social order (Walsh, 1972b) – an order which is shared by a social group, but always open to challenges and renegotiation. The individual is thus allowed some life-choices. The phenomenologists, however, largely fail to consider the importance of power in relationships. In the health sphere, for example, lay and professional ideas about health and illness are accorded equivalent status by phenomenologists because they are social constructions, but, in fact, professional ideas are dominant because of their monopoly of knowledge and, therefore, power.

It is perhaps germane here to consider the importance of the contribution of Schutz to the phenomenological paradigm (see also the discussion by Rose in chapter 9 and by Pickles in chapter 13). It is probably Schutz more than any other individual who has established phenomenology as an alternative to positivism and structural functionalism in sociology. Schutz claims that his writings draw directly on the philosophy of Husserl, although his critics claim that he has imposed his own ideas on Husserl's, and so his foundations are not truly phenomenological (Hindess, 1972; Gorman, 1975). Of particular importance here are Schutz's developments of some of the ideas first postulated by Weber, such as the role of consciousness in giving meanings to phenomena, the importance of commonsense interpretations of reality, and the role of ideal types in everyday interaction. Most of these developments are contained in Schutz's major work, *The Phenomenology of the Social World* (1972).

Schutz thought that the aim of the social sciences should be to interpret (that is, understand) the subjective meaning of social action. He saw action as defined through meaning. Schutz borrowed many of Weber's ideas about the importance of individual perceptions and the formulation of ideal types, but he thought the social world was much more complex than Weber did. Schutz believed that the social world was a complex system of perceptions, some held in common with others, some unique to particular individuals. To understand the social world and the behaviour of individuals, he believed researchers would have to examine the formation and structure of the life experiences which give meaning to actions. 'Meaning is a certain way of directing one's gaze at an item of one's own experience' (Schutz, 1972: 42).

The idea that experience could not be grasped as it occurs but only reflectively, once it has passed, is another of Schutz's important contributions to phenomenology. While it occurs, he postulated, behaviour is a 'pre-phenomenal' experience. Behaviour has meaning because it is an experience that has occurred and has been looked at reflectively. The meaning does not, therefore, lie in the experience, because experiences can only be meaningful if they have been grasped reflectively. Consequently, not all experiences are meaningful because they are not all reflected upon. It is the act of the reflective glance that singles out elapsed experiences and endows them with meaning.

This theory has implications for interpretation, because it means that one cannot interpret another's experiences directly but only through picturing the other's reasons and motives. The interpretation of reasons and motives is based upon previous experience and on cultural inheritance, but the context is also extremely important. The interpreter may use subjective meanings (and commonsense) to arrive at a reason for the other's action, or may try to find out what the other person means by putting herself or himself into the place of the other and imagining selecting the same motives to understand why the particular actions were chosen. The social scientist should aim to comprehend the deeper levels of understanding, beyond ordinary conversation.

Schutz believed that every time people meet each other, each brings to the encounter a stock of knowledge (see Rose, chapter 9 this volume), which are 'recipes' for action. Culture, through an individual's stock of knowledge, establishes recipes for action which enable individuals to know when they or others are ill, and the sort of behaviour that is expected of themselves or others who are defined as 'ill'.

Schutz was not only concerned with the theories of phenomenology; he also sought to outline an adequate methodology. He was aware that there is a danger that in observing the social behaviour of another person, the researcher may merely substitute her or his ideal-types for those in the mind of the subject. To avoid this, Schutz advocated a method which involved subjecting to detailed analysis everything that is normally taken for granted. Thus both the judgement of the researcher and the researched must be investigated so that the biases and pre-judgements of both may be exposed and described. The role of the researcher is crucial here, with the requirement of becoming immersed into the world of the subjects without preconceived ideas or theories, in order to understand fully what the life of the other is like without relying on commonsense.

The task of the social sciences is seen by Schutz to be the understanding of the subjective meaning of social action. This is to be achieved through the construction of ideal-types and second-order constructs. Second-order constructs are similar to scientific constructs and are modelled on ideal-typical situations. Methodological difficulties have, however, blunted the phenomenological critique. The critique proposes research which should focus on 'the meaningful character of social phenomena' (Walsh, 1972a), but which also avoids 'subjective excesses' (Louch, 1966). How to do research based on their theories has proved difficult for the phenomenologists. Weber proposes a 'value-free' social science based on *Verstehen* (total empathy with the subject) and ideal-types drawn from the social world. It is difficult to imagine how such a social science might be described. For others, the methodology should be left to the choice of the researcher, with the proviso that the technique should rest upon its ability to include the uniqueness of everyday life (Silverman, 1972). Positivistic methods are rejected because they are seen to be based on unrecognized commonsense beliefs, tend to force the data into preconceived models and theories, and obscure the 'sense' of the data by removing them from their contexts (Cicourel, 1964). The work of Schutz, adapted by others, calls upon the researcher to become fully conversant with her or his biographical situation and to tackle everything previously assumed within commonsense in order to get at the motives, thoughts, perceptions and meanings of the subjects being studied. This can be done through communication with the subject or subjects, usually by participant observation and/or detailed unstructured or semi-structured interviews (Douglas, 1971; Burgess, 1982), with the aim of studying the phenomena in their own terms and developing theories grounded in the data collected (Glaser and Strauss, 1967).

The work of Glaser and Strauss on grounded theory (1967) is worth considering here on its own merits. Their work is derived from phenomenology, but is concerned particularly with empirical work. 'Grounded theory' is generated by empirical data which fits everyday situations and is understandable both to professional sociologists and lay people. Unlike positivistic research, grounded theory does not begin with theories and hypotheses to be tested, but consists of gathering qualitative data and at the same time working out hypotheses and concepts in relation to the data being collected. Work is started by a researcher choosing a topic; thereafter, the research is not guided, but is directed by what is discovered and logistical difficulties.

Grounded theory is generated by comparative analysis, in which concepts which emerge from the data can be taken back to see if they are adequately representative. If the evidence changes, and a category no longer appears to 'fit', the data can be examined to see why this might be the case, thus either explaining an unusual case or modifying the category to include the new information. This ties in with the notion of the negotiable nature of people's stocks of knowledge. Glaser and Strauss focus on the idea of verifying the theory, not through numbers or questions of adequacy, but by its relationship with the data and its comprehensibility. It is assumed that the research comes to a conclusion when sufficient data have been collected to saturate the categories or concepts and when the theory appears to fit most cases. The data should be presented in order that the reader may understand from where the categories have arisen. Grounded theory can be verified if it fits the empirical evidence from the area, is general enough to apply to many situations, and is relevant enough to make it applicable to the fluctuations of daily life (Glaser and Strauss, 1967).

This study of black people's health, then, draws on phenomenology. The phenomenological critique, particularly as developed by Schutz, emphasizes the essential importance of studying phenomena in their own terms, without applying artificial constraints. Also emphasized is the need for the researcher to be able to empathize with the group under study while at the same time being critically aware of the influence she or he may be having on the research and on the group itself. As a white but Jewish woman, for example, I was able to share with the informants some experience of racism (anti-semitism). It is obvious, however, that because I am not black, there are some things that they could not share with me.

The importance phenomenology places on the meanings of health and illness and of their negotiability depending upon each individual's personal and cultural heritage and in the context of everyday events is crucial to this study. The concentration throughout is on the processes of experience, and the effects that commonsense and each individual's stock of knowledge may have on the choice of action are considered. Consequently, the research methods follow those of grounded theory (Glaser and Strauss, 1967) and the data are generated by in-depth interviews, organized into categories, and presented in depth elsewhere (see Donovan, 1986) to allow the reader's own assessment. Throughout the study, the emphasis has been on the importance of being able to understand the world as the subjects see it, and to try to examine and take account of the researcher's own biases and commonsense view of the world.

The variability of meanings of health and illness is due in a large degree to the negotiability of social order. An informant may, therefore, negotiate with others to convince them that she or he is ill and deserves attention. The negotiability of the meaning of ill-health depends on the context of each event. It is clear, for example, that not all episodes of feeling unwell become defined as 'illness'. Hence young Afro-Caribbean men in this study shrug off minor complaints so that they can go to work, whereas in similar straits one of the lonely Asian women may consider herself to be ill. In another case, an Asian woman ignores a painful slipped disc because she is obliged to make arrangements for visitors. It may be that these differences in perception are related to whether or not the individual feels responsible for a particular condition (see also Cornwell, 1984). The social context is also crucial. The women of Asian descent have more time to themselves and at home than the Afro-Caribbeans, most of whom have jobs as well as family responsibilities. Class may also be a factor, as some of the Asian women come from upper-class families in the sub-continent, whereas the Afro-Caribbeans are from working-class backgrounds.

Power is another important factor in the negotiability of meanings. Doctors, for example, hold power in their dealings with patients and often it is they who decide who is legitimately entitled to the label 'ill'. Doctors may, then, contend that a person is not ill and so social sanction to stay off work or to drop social obligations may be withheld from someone who is genuinely unwell. An example of this is the case of one of the Asian women who had TB, but whom doctors diagnosed initially as suffering only from marital problems arising from her arranged marriage (!). There are also several instances where informants maintain that doctors told them that they were pretending to be ill. The power exerted over black and women patients is inevitably a manifestation of larger race, class and gender relations.

Phenomenology allows that every individual has a unique state of knowledge, based on previous experiences and inherited ideas. These stocks of knowledge can be altered by interactions, through negotiation. Stocks of knowledge also seem to contain contradictory ideas, some of which may be imposed by the dominant meaning systems. The informants in this study have stocks of knowledge which contain theories and experiences from southern Asia, Africa and the Caribbean, some of which have been retained, some discarded, and some maintained alongside sometimes contradictory Western European theories. Many of the informants draw on their stocks of knowledge when they are ill and produce a wide range of home remedies or theories about the use of such things as heat and cold. In this way, they have some choice for action during ill-health. They can and do, of course, also make use of the National Health Service, and some also use private practitioners.

An offshoot from the phenomenological critique developed into a group of researchers known as the ethnomethodologists. Their focus of interest is on what goes on in everyday life, and they consider that commonsense and routines should be analysed closely. The basis of ethnomethodology comes from a fundamental idea that until we understand how we understand each other, all social enquiry is useless (Dreitzel, 1970). Their focus is on the process by which actors manage to produce and sustain a sense of structure in everyday life. Since language is the principal medium of social interaction, it is language that they examine in detail, particularly that held in common (Walsh, 1972a). According to Phillipson (1972a), everyone is seen to have access to the social world through commonsense reasoning, and so in interaction we tend to assume that others know what we mean and will fill out what we say to make sense of it. This is the 'inherent indexicality of accounts' – a sort of verbal shorthand. One of the aims of ethnomethodology, then, is better to understand the indexicality of language, not so that the indexical expressions can be changed, but so that the workings of society may be better understood (Agar, 1980).

An example from this study is the use by the Asian informants of the concepts 'hot' and 'cold'. A perception of something as 'hot' is not merely an indication of its temperature, but conceals a myriad of traditional ideas which need not be explained to those conversant with them, but seem incomprehensible to the ignorant. (A fuller description of the meanings of hot and cold may be found in Donovan, 1986.)

The methods of the ethnomethodologists are similar to those of the phenomenologists in that they advocate the use of tape-recorded interviews and participant observation so that discussions between participants may be analysed to reveal the nature of the language used, but they also utilize disruptive experiments (Garfinkel, 1967). Ethnomethodologists, unlike traditional sociologists, consider lay perceptions and opinions to be as valid as professional ideologies, and take as a subject for study the difference between public and private accounts of events (Cornwell, 1984).

Cicourel (1964) advocates the researcher deciding upon personal methodology to generate data. His only constraint is that the method must reveal the way in which members' theories combine with formal rules and practices, and expose the underlying patterns of social interaction. He was particularly concerned with, as he saw it, two types of rule held by everyone: basic rules, which are deep structures and enable the individual to make appropriate and even innovative responses to changing situations; and surface rules, which are shallow structures and constitute the tried-and-tested recipes used in everyday, 'normal' behaviour. Ethnomethodology should, therefore, study both types of rules – the surface ones which make up ordinary interaction, and the basic ones which give meanings and generate responses to the unexpected.

Ethnomethodology is of relevance to this study primarily because of its focus on everyday life and because its followers emphasize the comparable validity of lay and professional opinions and conceptions. In the field of health, this means that the neglected area of lay perceptions of health and illness can be considered as important as the dominant professional view of medicine. Some of Cicourel's ideas are also relevant, especially those concerning the use by individuals of surface and basic rules to cope with everyday life. In this study, some of the Afro-Caribbean informants draw on well-established home remedies such as mint tea or 'bayrum' (a poultice) to deal with minor illnesses such as colds or headaches (surface rules); but when faced with persistent or unusual problems may refer to others or make up new or more specific recipes (basic rules).

Ethnography is part of an anthropological tradition which draws upon symbolic interactionism, phenomenology, hermeneutics, linguistic philosophy and ethnomethodology. Ethnography is associated with the importance of understanding the perspectives of the people under study, and of observing their activities in everyday life (Hammersley and Atkinson, 1983). It emphasizes that the researcher should be faithful to the phenomena under study rather than to particular methodological principles (Znaniecki, quoted in Burgess, 1982). Ethnography has been used particularly in anthropological work, based upon the methods of participant observation, un- or semi-structured interviewing, or by the researcher becoming part of the society or social group being studied. In the interview, it is stressed that the informant should direct the discussion because the ethnographer becomes the learner. In this, as in many other projects, it was emphasized that the researcher was a student, desiring to learn from the informants (Agar, 1980).

The methodology of ethnography is usually dependent upon the constraints operating on whom or what the researcher wants to study. Initially, the ethnographer will try to gain access to the group chosen for study, either by approaching them through an intermediary, or without a prior introduction. The dress, appearance, accent, class, ethnicity, age and sex of both the informant and researcher are important here, and, unlike traditional social researchers, ethnographers do not, largely, ignore these issues. As Agar (1980) points out, the problem is not that biases exist, because they do exist in all types of social interaction, but how they can be documented and dealt with as part of the methodology. The effects of the researcher's personal characteristics, then, become an integral and beneficial part of the research (Easterday, 1982; Burgess, 1982).

In this study there was the not inconsiderable problem of a white researcher seeking out black people. The initial entry into one of the Afro-Caribbean groups was achieved through the help of a fellow student who introduced me to people with whom he worked. The other Afro-Caribbean group was reached through an introduction from another friend. The Asian women were contacted through a social worker who knew of a member of a local group who spoke English and might be willing to act as an interpreter.

After initial access is gained to the group under study, the next major problem is who is to be interviewed or observed? Ethnographers tend to use either non-probability methods of sampling, depending, for example, on who is available or to whom the researcher is introduced (Burgess, 1982); or theoretical sampling, in which the choice of informant is determined by theoretical development (Glaser and Strauss, 1967). Here, a combination of key informant and snowball sampling was used. Key informants (Tremblay, 1982) were used in the Asian and two Afro-Caribbean groups. These individuals help by providing information and advice about neighbourhoods, customs, unacceptable questions, language, etc. The key informant of Asian descent also acted as interpreter and arranged meetings with most of the other women. A few of the Asian women and most of the Afro-Caribbeans were obtained by snowball sampling (Burgess, 1982), where one informant introduces another. These techniques ensure that the researcher gains the trust of the group because she is known to others, and allow such things as the checking of stories in comparison with others, the assessment of the importance of family or other relations in health matters, the discussion of sensitive and confidential matters, and an analysis of the degree of retention of traditional ideas between generations.

Data are gathered in ethnographic research through interviews and/or observations that are recorded in the form of field notes and/or audio or video tapes. The interview has been termed a 'conversation with purpose' by Webb and Webb (1932; quoted by Burgess, 1982: 107). Ethnographers do not decide beforehand on the wording of the questions they want to ask, although they may well have a list of issues they want to cover, and they do not restrict themselves to a single mode of questioning (Hammersley and Atkinson, 1983). The interviewer becomes an active listener, building up a rapport with the informant. Expressions of interest in statements, encouraging gestures, probing questions and leading questions are all part of the repertoire of un- and semi-structured interviewing (Agar, 1980). The researcher must again take note of the influence she or he may be having, but the method allows the validation of some stories by comparisons with others (Whyte, 1982; Evans, chapter 11, this volume).

One of the major criticisms of ethnographic work concerns the question of the representativeness of a small number of cases studied in detail. Case studies have, however, been part of social research for as long as it has existed, but the method was discredited in social science circles during the quantitative revolution after the Second World War, principally because of the desire to quantify, but also because of the development of survey methods and sampling techniques based on statistical procedures. Since these techniques have been established, case-studies have been subjected to assessment by the same criteria as for statistically-derived samples, even though this betrays a confusion between the procedures. Questions about the validity of making inferences from a small number of cases have been asked, for example. Mitchell (1983) answers this challenge by showing that the inferences from statistics are based on correlations and are linked together by theoretical thinking; whereas inferences from case-studies are logical or causal and are based in the data collected (see Eyles, chapter 1, this volume).

Statistical inferences, based on correlations, do not explain associations between variables, only declare that a relationship may occur according to a particular probability. It may be that in some cases the presence of a strong correlation does not necessarily ensure that a causal relationship does exist between variables. Inferences from statistical samples require two steps: first, statistical inference, which makes a statement about the confidence one may have in a relationship; and secondly, the logical inference, which draws conclusions about the links between the data and a set of theoretical principles (Mitchell, 1983). In case-studies, only the second step is necessary.

Conclusion

The major characteristic of case-studies is that they capture the 'wholeness' of an individual or group. They can be focused on an individual through the life-history approach or on a group, but they are located in a wider context which should be taken into account. In this project, the focus is on the health and lives of black people, examined through their life-histories and discussions about their experiences of illness and the health services, but that their lives are located in the context of British society is never forgotten or ignored. Indeed, this context influences their lives and health as they themselves relate. As workers, for example, their jobs define their levels of income and prosperity and may limit their health through injuries and poor conditions. As black people, the actions of the state on issues such as immigration and 'stop and search' laws; the institutional forms of racism in the health service, the police, the housing departments, and the day-to-day reactions of people on the streets, all shape the lives that they have to live.

This is not to say that they cannot make their own decisions in life. They clearly can, but within the constraints of these larger social, economic and political forces. In the arena of health, for example, they can decide what sort of treatment to employ during each episode of illness – to 'work the complaint off', a home remedy, prayer or a doctor, public or private. But pressures of work, family responsibilities, lack of time and/or money, may constrain these choices. Each choice must be seen in its context, through the perceptions of the individual, to be comprehensible. People may behave in an apparently irrational manner, but it may be that they hold to a different kind of rationality. Two informants speak for themselves:

You have to get a balance in the bile of the body – the hot things cause you bile and heat in the body and then it upsets your stomach. . . . So to balance them you have to take cold things, oranges or orange juice or lemon. (Asian woman)

It's your problems that make the body sick, what give you all the aches and pains. You're not relaxed if you've got a problem . . . I smoke a cigarette or marijuana to soothe. It keeps me calm, comforts me. . . . I can't say it's bad for health because some people that don't smoke suffer with bad health. . . . Some say it gives you cancer, but my mother never smoked and she died of cancer. (Afro-Caribbean woman)

The eclectic nature of the methodology allows for the input of ideas from several sources. Admittedly, eclecticism removes ideas from their original context and may weaken their theoretical strengths, but it does allow the choice of theory and methodology that fit as closely as possible the subject-matter under study. As has been shown, parts, but not all, of phenomenology, ethnomethodology and ethnography contribute to this methodology. Similarly, theories surrounding culture and race have both been utilized. The concern throughout was not to produce a study designed in accordance with 'proper form' (Louch, 1966), but one which took due cognisance of the subject-matter and the lives of the informants. Such an approach cannot be said to be unproblematic, but the justification of the methodology and the interpretations of the data are related at length elsewhere (Donovan, 1986) so that the reader is able to make her/his own judgements as to their efficacy and validity.

Notes

This chapter is taken from my PhD research which was funded by the SSRC/ESRC, 1981–4, and undertaken at Queen Mary College, University of London, in the Health and Health Care Research Centre. I would particularly like to thank Dr John Eyles for his encouragement and supervision of the project, Professor David Smith for his helpful comments on drafts of the thesis and Prince, Humphrey and Pete. I must, of course, extend my greatest thanks to the informants, especially 'Naseem' and 'Delores'. The material on which this chapter is based was originally published in J. L. Donovan (1986) *We don't buy sickness, it just comes*, Gower, Aldershot.

1 For the purposes of this chapter, the term 'black' is employed to refer to people of Asian and Afro-Caribbean descent who share the common experience of racial discrimination because of the colour of their skin. It is a political term in common usage which emphasizes solidarity and unity among ethnic minority groups.
2 Racism is a term in common usage. In this context, racism is a theory which has grown out of xenophobia, uneven power relations and colonialism, and which encourages or allows the unequal treatment of some people on the basis that they are inferior or different. Racist theories are historically specific, moulding themselves to contemporary beliefs and demands. Their existence may be inferred from literary writing, vernacular language, historical documentation and contemporary press reports and social surveys.
3 An example of this phenomenon is rickets. The discovery of rickets among some Asian children in British cities in the 1960s and 1970s was postulated to have been caused by Asian diets being low in vitamin D or by Asian women not exposing enough skin to sunlight. In fact, the traditional Asian diet is close to the WHO ideal and it has been suggested that the fortification of a popular food would eradicate the condition just as it did among white children at the turn of the century (margarine was fortified). For a further exploration of these issues, see Sheiham and Quick (1982).
4 The specific reasons for dismissing positivistic and structural functionalist theories and methods are elaborated in Donovan (1986).

References

Agar, M. H. (1980) *The professional stranger*, Academic Press, London.
Ballard, R. (1982) in Rapoport and Rapoport (eds), *Families in Britain*, Routledge & Kegan Paul, London, 179–204.
Barker, M. (1981) *The new racism*, Junction Books, London.
Brent Community Health Council (1981) *Black people and the Health Service*, Brent CHC, London.
Brown, C. (1984) *Black and white Britain: the third PSI Survey*, Heinemann, London.

Burgess, R. (ed.) (1982) *Field research: a sourcebook and field manual*, George Allen & Unwin, London.

Centre for Contemporary Cultural Studies (1982) *The Empire strikes back*, Hutchinson, London.

Cicourel, A. V. (1964) *Method and measurement in sociology*, Collier-Macmillan, London.

Cornwell, J. (1984) *Hard-earned lives*, Tavistock, London.

Denzin, N. K. (1978) *The research act*, McGraw-Hill, New York.

DHSS (1980) *Inequalities in health – the Black Report*, HMSO, London.

Dingwall, R. (1976) *Aspects of illness*, Martin Robertson, London.

Donovan, J. (1984) 'Ethnicity and health', *Social Science & Medicine* 19, 7, 663–70.

Donovan, J. L. (1986) *'We don't buy sickness, it just comes'*, Gower, Aldershot.

Douglas, J. (ed.) (1971) *Understanding everyday life*, Routledge & Kegan Paul, London.

Dreitzel, H. P. (1970) *Recent sociology*, Macmillan, New York.

Easterday, L. (1982) 'The making of a female researcher', in Burgess, *Field research*, 62–7.

Eisenberg, L. and Kleinman, A. (eds) (1981) *The relevance of social science for medicine*, D. Reidel, Dordrecht.

Fabrega, H. and Tyma, S. (1976) 'Culture, language and the shaping of illness', *Journal of Psychosomatic Research* 20, 232–17.

Filmer, P. et al. (1972) *New directions in sociological theory*, Collier-Macmillan, London.

Freidson, E. (1970) *Profession of medicine*, Dodd Mead & Co, New York.

Garfinkel, H. (1967) *Studies in ethnomethodology*, Prentice-Hall, Englewood Cliffs, New Jersey.

Glaser, B. G. and Strauss, A. L. (1967) *The discovery of grounded theory*, Aldine, Chicago.

Gorman, R. A. (1975) 'Alfred Schutz', *British Journal of Sociology* 26, 1–19.

Hall, S. (1978), in Lane, D et al. (eds), *Five views of multi-racial Britain*, CRE and BBC, London, 23–35.

Hall S. et al. (1978) *Policing the crisis*, Macmillan, London.

Hammersley, M. and Atkinson, P. (1983) *Ethnography*, Tavistock, London.

Hindess, B. (1972) 'The "phenomenological" sociology of Schutz', *Economy & Society* 1, 1–27.

Khan, V. S. (1977) in Watson, J. L. (ed.), *Between two cultures*, Basil Blackwell, Oxford.

Kohn, R. and White, K. L. (eds) (1976) *Health care: an international study*, Oxford University Press, London.

Louch, A. R. (1966) *Explanation and human action*, University of California Press, Los Angeles.

Manning, P. K. (1967) 'Problems in interpreting interview data', *Sociology and Social Research* 51, 302–16.

Mechanic, D. (1978) *Medical sociology*, Free Press, New York.

Mitchell, J. C. (1983) 'Case and situational analysis', *Sociological Review* 31, 187–211.

Parkin, F. (1982) *Max Weber*, Tavistock, London.

Parsons, T. (1951) *The social system*, Routledge & Kegan Paul, London.

Pearson, M. (1986) 'The politics of ethnic minority health studies', in Rathwell, T. and Phillips, D., *Health, race and ethnicity*, Croom Helm, London, 100–16.

Phillipson, M. (1972a) 'Theory, methodology and conceptualisation', in Filmer et al., *New directions in sociological theory*, 78–116.

Phillipson, M. (1972b) 'Phenomenological philosophy and sociology', in Filmer et al., *New directions in sociological theory*, 119–163.

Schutz, A. (1972) *The phenomenology of the social world*, Heineman Educational Books, London.

Sheiham, H. and Quick, A. (1982) *The rickets report*, Haringey CHC and CRC, London.

Silverman, D. (1972) 'Methodology and meaning', in Filmer, *New directions in sociological theory*, 183–200.

Sivanandan, A. (1982) *A different hunger*, Pluto, London.

Smith, D. J. (1977) *Racial disadvantage in Britain*, Penguin, Books, Harmondsworth.

Tremblay, M.-A. (1982) 'The key informant', in Burgess, *Field research*, 98–104.

Walsh, D. (1972a) 'Sociology in the social world', in Filmer, *New directions in sociological theory*, 15–35.

Walsh, D. (1972b) 'Functionalism and systems theory', in Filmer, *New directions in sociological theory*, 57–74.

Whyte, W. F. (1982) 'Interviewing', in Burgess, *Field research*, 111–22.

11

Participant Observation
The Researcher as Research Tool

Mel Evans

Introduction

The most commonly adopted method of study of local communities is
that of participant observation, and yet the techniques of this method
remain ill-defined and, to many, tainted with mysticism. Although texts
which endeavour to explicate the participant observation method do exist
(see for instance, Bruyn, 1966; Jacobs, 1970; Spradley, 1980; and
Hammersley and Atkinson, 1983) the tendency has largely been to counsel
prospective participant observers to 'go forth and do likewise' by
reference to certain classic examples (such as Vidich et al., 1964;
Whyte, 1981). Such a tendency has contributed to the dismissal of
participant observation by some researchers as being idiosyncratic, not
sufficiently objective and 'unscientific'. But by its very application
participant observation (in common with other qualitative methods) has
led to the very questioning of the objectivity of the researcher, the status
of the observation of social phenomena, and indeed the scientificity of
social research.

In this contribution I shall provide an account of the use of participant
observation in a particular research setting, which I hope will illustrate
the kinds of consideration that the participant observer must inevitably
encounter. This may appear to be yet another addition to the catalogue
which directs to go forth and do likewise, but as I shall argue, the success
of participant observation does not primarily depend upon the casual
adoption of one set of rules as against another but upon a profound level
of introspection on the part of the researcher with respect to his or her
relationship to what is to be (and is being) researched. For this reason
illustration is perhaps the best mode of instruction.

A methodological framework

In approaching the study of social and community life, of which we as researchers and individuals are a part, we cannot ignore the competing tensions active in the array of social research methods. Broadly, these tensions result from two diametrically opposed approaches to social research – positivism and naturalism. For some considerable time positivism, the endeavour to construct a science of society modelled on the logic of experimentalism in the natural sciences, has been dominant in empirical method. The positivist method operates by the categorization of directly observable social phenomena into variables which are tested in their causal relationship to certain independent variables in an attempt to produce testable laws and theories. The logic of the model relies upon quantitative manipulation. Thus in community study a positivist would approach social phenomena by the use of questionnaires and attitude surveys, which test the incidence of certain responses to attitudes or questions against independent variables such as social class (e.g. Young and Willmott, 1957). The shortcomings of such an approach lie in the preoccupation with social phenomena which are directly observable. Such a preoccupation is evidenced in the positivist obsession with sampling and standardizing techniques in an attempt to create categories of data generalizable across all situations and research circumstances. By restricting the extent of social phenomena to that which is directly observable there is a tendency to extract the phenomena from the social context in which they are observed and measurable. This in turn leads to a tendency to omit consideration of the largely non-observable values, meanings and intentions whch may be present in such situations. Finally, there is an inclination to presume a neutrality of observation and to ignore (for instance) a cultural perspective on the part of the observer. As Charles Darwin once said, 'How odd it is that anyone should not see that observation must be for or against some view, if it is to be of any service' (quoted in Selltiz et al. 1959: 200).

In following the imported logic of the model of the natural sciences, positivism strives to create a neutral observation language and artificial experimental settings in an endeavour to counter the real possibilities of researcher bias which exist in social research. However, to consider, as positivism taken to its logical extremity must do, that observation can be carried out in a value-free vacuum, is unrealistic.

Naturalism (not to be confused with natural science) on the other hand, differentiates the social disciplines from natural science on the basis that social phenomena are different in character from natural phenomena. Furthermore the naturalist stance proposes that the social realm should be approached in its natural state, and its first requirement is that the integrity of phenomena should remain unimpaired. Thus whilst the naturalist accepts that social phenomena do appear as directly observable, that characteristic alone (and the isolation and measurement of them on that basis) is insufficient to understand and explain their existence. All variations of naturalism place emphasis on the social meanings, intentions and attitudes which are the underlying basis of the appearance of social phenomena. To understand appearances we must therefore employ a method which gives us access to the underlying meanings, etc. The point of access which naturalism identifies is that we are all, as members of society, able to participate in the social phenomena we observe and thereby learn the underlying meanings (etc.) which produce them. One such approach is termed participant observation. However, the tendency with most forms of naturalism (e.g. ethnomethodology (Garfinkel, 1967), sociological phenomenology (Schutz, 1970) and transcendental phenomenology (Wolff, 1964)) is to place such a high premium on the retention of the integrity of phenomena as to isolate the researcher to an extent that participation becomes largely meaningless. For example, Kurt Wolff's method of 'surrender to' (Wolff, 1964) relies upon the manipulation of the researcher by the phenomena to such an extent that the focus is upon the contortions of the transcendental acts of the researcher rather than the community being studied. The ultimate effect of naturalism is that because 'the naturalist resists schemes or models which oversimplify the complexity of everyday life' (Denzin, 1971), we are left with what amounts to descriptions rather than explanations of social phenomena. The appearances of social phenomena become so highly valued as 'reality' that they become conflated with 'truth' to the extent that to delve beneath the surfaces of observed phenomena in order to seek the meanings and intentions which produce it becomes sacrosanct on the grounds that it would somehow distort 'truth'. Thus naturalism leaves us with little more than positivism; an emphasis upon the directly observable and a divorce between the researcher and the researched which ultimately amounts to an artificial separation of theory from method.

Yet the essential advantage of participant observation remains that the researcher as a member of society has access to participation in social phenomena which in itself constitutes a method: the use of the researcher as methodological tool. Traditionally such an approach has developed from Dilthey and Weber's use of the concept of *Verstehen* (Outhwaite, 1975) as an endeavour by the researcher to achieve an empathic knowledge of the state of mind of the actor in order to reconstruct social phenomena. In recent years *Verstehen* has been developed as the principle of reflexive explanation; that each of us as members of society are able to participate via certain roles and come to reflect on the products of that participation. But this in itself is insufficient to develop the objective interest that researchers have as participants. To rely on reflexivity alone (as Wolff, 1964) is to divorce the researcher from the researched. Self-interrogation to calculate the extent to which we change during the research procedure is a measure of the reaction of the subjective realm upon oneself and would depend ultimately upon this in relation to what we were like prior to entering the research setting. Furthermore, just because we as researchers have made explicit by a process of reflexivity our meanings and intentions, and gained a knowledge of the way that they translate into actions, does not necessarily entail us understanding that same process in others; all we see in fact are appearances, the results of the process. For this reason interpretation becomes necessary, and in that we do not accept social phenomena at face value (i.e. are interested in underlying processes) such interpretation is of a critical persuasion. Thus as opposed to the phenomenological dictum of the suspension of received notions, as participant observers we must suspend belief in the reality of appearances. In fact, in contradistinction to the suspension of received notions, participant observers become informed and employ theories and hypotheses in the very act of research; an experimentalist attitude is adopted in the sense of 'trying things out'. By introducing theorization to the research situation we are, of course, conjoining theory and method. But it should be borne in mind that theory is after all, like any knowledge, produced by social practices and reflection on those practices. Knowledge is in turn transformed by practice, just as practice is altered by knowledge.

The suspension of judgement as to the reality of appearances, the adoption by the participant observer of a critical, interpretative stance, necessitates an evaluation of the relation of the researcher to the researched. This is perhaps best considered in the context of Simmel's formulation of the role of the stranger (Simmel, 1971). The researcher may in fact be a stranger to the social phenomena in question by virtue of not being a recognized participating member within it. But more importantly the researcher as a marginal individual, by the suspension of belief in the reality of appearances, is also adopting the role of the stranger and achieves a level of objectivity by it.

Because he is not bound by roots to the particular constituents and partisan dispositions of the group, he confronts all of these with a distinctly 'objective' attitude, an attitude that does not signify mere detachment and non-participation, but is a distinct structure composed of remoteness and nearness, indifference and involvement. (Simmel, 1971: 145)

In adopting such a reflexive, critically interpretative stance as participant observers and thereby conjoining theory and method, there would appear to be problems of both validating and verifying research. A research method achieves a level of validity when the knowledge which it constructs is considered to be an adequate articulation of the social phenomena which it purports to understand and explain. The verification of the method thereby becomes the extent to which it is able to achieve a level of adequacy in other research situations, i.e. is repeatable. Participation is in essence really only a refinement on the methods used to reflexively understand and interpret in everyday life. To this end, the measure of adequacy of the articulation of the social phenomena researched is the success of the participation by the researcher in the 'collective contract' (Barthes, 1970; Eyles, 1985) of the everyday life being studied. As George Herbert Mead points out, participation is the very essence of meanings which form a collective contract; indeed he identifies two characteristics of what we term meanings:

One is participation and the other is communicability. Meaning can arise only insofar as some phase of the act which the individual is arousing in the other can be aroused in himself. There is always to this extent participation. And the result of this participation is communicability, ie. the individual can indicate to himself what he indicates to others. (Mead, 1956: 183)

Validation is, therefore, by the very act of participation, internal to the research in that whilst interpretations must be justifiable in terms of the cited evidence, they are still the product of the ability of the observer to participate meaningfully. In terms of verification,

What is necessary is that the participating observer be able to provide other potential participating observers with a set of explicit instructions (which are at present taken for granted) on how to put themselves in the same situation so as to have the same or similar experience. (Phillips, 1973)

I shall shortly turn to consider such a set of explicit instructions. However, it should be noted that if the aim of repeatability is to assist potential participant observers to put themselves in similar situations, then heed must be paid to the considerations of methodological framework we have thus far made in this section. Other researchers should be made aware of the hurdles which the dominance of positivism and the challenge of naturalism present, the relation that they as individuals have to what they research and the reflexive and critical character of the interpretative process.

202 Participant Observation

Ideology in the local community: a research problem identified

The manner in which research problems come to be identified is a matter which is rarely given consideration. In the natural sciences there is still a widely-held belief (although less common today) that the agenda is established externally by the logic inherent in natural phenomena. But social influences, and in particular the imperatives of technological change (e.g. the influence of the Cold War on the development of nuclear science) cannot be ignored. In so far as social research has been modelled along the lines of natural science by the influence of positivism an emphasis has been placed upon the rigour of an imported logic to the detriment of the subtler qualities of social processes. As argued earlier, positivism produces a concentration upon observable phenomena and its categorization at the expense of ignoring the underlying motives and intentions guiding human action. Furthermore in trying to create a neutral observation language positivism attempts to discount the fact that the researcher is a participant in society, and therefore a tool of research, in his or her own right. Yet it has for some time been recognized that social scientists as interacting communities have endeavoured to establish paradigms of problems and methods of investigation (Kuhn, 1970), but it is only recently that a recognition of the researcher's place in a wider community of everyday life, and its influence upon the researcher, has come to be recognized.

The problem which my research addressed was influenced by an academic community in which neo-Marxist and structural theories of the city were in the ascendant (Harvey, 1973; Pickvance, 1976; Castells, 1977). In particular, however, the absence of an ability in this framework to account for human motivation and action in anything other than a mechanistic way, directed my attention towards the Marxist conception of ideology. Nevertheless, it seemed to me that the prevailing accounts of how ideology operated (Althusser, 1971; Poulantzas, 1973) placed an overemphasis on the power of institutions (eg. factory, school, church and media) and in the last analysis, the economic base, to determine consciousness. The word 'seemed' is important here; what was the source of my dissatisfaction? Although the structuralist contortions of Althusser (the major influence on neo-Marxist conceptions of the city) were receiving a severe mauling at the hands of E. P. Thompson (1978) and other humanist Marxist representatives, the academic community was not the sole source of my scepticism. Perhaps more influential was my participation in the everyday life of the area where I resided. Socializing and listening to people there revealed concoctions of fragmented values, beliefs, stereotypes, cliché, myth, superstition, prejudice, humour, pathos and drivel, little of which could be directly attributed to the supposed institutional bearers of ideology. Even if elements of such dialogue could in some way be seen as determinations of power structure, it was usually juxtaposed with other contradictory elements. The concrete basis upon which the assertion of ideology as functional to the maintenance of social order was founded therefore began to interest me.

The identified theoretical problem (arising from a dialectical relationship between the researcher as member of an academic community and as a member of a society) then became a problem of how to research it. The positivist paradigm of social scientific research offered the possibility of survey techniques including questionnaire and attitude sampling. Whilst this offered the attraction of data which was accessible, verifiable and quantitatively testable, such an approach was rejected on two grounds. First, the items which I would have had to choose for subjects to respond to in attitude surveys would necessarily involve me in *a priori* assumptions of what ideological values were. The research would take the form of a self-fulfilling prophecy. Secondly, and more importantly, the interview situation necessary to attitude testing takes respondents out of an everyday, concrete setting and places them in an abstract situation where their responses are likely to be different. Although an interview situation is still a social situation (and notably, with its own roles and power structures) it is a world apart from everyday life. From my own experience of everyday life it was obvious that the ideological, as identifiable in values, beliefs, etc., was not necessarily a directly observable phenomena but operated on a largely unconscious plane. To place so-called ideological items in an attitude survey and present them to respondents would elicit attitudes towards them not typical in everyday circumstances. Having said that, however, an attempt at an attitude survey was made at the end of my research, although never to be used in the written-up form. The items used were derived from data from participant observation, and therefore constituted a re-presentation of items to the community. The reason why this attitude survey never became part of the final research are those of the second ground given above. Why the survey was carried out in the first place says more about the standing of and attitude towards qualitative techniques as a supposed poor relative of positivist social science than anything else (see Conclusion; and Silverman, 1986).

The method of study finally chosen was that of participant observation of a community for an eventual period of twenty months. This appeared the most appropriate method with which to tackle the study of the workings of what were not essentially considered a directly observable phenomenon. Because the method of participant observation relies heavily upon the 'social skills' of the researcher, it is also a method which requires a considerable amount of introspection, questioning and (sometimes) self-doubt. The very fact of participation means that there is little in the way of objective techniques that the researcher can employ to assess the consistent quality of data. Subsequently data are apt to vary throughout the process of the research. Nevertheless there are initial considerations that all participant observers make to some extent prior to entering and during fieldwork.

The practice of participant observation

There are basically six areas of consideration to which the researcher should pay some attention. These are research design, access to the community, field relationships, questioning and listening, recording data, and analysis and presentation. The final area will, of course, mainly come under consideration upon the completion of fieldwork, but it should be stressed that the remaining five are also likely to alter in substance during the course of research. Participant observation by its very nature is a fluid process involving changes in the researcher and his or her relation to the subject community in the course of the research. The point is not to resist such change, but to be aware of it, understand and accommodate it and utilize it in the direction of the research problem. In the following pages I shall assess the effect of these considerations upon the course of my research. This will also serve to highlight aspects of the choice of methodological framework.

Research design

In terms of this research, this covers much of what we have already dealt with in the previous section of this chapter, and what Malinowski referred to as the 'foreshadowed problems' of the research: 'Good training in theory, and acquaintance with its latest results, is not identical with being burdened with "preconceived ideas" ' (Malinowski, 1922: 8–9). In fact, it is the very accommodation of reflexive interpretation that participant observation allows which enables theory to develop in a dialectic with method, thus escaping such charges of preconception.

Further considerations of research design include the setting of the research and its timespan. The setting of this particular research was that of a local community (conceived as a *place*). This setting was chosen (as against, for example, a factory or a hospital, both of which possess an everyday life) largely on the grounds of theoretical concern. If it was claimed that ideology maintained social order, surely it did so in an all-embracing way, encompassing all aspects of everyday existence. The local community where many different social interactions and practices occur, it was thought, would reflect such a holism at a microscopic level and enable such a focus as I desired. Furthermore, such holism would be reflected in the context of interaction, whereas a factory or a hospital would under-represent certain segments of experience in favour of others. I was not interested in the possibility of the local community as an ideological structure *per se*, but as a localized basis of interaction; a setting in which to examine the workings of ideology in a concrete manner. I was therefore particularly keen not to choose a locality in which a community spirit was celebrated (e.g. Young and Willmott, 1957) or where particular forms of solidarity were of notoriety (e.g. a mining village; Dennis et al., 1957).

After some considerable thought I decided that the research setting should be that of the community where I had resided all my life. The reasons for this were largely those of familiarity; there were no problems of access (see below) or of adopting a participating role, since these were already defined by the researcher's own background in the area. Such a choice however stresses the importance of an account of the researcher's background, of my own upbringing in this community, and thus necessitated the inclusion within the written research of a biographical section. Nevertheless, it could be considered that an account of the background of the researcher is important in any participant observation research, if only that it may be indicative of any biases contained within the researcher's world-view (e.g. class bias).

A possible failing of such a 'personal' choice of setting could be that the researcher is over-familiar with the community; too much participation at the expense of observation. However, as noted earlier, the advocated stance of the participant observer is very much that of the stranger. This is not necessarily characterized by one who is 'not of the locality' but more by one who is 'marginal to the locality', a description of a quality that the individual bears in relation to the community. In my particular case the researcher's background as somebody of the locality who is 'differently marked' by virtue of a higher education, developed such a marginality; a natural observer as well as participant. This comes across in the biographical section of the research, but it should be borne in mind that membership of an academic community as well as of a local community inevitably leads to such a marginality.

There was also a theoretical reason for the choice of my own community for study; and this lies in the very type of community which the research problem required. The relationship of ideology to the local community was not posited in such a manner that the community was considered to be an ideological structure in itself, but rather a setting for ideological processes. It was the local quality of interaction that was to be examined, and not anything particular to the community itself. This is not to suggest that the social history of any community is unimportant (a social history of my community was indeed provided in the final written form of my research) but rather that ideological processes would manifest social order wherever there existed the necessary local social interaction. Neither does this deny the possibility that local community can indeed be an ideological structure in itself.

Access

The participant observer also has to surmount the problem of gaining entry to the field setting chosen. This largely amounts to the problems involved in making contact with people with whom to participate, and these may be considerable depending upon the setting. One of the commonest ways in which the participant observer approaches the problem is by identifying significant individuals and attaching themselves to them. These individuals become 'gatekeepers' to the research setting for the participant observer, as for example 'Doc' was for William Whyte (1981). An attempt at this was initially made in my research, however data derived in this manner did not form a significant part of the final written form of the research. Although important for checking out certain qualitative impressions of the local community, I found that such gatekeepers were often by their role and its power content also marginal to the community and their values reflected such power however minimal. Association with such gatekeepers also seemed to affect the field relationship with other community members, in that I was seen as part of 'that crowd'. More important to me was that as a participating member of my own community I had as it were, 'natural access' by virtue of my own local social network which acted as the basis for the development of participant observation. The settings of the research reflected aspects of the social network of the researcher (i.e. pubs, clubs, friends' houses, socials, doctors' waiting-rooms, and meetings, etc.). For participant observers generally, attachment to gatekeepers may be necessary depending upon their status as community members; the problem then becomes one of not over-identifying with such gatekeepers and carefully monitoring the degree of this.

Field relationships

Allied to the problems of access are those of the field relationship
that the participant observer establishes once within the setting. The
role that the researcher plays (and the extent of choice in adopting that
role, and whether indeed it is the role of researcher) will define the
character of field relations. In particular the researcher must be aware of
the definitions made by 'others' of 'self' (Laing, 1961). Much of the
parameters of roles are ultimately beyond the direct control of the
researcher and concern the physical, biological and existential characteristics of the researcher (e.g. gender, age, race, education, religion, etc.).
However within such parameters the researcher is able to 'manage' his or
her impression to others (e.g. in terms of dress, speech, mannerisms,
affability, etc.). In my particular research little consideration needed to
be given to such aspects, as in large measure my role was circumscribed
by my membership of the community. Although in fact, in terms of
field relationships, my involvement in the community was extended and
I became noticeably more gregarious. Generally however, the management of impressions on the part of the researcher is guided by the type of
community under study (e.g. a three-piece suit, briefcase and clipboard
will appear incongruous and suspicious in a working men's club). This
raises a wider issue in respect of participant observation in that it is often
claimed that this technique is most often used in the study of working-
class communities because it is much easier to operate there as researchers
are dealing with people less powerful than themselves.

Access to society's underdogs generally proves relatively simple, partly because it
involves the sociologist in intrusions upon people who are less prestigious and
powerful than himself . . . it is somewhat simpler to infiltrate a working men's
club than it is to gain entry to the Masonic Lodge, and the difficulties of
participant observation on the factory floor are likely to pale into insignificance
when the sociologist moves into the boardroom. (Saunders, 1979: 325–6)

This is obviously both a valid criticism and limitation of participant
observation and one which should be borne in mind by potential users of
the technique, both in its practical and ethical overtones.

   A further consideration which has bearing on field relationships is the
extent of participation on the part of the researcher. Much discussion has
ranged around degrees of participation or observation along a continuum
extending to either extreme, from total observer to total participant
(Hammersley and Atkinson, 1983: 93). It is clear, however, that both
extremes do not reflect the spirit of the method of participant observation,
and each leads to problems of objectivity on the part of the researcher.
The advantage of the method lies in the use that researchers make of

their access to meaning systems, and the success of reflexive understanding in observation. Both involvement and detachment are necessary components, and the dynamics of changes in the research process which may arise should not be resisted.

An important aspect of considering total observation or participation as ideal types is the overtness and covertness of the researcher implicit in each. Covertness is a matter for the conscience of the researcher, but it is one that will have bearing on how data are recorded and will ultimately depend upon the nature of the research design. In most cases involving participant observation it is the case that

If the researcher is completely honest with people about his activities, they will try to hide actions and attitudes they consider undesirable, and so will be dishonest. Consequently the researcher must be dishonest to get honest data. (Gans, 1967; 440)

The ethical kernel of this stance is stated by Vidich (1964) as the researchers' maxim: deceiving the society so as to study it and wooing the society to live in it. Such a position has led the method to be levelled with the charge of voyeurism by the critics of covert participant observation. However, it should be remembered that the researcher is responsible in large measure for the situations in which he or she records data in so far as the method involves the very act of participation. To such an extent researchers are no different from writers who doubtlessly draw upon their experience and contacts for material, and as long as identities remain well concealed there should be no real cause for pangs of conscience.

In my own research field relationships were built upon pre-existing roles and relationships. I was really doing no more than I would normally do in the course of my everyday life, except that I was writing about it and the people I encountered. My role was a covert one, however, and the reason for this was the nature of my research problem. It was felt that in order to examine the concrete workings of meanings and ideology it was necessary to participate and observe within concrete situations. Should the field relationships have been overt, settings and context would have been abstract as respondents adjusted their attitudes according to what they felt my role as researcher was. This is not to say that my field role was a passive one, which brings us on to the matter of questioning and listening.

Questioning and listening

The practices of questioning and listening are central to obtaining data in participant observation; they are the routes of access to subjective meanings. By their use we obtain data and in this respect they have an informative function. However we are also able to use questions and our ability to listen to accounts as a means of acquiring the perspectives of respondents, at which point we tap the underlying processes of social phenomena – the essence of empathy. At all times, nevertheless, the researcher is a methodological tool; it is the fact of participation, of being part of a collective contract, which creates the data. Much has been made of the benefits of listening as opposed to questioning: 'The central paradox of the participant observation method is to seek information by not asking questions' (Frankenberg: 1963). Whilst this may well give researchers answers to questions that they may not have considered asking, it is at the same time a step towards complete observation and the method suffers by the loss of its essential impetus; participation. One suspects that listening is favoured amongst some researchers since questioning can be considered manipulative. For example, a leading question may take the respondent outside the bounds of the context of everyday life. Yet by their very use leading questions illustrate the benefits of the participant observation method; the researcher as methodological tool testing hypotheses and theories acquired by reflecting on fieldwork so far. Having said that, however, the major use of questions in the context of participant observation are largely of the qualification variety (e.g. 'Why do you think that?' and 'What do you mean?') in order to prompt the respondent to proffer further information. This was the case in my own research; however as community member and participant I was aware of the need to maintain my normal role in the community and was able to use that to good effect in questioning.

Recording data

The major considerations behind what to record, how to record it and when to record it depend upon research design (the problems being researched) and whether the research is carried out covertly or overtly. Even if the research is being carried out overtly the nature of participation is such that it is not often done with one party constantly using a pencil and notebook; this would be disruptive, to say the least. Therefore most data are retrieved on reflection as soon after the situation as possible, and thus are very dependent upon memory. It is in the best interests of research that the data be concrete in nature, with the researcher making every effort to record speech and accounts as verbatim as possible. This has led to some use of mechanized assistance in the form of recording equipment, and whether this is used overtly or covertly again becomes an ethical issue. In my own research, some covert use was made of a micro-recorder and tapes were later transcribed. Its use was the subject of much conscience-seeking on my part. I eventually reasoned that as the machine was in fact an *aide-mémoire*, the burden of the ethical problem lay in the fact of the covertness of the research. If I were possessed with a perfect memory, the problem would have remained. The ethical issue therefore reduces to that dealt with above. In the end the use of the micro-recorder was abandoned since the quality of the recording was poor and in most cases the memory of the researcher had to be relied upon.

Two further considerations need to be made in respect of recording data. First, it is important to record background information about respondents (if known), the place the situation occurred, others present, what people were doing and anything else which may be relevant, as this may not be apparent in the speech. It is seemingly incidental factors such as these which are important in defining the situations which people are in and they will have a bearing on the meanings and attitudes offered. Secondly, the storage of data should be given some prior thought as this is often overlooked. Having said that, it is likely that categorizations under which data are stored are likely to change as themes and research directions fade and emerge. In my research a major reclassification occurred when the typifications referred to in the developed model (see 'Analysis and presentation' below) emerged. Prior to this, data were stored according to subject-matter of responses (e.g. politics, education, family, health, etc.); that is, what people were referring to in their speech. This was cross-referenced for access purposes. Reclassification and final storage form of the data ultimately depends upon how theory develops in the course of application of the method. It should eventually be in a form which resembles the way in which the research will be presented.

Analysis and presentation

Participant observation presents at least one great advantage to the social researcher. In pursuing the universal validity of reflexive interpretation (that is, its applicability to both 'lay' and 'scientific' explanations of social phenomena), it avoids an artificial divorce between theory and method. The positivist will test the validity of a theory by the application of research methods, and will only return to examine the components of the theory if the theory fails to prove its applicability to the particular situation researched. Theory and method have essentially separate existences according to positivism. A follower of the naturalistic school of methodology claims that the integrities of the appearances of social phenomena are sacrosanct. Theories can be made *of* them but never *about* how they came to appear that way. In placing such an imbalanced weight upon the integrity of phenomena we are only left with subjective accounts: descriptions of phenomena. We cannot go objectively beyond them as such, which makes both our theory and method subservient to them. The participant observer in such a naturalistic framework really only observes.

On the other hand, if the participant observer accepts the universality of reflexive explanation, and applies it critically within the research, theory and method develop in a dialectic. The process is one of trying out (experimenting with) hypotheses in the research situation. In this way the patterns and interpretations of the data develop due to the introspection and critical reflexivity of the researcher.

Ultimately the manner in which the researcher chooses both to analyse and present the data will depend upon the features of it which highlight the hypotheses and research problems investigated. That a basic grounding in relevant theory is important is borne out by the extent to which every possible theoretical avenue is explored in analysis, and the success of endeavours to explain phenomena which do not fit such theories by the development of new theory, models or typologies. Likewise presentation will vary according to the research problems (e.g. if temporal change is important, chronological presentation may be appropriate).

In my research into ideology, social order and local community a typological model was developed employing components of the work of Ardrey (1967), Fraser-Darling (1952), Soper (1981) and Heller (1974) on human needs; Therborn (1980) on ideological interpellation; and Heller (1984), Weber (1970), Gramsci (1971) and Collier (1974) among others on aspects of everyday life. The result was the typological model in table 11.1.

Table 11.1

Communal needs	Mode of interpellation		
	What exists	What is good	What is im/possible
Security	Routinization	Tradition & moral law	Common sense
Identity	Roles	Reference groups	Values and beliefs

Source: Evans (forthcoming).

The model developed out of the dialectical process which exists between theory and method, and with particular regard to two theoretical problems which my research identified. These were, first, what human psychic needs does a sense of community arise to satisfy? Secondly, how could ideology be said to function as a social process, or, how does it operate in everyday life? Drawing on the work of Robert Ardrey (1967) and Frank Fraser-Darling (1952) on the social psychological needs met by territory, and applying them to the conception of local community as a symbolic construction, the major needs identified were those for security and identity. My reasoning ran that as these were fundamental human needs they would require to be met in some way, if not by a sense of community. The notion of ideology as a social process serving to interpellate subjectivity (as developed by Goran Therborn, 1980) seemed most appropriate to explain how individuals make sense of the world, create social order and satisfy their needs for security and identity therein. According to Therborn, the three fundamental modes of interpellation are: (1) what exists and what does not exist; (2) what is good, beautiful, etc. and what is not these things; (3) what is possible and impossible (see Therborn, 1980: 18). The underlying rationale of the process by which ideological interpellation emerges to meet needs in the absence of their satisfaction by local community was derived from Marx's early work on the notion of alienation (Marx, 1975), and more especially from his concepts of real and illusory community (Marx, 1965), whereby illusory community is the alienated, represented ideological form of community. Such a conception has more recently been utilized with regard to the state by Alan Wolfe (1974).

The contents of the grids are the phenomenal forms, the ideological effects, which emerge on the basis of ideology functioning to satisfy the stated needs in the absence of a sense of community. It should be stressed that the categories of the model are not mutually exclusive and overlap considerably. The final section of this chapter is devoted to two brief examples of presented analysis on the basis of the typological model outlined above.

Excerpts from participant observation research

The following are extracts from data derived by the use of participant observation in my research. In each case the data are followed by interpretative passages and are analysed in the context of the typological model previously referred to. The first extract displays how routinization and role expectations serve to meet security and identity respectively through the ideological interpellation of what exists (and does not exist).

In the final form of the research the passage links sections on routinization and roles and shows the extent of overlap between the various
categorizations of figure 11.1.

An important aspect of routinization is in the role that significant
others play for the individual, in this respect the interpellation of what
exists (and does not exist) provides both identity and security in a
community context. Naturally, if the world were full of totally unpre-
dictable people (in terms of their activity) the individual would feel
insecure in the knowledge of what exists, and it would be very difficult to
establish any kind of order in the personal everyday life world. It is in not
having to anticipate the attitudes of certain others (reinforced by certain
linguistic protocols, e.g. 'you know what I mean?', 'tell me I'm wrong',
'agreed?', 'you see', 'right?', and so on) that routinization arises in
human relationships and thereby enables a sense of security. When the
routines which are implicit in role relationships are altered a challenge to
the values and assumptions contained in those routines will arise, anxiety
is evident and a re-evaluation must take place. To exemplify, this is a
conversation with a married man (Benny) in his early sixties, who has
a son (Phil) of seventeen; R. is the researcher.

Benny 'I've always said you've got to learn by experience, books tell you
nothing, you live and learn, right?'

R.   'So what would you do if you found that your Phil was taking heroin?'

Benny 'He wouldn't! I'd see to that! Phil wouldn't touch it!'

R.   'But I'm saying *suppose* he did – just suppose – what would you do?'

Benny 'I'd f_____ well kill him! He'd be out on his arse!'

R.   'So you see what I'm saying is you can't learn by experience all the time
can you?'

Benny 'Agreed . . . but you're talking about drugs, all that shooting in the arm
stuff. . . . They've got to be sick anyone that does that. My Phil hates
things like that.'

R.   'But if you're telling him to learn by experience then surely he'll think it's
okay to go ahead and try –'

Benny 'But you don't know my Phil. He's like me, he thinks drugs are evil.'

Although this is merely a scenario that the researcher puts to Benny, it
clearly exemplifies how in reality it would lead to the necessity for a redefinition of the role relationship he had previously taken for granted, that
had in fact become routine, a part of what exists. The general assumption
we make is that until circumstance, fate, chance, or however we symbolize
it, takes a hand to alter the situation then our relationships remain in
aspic. Furthermore to remain suspended in this way must mean to us that
they constitute good relationships – so good that we identify them in
relation to ourselves. We are also able to make stereotypifications about

roles that we do not like, in order to characterize our non-identification with them. In becoming routinized, however, roles and relationships carry an essential ideological function in the fact that what exists remains unquestioned.

The illustrative importance of the dialogue above lies not so much in the interpretation and analysis; in that sense it forms part of a wider argument regarding routinization (see Evans, forthcoming). More important is the way in which it illustrates the role of the researcher in participation as a methodological tool, trying out hypotheses within the research situation and not remaining a passive recorder of an appearance of everyday life. The style of the questioning is leading in order to extend the respondent beyond the immediate situation and gauge the resulting response.

By way of comparison, the following extract highlights the use of reflexive critical interpretation in the analysis of the data. The researcher is not a participant here. Its place in the overall research is within a section on how reference groups meet the needs of identity in the ideological interpellation of what is good, beautiful, right, attractive, etc. and its opposites. The extract involves a lunchtime conversation in a local pub between Gerry (a middle-aged unemployed man), Albert (a night-worker in his late fifties) and Doris (a barmaid in her late forties).

Albert 'Well let's get things into perspective, let's face up to facts. If you throw out the foreigners in this country that means your Paddies have to go too.'

Gerry 'Oh yea! Well certainly the southern Irish . . . well I mean look at what they did to Lord Mountbatten . . . that just weren't on and what do we do? Pat them on the head and say "you've been naughty boys"! It's all out of order, that man was a gentleman in my book – I don't know about yours.'

Albert 'Oh yes!'

Doris 'Well I think that all this could have been avoided – this coloureds problem is a flashpoint, it's an outcome not a cause of all the trouble. It's like something you fasten onto in times of confusion and it snowballs out of hand. I mean they could so easily have been absorbed, let's face it.'

Albert 'Oh yea, they *could* have been absorbed and the whole thing avoided, but that's not what *they* want is it? It ain't worked out like that has it?'

Gerry 'Well I don't know what the old King would have said!'

(*pause*)

Albert 'Ten months you say you've been out of work?'

Gerry 'Yea, ten months and I've not had a stroke of work and believe me I've looked all over the place. . . . I'm getting right browned off.'

(*pause*)

Albert (to Doris) 'See, no one really cared when it was all up North, they've
    always had it, but it's down here now. It's a crime all these people
    unemployed.'
Gerry 'Well I'm not unemployed really, I'm redundant . . . I was laid off.'

Gerry and Albert share a reference group (despite their being a non-
worker and a worker, respectively) which serves to interpellate what is
good (etc.), and confers identity thereby, in the face of what is perceived
as existing (i.e. rising unemployment). The major referrent shared is a
characteristic xenophobia, an out-grouping, clearly local in its origin and
reinforcement. The reference group serves a moral identificatory
purpose, a repository of shared myth, where what exists cannot give such
identity. The group is filled with characters who represent points of
reference (e.g. Lord Mountbatten, the old King). The possibility that it
may be based on a misrecognition (i.e. Doris's observations) is swiftly
dismissed by reference to the perceived roles and reference groupings of
others outside the group (i.e. 'foreigners'). Gerry in particular draws
from a nationalistic frame of reference, of tradition and the characters
who belong to and epitomize it, to identify himself as part of a shared
reference group and endeavours to define further his identity within the
proximate reference group in classing himself as redundant rather than
unemployed. This enables some association with a shared work ethic.
The conversation betwen Gerry and Albert indicates a shared reference
group. When Gerry says, 'I don't know what the old King would have
said', he is not only pulling symbols into the situation but expressing
values relating to social change and tradition. Albert fully understands
these and responds. A reference group is more than a collective contract
in that it indicates an agreement as to the symbols, values and myths
which constitute it. A collective contract requires a common understanding of communicated meanings but not necessarily agreement with the
values that they express.

Conclusion

It may appear that by choosing a community that I was familiar with I
was able to avoid much hard work and short-cut the circuit to
community study. The problems which I faced in participant observation
were therefore in many ways rare in that I had to confront over-
identification as opposed to the more common problem of access and
participation. Nevertheless I feel that both membership of an academic
community and a growing realization of my marginality enabled me to
achieve an adequate distance so as to view the everyday with a critical

gaze. An awareness of the researcher's role as a stranger to a community cannot be overstressed in its importance to participant observation. The use and awareness of a critically interpretative stance reinforces the marginality of the researcher as stranger.

The very term 'participant observation' should really indicate to us all an approach which conjoins theory and method. Perhaps it is indicative of the dominance of positivism, and the 'headiness' of the reaction against it (naturalism), which has forced many social researchers to over-look the possibility of a methodological framework founded upon the principles of *Verstehen*. It is perhaps inevitable that in a modern social science equipped with the impressive gadgetry of statistical techniques and computers that the essentially 'human' techniques of participant observation look paltry and insignificant. The disregard for qualitative techniques in general has of course been assisted by the new realism of the ESRC and their obsession with quantitative data and 'relevant' research. This has moulded a dominant conception of what social research should be. Yet even with this new realism, the inevitable intrusion of participation and observation (however involuntary) on the part of researchers in the social realm must exist, if only in the form of the now famous 'hunches'. An awareness of the natural extension of this partici-pation into fieldwork will lead to the re-emergence of qualitative techniques and the inevitable rebirth of theorization will be very welcome.

References

Althusser, L. (1971) *Lenin and philosophy and other essays*, New Left Books, London.

Ardrey, R. (1967) *The territorial imperative*, Fontana, London.

Barthes, R. (1970) *Elements of semiology*, Beacon Books, Boston.

Bruyn, S. T. (1966) *The human perspective: the methodology of participant observation*, Prentice-Hall, Englewood Cliffs, N.J.

Castells, M. (1977) *The urban question*, Edward Arnold, London.

Collier, A. (1974) 'The production of moral ideology', *Radical Philosophy* 9, 5–15.

Dennis, N., Henriques, F. M. and Slaughter, C. (1957) *Coal is our life*, Eyre and Spottiswood, London.

Denzin, N. (1971) 'The logic of naturalistic inquiry', *Social Forces* 50, 166–82.

Evans, M. (forthcoming) *Ideology in the local community*, Unpublished PhD thesis.

Eyles, J. (1985) *Senses of place*, Silverbrook Press, Warrington.

Frankenberg, R. (1963) 'Participant observers', *New Society*, 23.

Fraser-Darling, F. (1952) 'Social behaviour and survival', *Auk* 69, 183–91.

Gans, H. (1967) *The Levittowners*, Allen Lane, London.

Garfinkel, H. (1967) *Studies in ethnomethodology*, Prentice-Hall, Englewood Cliffs, N.J.

Gramsci, A. (1971) *Selections from the prison notebooks* (ed. Q. Hoare and G. Nowell-Smith), Lawrence and Wishart, London.

Hammersley, M. and Atkinson, P. (1983) *Ethnography; principles in practice*, Tavistock, London.

Harvey, D. (1973) *Social justice and the city*, Edward Arnold, London.

Heller, A. (1974) *The theory of need in Marx*, Allison and Busby, London.

Heller, A. (1984) *Everyday life*, Routledge & Kegan Paul, London.

Jacobs, G. (ed.) (1970) *The participant observer*, George Braziller, New York.

Kuhn, T. S. (1970) *The structure of scientific revolutions*, University of Chicago Press, Chicago.

Laing, R. D. (1961) *Self and others*, Penguin Books, Harmondsworth.

Malinowski, B. (1922) *Argonauts of the Western Pacific*, Routledge & Kegan Paul, London.

Marx, K. (1975) *Early writings*, (ed. L. Colletti), Penguin Books, Harmondsworth.

Marx, K. and Engels, F. (1965) *The German Ideology*, Lawrence and Wishart, London.

Mead, G. H. (1956) *The social psychology of George Herbert Mead* (ed. A. Strauss), University of Chicago Press, Chicago.

Outhwaite, W. (1975) *Understanding social life: the method called Verstehen*, Allen and Unwin, London.

Phillips, D. (1973) *Abandoning method*, Jossey-Bass, London.

Pickvance, C. (ed.) (1976) *Urban sociology; critical essays*, Tavistock, London.

Poulantzas, N. (1973) *Political power and social classes*, New Left Books, London.

Saunders, P. (1979) *Urban politics: a sociological interpretation*, Penguin Books, Harmondsworth.

Schutz, A. (1970) *Alfred Schutz on phenomenology and social relations* (ed. H. Wagner), University of Chicago Press, Chicago.

Selltiz, C., Jahoda, M., Deutsch, M. and Cook, S. (1959) *Research methods in social relations*, Holt, Rinehart and Winston, New York.

Silverman, D. (1986) 'Six rules of qualitative method', in J. Eyles (ed.), *Qualitative approaches in social and geographical research. Queen Mary College, Department of Geography and Earth Science. Occasional paper* 26.

Simmel, G. (1971) 'The stranger', in D. N. Levine (ed.), *Georg Simmel on individuality and social forms*, University of Chicago Press, Chicago, 143–9.

Soper, K. (1981) *On Human Needs*, Harvester Press, Brighton.

Spradley, J. P. (1980) *Participant observation*, Holt, Rinehart and Winston, New York.

Therborn, G. (1980) *The power of ideology and the ideology of power*, Verso, London.

Thompson, E. P. (1978) *The poverty of theory*, Merlin, London.

Vidich, A. J., Bensman, J. and Stein, M. (eds) (1964) *Reflections on community studies*, Harper and Row, New York.

Weber, M. (1970) *From Max Weber*, ed. H. H. Gerth and C. Wright Mills, Routledge & Kegan Paul, London.

Whyte, W. F.(1981) *Street corner society: the social structure of an Italian slum*, University of Chicago Press, Chicago.

Wolfe, A. (1974) 'New directions in the Marxist theory of politics', *Politics and Society* (Winter), 131–59.

Wolff, K. (1964) Surrender and community study, in Vidich et al., *Reflections on community studies*.

Young, M. and Willmott, P. (1957) *Family and kinship in East London*, Routledge & Kegan Paul, London.

12

A Case-Study Approach to Lay Health Beliefs
Reconsidering the Research Process

Jocelyn Cornwell

Introduction

The accounts researchers give of their work in academic papers are much like other accounts: they reconstruct the past to make it fit with and seem to have logically led to the present. As a result, certain aspects of the research process tend to go unmentioned. One is presented with a process of steady, linear progression from one step to the next, and there is no suggestion that the researcher might have experimented with concepts, methods or avenues of study which were later abandoned. There are exceptions to this rule, but they tend to appear in collections of papers explicitly concerned with research methods and the research process (see, for example, Bell and Newby, 1977; Bell and Roberts, 1984) or in the autobiographies of social researchers (Bowen, 1964), and are not routinely included in research reports.

Given the constraints governing written and verbal presentations and the literal impossibility of recording every moment of a project which may take years to complete, researchers have to be selective in their accounts of their work. Nevertheless, it is perhaps worth asking why they very rarely choose to describe periods of relatively little headway or ideas which led up blind alleys. It seems not to be assumed that it is possible to learn from one's own and others' mistakes.

The work to which this chapter refers is a recently completed study of health beliefs in East London. The fieldwork took place over two years (1980–2) and the project was completed as a PhD thesis and published in 1984 (Cornwell, 1984). Since that date I have been working on a study of health beliefs of elderly people in the Oxford area using broadly similar research methods.

The chapter is divided into three sections. The first two are about the initial stages of the project and have been reconstructed from the original research proposal, papers written in the early stages of the project, field-notes and the research diary. The third section attempts to reassess the original analysis and interpretation of data in the light both of further research using the same methods in a different type of community, and of discussions in academic departments of community medicine and sociology and the reviews which followed the publication of the report.

What I should like to do, therefore, is to illustrate the argument that at every stage the research process is determined by the social relations of the academic institution and of the field. To take the first of these two instances: clarifying the research problem and selecting research methods are intellectual tasks, but they are carried out within, and to some degree shaped by, the social context of the academic institution. In this case the institutional environment was that of an academic geography department with a strong tradition of quantitative research in which qualitative methods were perceived as 'unscientific' and 'anecdotal'. The first two sections of this chapter describes what was in fact a prolonged but ultimately unsuccessful attempt to incorporate concepts from social administration and standard survey methods into a study in which they were singularly inappropriate. In retrospect, it is apparent that the effort was entirely misplaced but it arose out of the need to have the study accepted and legitimated by its institutional context. The third section of the chapter is concerned with the problem of theorizing the relationship between social contexts and the meanings they contain. It suggests that the original analysis of the East London data needs to be refined further and identifies a direction for the theoretical work to take.

The research problem

The diary, the original research proposal, the schedules of interviews used in the pilot study and the papers written in the first year of the study are all records of the assumptions and influences which shaped the project. One thing the diary shows but which the other sources cannot is how much time was devoted to ideas and impulses, stimulated either by the literature or from the field, which were later abandoned. For example, one of these was the idea, which came from interviews with two women in the pilot study, of looking in detail at the practice and significance of illegal abortions prior to the 1967 Abortion Act. Both women had talked about their own experience of illegal abortion and one had offered to put me in touch with the woman who had performed her own abortion and who had later been given a gaol sentence for her involvement in this activity. The woman in question deliberated for some time before finally refusing to be interviewed for the study and despite the fact that by now a considerable amount of time had been spent reflecting on the significance of illegal abortion for the study as a whole, preparing a schedule to interview her and pursuing the contact, that theme in the work then disappeared altogether. None of the women who were subsequently interviewed mentioned illegal abortion and the final report ignores the topic.

From the perspective of the completed project it is possible to look back to the period in which the research objectives were formulated and separate out three strands of thought as particularly significant. It has to be said, however, that it is a great deal easier to identify each of the strands and to see the connections between them *in retrospect* than it was at the time when I was struggling to define the research problem.

The first strand came out of a rejection of mainstream medical sociology for being too preoccupied with medicine, the medical profession and medical perceptions of sociological problems. This general criticism was closely linked to the second strand – a more specific criticism of the sociological literature on 'illness behaviour' and the use of services for making inappropriate and ill-founded judgements about the relationship of working-class people to health services (see Tuckett (1976), chapter 4 for a review). Since the research began there has been the initiation of serious public debate about the reasons for social differences in health and the use of health services (Townsend and Davidson, 1982; Blaxter and Paterson, 1982; Open University, 1985; MacIntyre, 1986), but at the time there was very little to explain why, despite generally higher rates of morbidity and mortality, semi-skilled and unskilled manual workers and their families make relatively less use of primary health and preventive services and more use of accident and emergency services than other occupational groups. The most frequent explanations for this phenomenon have taken Oscar Lewis's (1967) 'culture of poverty' thesis as their starting point and argued that the sub-culture of the manual working class produces a 'fatalistic' approach to illness which makes people feel there is nothing they can do to prevent themselves becoming ill or improve their position once they are ill. The notion of fatalism in the literature has also been linked to the idea that these same people have a 'crisis mentality' and live in a 'crisis economy', such that they only take action and respond to events if a situation (or an illness condition) becomes desperate and threatens the family economy.

My own interpretation of these explanations for social differences in the use of health services was that they were not explanations but labels which re-described patterns of behaviour without offering any particular insight into the reasons for them. Furthermore the labels themselves had negative connotations which had more to do with the fact that the people to whom they were applied were not using health services in the way that the professions responsible for the services wanted them to be used. It seemed to me that this was a classic example of social scientists adopting a medical point of view and interpreting professionally approved behaviour as normal and rational (and not worth researching) and 'deviant' behaviour as problematic (and worth researching) (Dingwall, 1976). Furthermore, it seemed that the medical sociological view of lay behaviour in general paid too much attention to medicine and health services and too little to the broader material and ideological forces which shape people's lives and their approaches to health matters. Together, these criticisms of sociological approaches to health and illness pointed to a gap in knowledge and understanding of the relationship between patients and health services which I was motivated to try to fill.

However, the third strand in my thinking at the time involved trying to link this research project into the social administration literature on definitions of 'need' and to define the research problem in the terms of 'felt needs' (for examples of the literature see Davies, 1968; Bradshaw, 1970; Culyer, 1976). This was unfortunate. The social administration literature refers to 'felt needs' but it is, as it were, 'paradigmatically opposed' to their investigation on the grounds that it is not possible to conduct a scientific examination of subjectivity. This literature was therefore the wrong place to be looking for the concepts and methods needed in the study and I wasted far too much time trying to resolve the problem of how to produce 'objective' measures of felt needs.

The key difference between the position I have characterized as a social administration or social policy type of approach and the one I later developed lies in the way that the former assumes that 'subjective depositions' means that every person has a deposition of their own needs which is unique to them, whilst the latter is concerned with ideologies – sets of ideas and beliefs – which people have in common. The former reduces and narrows subjective definitions of need to the level of individual psychology whilst the latter focuses on the social processes which produce a common culture. In this study it took over a year before I eventually abandoned the attempt to solve the problem of how to measure individual subjectivity and redefined the study objective as that of researching commonsense meanings of health and illness.

Once a conceptual shift of this kind has occurred it is not easy to retrace the steps which led to it as single moments in a process of inter-action which goes on continuously between the concepts and ideas which are being developed and the empirical data which are being collected. In this case the research had started from the simple aim of finding out how people felt about the health service and what they wanted from it, with an underlying commitment to the principle that whatever was said and however people felt would be treated as rational from their point of view. Despite being ambushed by concepts developed in social administration, it soon became apparent that in order to understand what was being said about health services I needed to know more about the research subjects' concepts of health and illness, their ideas about the causes of illness, their views of medical treatments, and so on. Shifts in the definition of the research problem continued to occur gradually to the point where it became obvious that the aim of the project must be to grasp all the commonsense meanings which people taking part in the research took for granted. The final formulation of the objective of the study then became that of inquiring into the lives of a selected group of people who live in East London and into their commonsense ideas and theories about health and illness and health services and to do so in the context of much more general inquiry into their lives as a whole.

Research methods: Choices and difficulties

Interviews

It is an obvious point to make to say that the methods chosen for the research have to be appropriate to the topic under investigation and functional. In the case of this study of lay health beliefs in East London, the research methods had to fulfil the following criteria. They had to:

1 allow the research subjects to speak for themselves, in their own words, and forms of words, about the subjects under consideration;
2 permit a wide-ranging investigation of areas of their lives other than their health including their work; family relationships; and involvement in the wider community;
3 provide access to their interpretations of the subjects under discussion and a means of exploring their system of values;
4 collect biographical and health data for each person and for the members of their social networks;
5 provide information about the research subjects' informal social relationships and their perceptions of the quality of those relationships.

Once the criteria for the research methods were established it was possible to rule out certain types of approach. These were formal survey methods using questionnaires or standardized and tightly scheduled interviews which restrict research subjects to a limited range of responses. This study was intended to be exploratory; it was not possible accurately to predict what people might say and the whole point of the exercise was to encourage them to talk about themselves and their concerns in a way they found easy.

The research methods which suggested themselves for the study were either some kind of loosely structured techniques of interviewing or participant observation. It is generally true that participant observation is ideally suited to the discovery of how people live their lives and give them meaning but in the case of this study it did not seem the most appropriate method of investigation. On a purely practical level it was difficult to envisage how to do participant observation since finding a room to stay with a family would have been unusual in this part of London. Families in the area do not, as a rule, take in lodgers and in any case the position of lodger might not permit access to the intensely private material I was interested in collecting.

The method I chose to use therefore was a case-study approach based on tape-recorded interviews, returning repeatedly to the same households and individuals to do further interviews. In this way I hoped to build up a sufficient degree of familiarity with the research subjects – and they with me – for them to be able to speak freely about the subjects which concern them and for me to direct the conversation to topics of interest to me.

The content of the interviews was loosely based on a schedule of topics drawn up in advance and designed to reflect the study objectives. The first schedules were immensely long – too long, as I discovered in the pilot study. They covered various aspects of the person's biography: housing, education, employment history, marriage, family life and full medical history. After the pilot, the schedules were redesigned so that roughly half the time was spent looking at the person's background and biography and the other half was spent discussing health and health services. In theory each person was to be interviewed at least twice and if they had a great deal to say that was relevant, as many times as seemed necessary. In practice two men stipulated in advance that they would do no more than one interview and the number of interviews with other people ranged between one and five.

In addition to the basic schedule of topics which was covered with everyone I developed special questions and rescheduled parts of interviews to fit the immediate circumstances of the person being interviewed. For example, one of the women mentioned in the first interview that her father was about to be admitted to hospital for surgery, and so in later interviews with her and with her sisters and her adult daughters I followed the story of his operation, his discharge home, the care he received from the GP and district nurses, the problems with obtaining adaptations for his flat, and so on.

The original schedules used in the pilot study included a check-list of indicators of material wealth adapted from Townsend's study of poverty (Townsend, 1979) which was designed to permit the people in the study to be rated according to Townsend's measures. This meant that the pilot interviews ended with a whole series of questions about household amenities – access to an indoor bathroom and toilet, hot water, fridge, washing machine, etc., cars and money. The design of these schedules was in keeping with the social policy perspective I was still trying to integrate into the study, but from the point of view of the main research objectives the check-list was a disaster. It introduced a new note into the interviews and one which went entirely against the relationship I had been trying to develop with the person I was interviewing. One reason for this was that it included questions about money which people were reluctant to answer, but it was also because it changed the atmosphere from one which was relatively informal and relaxed where the interviewee had a degree of control over the topics, to one which was comparatively tense and hostile in which I asked questions they were expected to answer. As a result of this experience in the pilot study I made the decision to prioritize the quality of the relationships with the study subjects and abandoned the check-list.

Recruitment

Recruitment to the study was based on two guiding principles: the need to avoid identification with service providers lest it affect people's willingness to talk about the health service; and the need for first-hand information about relationships in informal social networks. Since the aim of the study was to explore people's lives as fully as possible it was necessary to establish whom they saw regularly and the content and quality of their relationships with other people. The literature on informal social networks noted frequently and with regret that most such studies have been 'ego-centred' that is, have relied on one informant for information about all the relationships in the network (Bott, 1957; Friedson, 1961; Barnes, 1969a; 1969b; Mitchell, 1969). In view of this it seemed important to break with tradition and despite the practical limitations this imposed on the breadth of the sample and the methods of recruitment to make a study of only one or two social networks but collecting information from more than one member of the network.

The empirical research was organized in three stages: the pilot study which involved six people (four women and two men) all of whom knew one another and were neighbours and friends in the same street; Stage I, which involved seven people (six women and one man all in the same extended family); and Stage II, which involved eleven people (six men and five women) six of whom were related whilst the remaining five were friends and neighbours from the same housing estate.

In the same way that the interview schedules were modified after the pilot study, in the second and final stage of interviewing *the principle* of recruitment to the study through networks was abandoned because on balance and *as a principle* it no longer seemed of practical benefit to the project. The chief advantage of this method of recruiting had unexpectedly turned out to be that each person who was interviewed provided an introduction to someone else, and this made it easier to establish an informal relationship with the new person. But for the specific purposes of the research, the term 'network' had proved something of a misnomer; the 'networks' were much less general networks than they were sets of relationships between women. Furthermore, the importance of the network as a medium for the exchange of ideas, advice and information about health seemed to have been greatly exaggerated (Friedson, 1961; McKinlay, 1970; 1973). There were exchanges of this kind but they rarely involved more than two or three people and never the entire social network.

Most importantly, it became clear from the pilot and Stage I interviews that women were much more actively involved in the relationships which held the networks together than men and this had unwelcome consequences for the research. Being female myself, and given the women's role in relation to their networks, it was relatively easy for me to be 'taken up' by a network of women and passed from one contact to the next. But I also wanted to involve men in the study and having become part of a network of women this became virtually impossible. In the family network (Stage I) the women were not at all enthusiastic about asking husbands and male partners to take part in the study and rather than risk jeopardizing my relationship with them I stopped asking them if this would be possible. In the second and final stages of interviews I therefore concentrated on finding men who would agree to be interviewed. This led to a meeting of the Residents' Association on the estate where most of the research was done and it was from that meeting, rather than through one initial contact which snowballed to others, that I managed to recruit the six men and their friends, wives and relatives who agreed to participate in Stage II of the study.

Reassessing the analysis and interpretation of data

Analysis and interpretation of qualitative data of the kind collected in this study do not necessarily end with the writing of the report. The analysis in the report already had a short history in the sense that it had moved through different stages, and after the report was published, partly in response to criticism and partly through discussion and further empirical work, it has continued to develop.

There is a direct relationship between the methods of data collection and the way in which the data were interpreted in the study. The methods of recruitment and the collection of data – obtaining introductions through family and neighbourhood networks, doing multiple interviews with more than one member of the network – meant that for a period of six months to two years there was regular and frequent contact with the same small circle of people. The opportunity this created to go back over the same ground both with the same person and with different people, created an interview text which is multilayered and complex. People contradicted themselves; they said one thing on one occasion and a different thing the next; they gave different versions of stories they or other people had already told previously and they repeated themselves and each other.

It was the element of repetition which first drew attention to the different types of account contained in the interviews. The schedules for the first interviews contained a question about how Bethnal Green had changed in the person's lifetime and, regardless of the age differences of up to fifty years between them, everyone answered that question in much the same way and some people answered using the same words and phrases as other people had used already. The changes they outlined were invariably negative: they associated 'the past' with 'real community' life and spirit and talked of people trusting one another and being all the same as each other; they saw the present as marked by an absence of community, mistrust and by substantial material and financial differences between close neighbours.

In the first extended analysis of interview material which took place between the first and second stages of interviewing, I used the terms *repertoire* and *dynamic* to distinguish between the types of account the interviews contained. Repertoire accounts were identified by their predictability – I often knew in advance what the answers to certain questions would be – they were routine, and everyone gave them. There were repertoire accounts of most topics including families, husbands, children, black people and Asians, poverty and material wealth, education, and the topics in which I was most interested, health, illness, doctors and health service. The term dynamic was used to contrast with repertoire accounts. Dynamic accounts were identified by their fresh quality of people thinking new thoughts and saying things they did not appear to have said many times before. There was a sense of their responding directly to the interview situation and using it to explore new territory, or old territory from a new perspective.

After the second round of interviews I replaced the terms repertoire and dynamic with those of *public* and *private* accounts. It seemed to be the case that the different types of account which had been identified were linked to two interconnected sets of social relationship: the relationship between researcher and research subject, and the relationship between professionals and experts with the lay public as it is reflected in the legitimacy accorded to professional as opposed to lay knowledge. In parts of the interviews, the relationship between researcher and research subject was an unequal relationship – a relationship of strangers from different social backgrounds and statuses – and in those parts the people being interviewed appeared to give 'public accounts' of themselves and their experience. These were accounts which I defined as 'sets of meanings in common social currency that reproduce and legitimate the assumptions people take for granted about social reality', as conforming to 'least common denominator morality' (Douglas, 1971; Cornwell, 1984). If the issue being discussed was connected with health, the public account was one which the person presumed would be acceptable to the relevant experts in the field, i.e. the medical profession.

The length of the interviews and the fact that people were interviewed more than once meant that at least some of the time the research relationship became closer and more personal, and as that happened the social differences between myself and the people I was interviewing were forgotten. It was on these occasions that people gave what I termed private accounts which expressed the way they would respond 'if thinking only what (they) and the people (they) knew directly would think and do', and which seemed to spring more directly from their own experience and the thoughts and feelings which accompanied it (Cornwell, 1984). Private accounts of health matters were ones in which people gave their own opinions and made it clear that what they were saying was based on personal experience rather than medical authority.

The distinction between public and private served a useful purpose. It directed attention towards and helped to clarify the significance of both the social context (i.e. the research relationship) and structures of authority and legitimation in the wider society for the meanings contained in the interviews. With hindsight, and having acquired some distance from the project since its completion, the distinction seems both overly simplistic and somewhat rigid. It has, for example, rightly been said that people sometimes tell their most intimate thoughts and private stories to strangers and that the currency of the small circle of social intimates is frequently that of the public 'least common denominator morality' (Frankenberg, 1986). The experience of using similar research techniques with a socially mixed sample in a suburban community has also been instructive because there the repertoire of public accounts has been much less striking. One reason for this may be that the predictability and consistency of the public accounts in Bethnal Green is specific to that particular community or to communities with an equally powerful sense of local identity.

Instead of persisting with the dichotomy between public and private in the analysis of the case material from the most recent study, I shall be treating the text of the interviews as one which mediates between various kinds of knowledge. This is the analytic approach Allan Young has advanced, and he has set out a schema of analytically distinct kinds of knowledge – theoretical, empirical, rationalized, intersubjective and negotiated knowledges – which can be applied to empirical data (Young, 1981; 1982). These five kinds of knowledge are a useful starting point for looking more closely at the constitutive elements of what I had previously termed public accounts. Young has also developed the concept of 'proto-typical knowledge' which will refine the interpretation of the content of private accounts. He defines 'prototypical knowledge' as empirical knowledge based on observation of 'things which occur together', which he also refers to as 'congeries of elements' – these may be symptoms, or psychological states, events or relationships – which people perceive as grouped together in some way without ordering them into causal or func-tional relationships. Young identifies this lack of systematicity as the reason why people give accounts of their own and others' direct experi-ence which are not consistent. They introduce new elements and omit elements they had previously mentioned because they do not perceive them in an ordered way as interdependent, a characteristic also associated with private accounts.

Young's scheme is theoretical; it has not yet been applied to the analysis of case material from this country. There are problems with conducting a *post hoc* analysis using a scheme like this on material which has already been collected as opposed to working with such a scheme during the process of data collection. Nevertheless, the distinction bet-ween prototypical knowledge and the other five kinds of knowledge is especially helpful and seems to offer a way of taking further the analysis of lay health beliefs particularly because it seems to provide a way of thinking through the problem of how structures of authority and power impinge upon what is known and what is said in different social contexts.

Conclusion

The aim in this chapter has been to direct attention to aspects of the research process which are not featured sufficiently often in published accounts of sociological research methods. The chapter has examined problems and difficulties ranging from that of spending time which, from the point of view of the final report, can appear to have been wasted, to the theoretical inconsistencies and contradictions which impede progress, to the difficulties posed by research methods and interpretative frames of reference. Techniques that are ill-judged and inappropriate can put to waste the investment in recruiting and getting to know research subjects, and for a study such as the one reported here where the researcher is dependent on establishing relationships with research subjects which must last some length of time, this can be serious.

There can be difficulties that arise out of the researcher's own attributes. In this case, the fact that I was female and relatively young had consequences for the data which could be collected and for the interpretation of the material. It determined whether or not I had access to particular people (in this case male partners) and the kinds of material I was able to cover. The women, for example, talked in detail about married life, but the men would not; the women were also much more comfortable in discussions about illness than were the men and in general, more willing to speak about personal experiences and feelings than were the men. The latter were evidently unused to talking about themselves and about personal matters, especially to a young woman to whom they were not related. Clearly too the material from the interviews with the women and men is not comparable and this presents problems in the interpretation of data which Young's analytic approach will help to unravel.

In drawing attention to aspects of this particular piece of research which were difficult or problematic I am not trying to suggest that this study was unusual or different from other qualitative studies. On the contrary, I am suggesting that all studies are shaped by social relations which can pose theoretical and practical difficulties of obstacles to the work, and that researchers should make this explicit in their accounts of the research process. This is partly in order to present a more realistic account of what it is like doing sociological research, but it is also because the difficulties and obstacles are in themselves rich sources of data. To the measure that they are ignored our understanding of social processes will be impoverished.

References

Barnes, J. A. (1969a) 'Graph theory and social networks: a technical comment on connectedness and connectivity', *Sociology* 3, 215–32.

Barnes, J.A. (1969b) 'Networks and political Process', in Mitchell, J. Clyde (ed.), *Social networks in urban situations: analyses of personal relationships in central African towns*, Manchester University Press, Manchester.

Bell, C. and Newby, H. (eds) (1977) *Doing sociological research*. Allen and Unwin, London.

Bell, C. and Roberts, H. (1984) *Social researching: politics, problems, practice*, Routledge & Kegan Paul, London.

Blaxter, M. and Paterson, E. (1982) *Mothers and daughters: a three generational study of health attitudes and behaviours*, Heinemann Educational Books, London.

Bott, E. (1957) *Family and social network. Roles, norms and external relationships in ordinary urban families*, Tavistock: London. (Revised edition 1971.)

Bowen, E. S. (1964) *Return to laughter*, Anchor Books in cooperation with the American Museum of Natural History, New York.

Bradshaw, J. (1970) 'A taxonomy of social needs', in McLachlan, G. (ed.), *Problems and progress in medical care 7*, Nuffield Provincial Hospitals Trust, Oxford University Press, London.

Cornwell, J. (1984) *Hard-earned lives: accounts of health and illness from East London*, Tavistock, London.

Culyer, A. J. (1976) *Need and the National Health Service: economics and social choice*, Martin Robertson, London.

Davis, B. (1968) *Social needs and resources in local services. A study of variations in standards of provision of personal social services between local authority areas*, Michael Joseph, London.

Dingwall, R. (1976) *Aspects of illness*, Martin Robertson, London.

Douglas, J. D. (1971) *American social order: Social rules in a pluralistic society*, Free Press, New York.

Frankenberg, R. (1986) Review of *Hard-earned Lives, Sociology of Health and Illness 8*.

Freidson, E. (1970) *Profession of medicine: A study of the sociology of applied knowledge*, Dodd, Mead and Co., New York.

Lewis, O. (1967) *The children of Sanchez*, Random House, New York.

Macintyre, S. (1986) 'The patterning of health by social position in contemporary Britain: Directions for sociological research', *Social Science and Medicine 23*, 393–414.

McKinlay, J. B. (1970) 'A brief description of a study of the utilization of maternity and child welfare facilities of a lower working-class sub-culture', *Social Science and Medicine 4*, 551–6.

McKinlay, J. B. (1973) 'Social networks, lay consultation and help-seeking behaviour', *Social Forces 51*, 275–92.

Mitchell, J. Clyde (1969) 'The concept and use of social networks', in Mitchell, J. Clyde (ed.), *Social networks in urban situations: analysis of personal relationships in central African towns*, Manchester University Press, Manchester.

The Open University (1985) *The health of nations* (U205 Book III), The Open University Press, Milton Keynes.

Pill, R. and Stott, N. C. H. (1982) 'Concepts of illness causation and responsibility: some preliminary data from a sample of working class mothers', *Social Science and Medicine* 16, 43–52.

Townsend, P. (1979) *Poverty in the United Kingdom. A survey of household resources and standards of living*, Penguin Books, Harmondsworth.

Townsend, P. and Davidson, N. (1982) *Inequalities in health. The Black Report*, Penguin Books, London.

Tuckett, D. (ed.) (1976) *Introduction to medical sociology*, Tavistock, London.

Young, A. (1981) 'When rational men fall sick: an inquiry into some assumptions made by medical anthropologists', *Culture, Medicine and Psychiatry* 5, 317–35.

Young, A. (1982) 'The anthropologies of illness and sickness', *Annual Review of Anthropology* 11, 257–85.

13

From Fact-world to Life-world
The Phenomenological Method and Social Science Research

John Pickles

The typical working scientist is like an artist who creates without being particularly aware of the theory behind his performances. This one-sided brilliance is even to a certain extent necessary for the advance of the sciences. He who goes forward cannot look over his shoulder for long. But without intrinsic rationality and clarity in foundations, a working science is just that, i.e., a technology whose 'theoretical techniques' permit the prediction of future events and the technical control and domination of nature, which makes the world more useful but not more understandable.

Kisiel, 1970

Introduction

Geographers would generally agree that the meteoric rise to prominence in the past decade of alternative research methodologies has been attended by the rather limited development of one of their intitial major conceptual underpinnings – that of phenomenology. The application of phenomenological principles in geography has been limited and few substantive contributions have been made. Even as early as 1976 Entrikin suggested that the role of the phenomenological method itself has been reduced in the work of geographers such as Buttimer and Tuan, and that, as a result, the phenomenological perspective can best be seen as criticism of positivistic conceptions of science. For many geographers, the failure of phenomenologists to produce rigorous empirical phenomenologies casts a dark shadow over the whole enterprise, and other qualitative research approaches are to be sought (Jackson, 1981; Eyles, 1985). Among those geographers who still find the phenomenological project of interest, many have begun to argue that we need practical examples of phenomenological geography carried out in concrete situations (Seamon, 1980; Relph, 1981a).

In this chapter I shall not be concerned with a detailed examination of claims about phenomenology made by geographers, nor about the varieties of phenomenology (descriptive, hermeneutic, mundane or transcendental) that we may adopt. (These claims are available elsewhere, and the interested reader is referred to them: Relph, 1981b; Pickles, 1985.) The present chapter will concentrate on clarifying the central claims and underlying rationale for a phenomenological approach. Its conclusions might be surprising, for in them I shall argue that for the most part scientists already do phenomenology, but that they need to do it rationally and explicitly (descriptive science of regional ontology) *and* that the adoption of phenomenological principles does not challenge or necessarily say anything about the empirical concerns of scientists or the approaches and methods they choose to adopt.

In part the slow development of sound exemplars of phenomenological method is a product of the difficulty involved in understanding the complex and varied claims made about it, and in part the difficulty of the method itself. But there is another reason why we have seen only limited application of the phenomenological method in the discipline: this has to do with what we normally think 'method' entails, and what 'the phenomenological method' actually is. In this chapter I shall show why the phenomenological method is not a method like many others, but how it underpins all claims to valid method. The chapter is in two sections. The first clarifies the aim of phenomenology; the second addresses its value and application. Before turning to these issues, however, it will be necessary to make some preliminary comments about language.

The internal problem of language

Despite the apparently limited success of phenomenological approaches, phenomenological terminology and much of the spirit of its early advocates have found acceptance and continue to exert a strong influence on a discipline which now takes the life-world and the taken-for-granted world as important areas of study, and qualitative or interpretative methods as serious alternatives to naturalistic methods. Such claims alone suggest that something important is embedded here. But what could it be?

Previous attempts to give an account of the phenomenological method have encountered severe difficulties. Central among them is the need to use language which presupposes the phenomenological project, but which is either uncommon or now means something very different in everyday language. Thus, in commenting on my *Phenomenology, Science and Geography*, Johnston (1986) complained that some of the words used – apodictic, factical, incompossible – were neither in his personal vocabulary nor his dictionary. This points to a basic requirement for the student of phenomenology. These words are in the *Oxford English Dictionary*, and the reader of phenomenological works must be prepared to keep a vocabulary list of such words. Partly this is a necessary condition of beginning any new scholarly endeavour. Partly it is because in the phenomenological project, in trying to overcome the traditional metaphysics of subjectivism and objectivism, everyday language use often is not appropriate. Translators of phenomenological works have been forced to use terminology which is exact, but which does not evoke this traditional metaphysics.

This attempt at careful language use has not been entirely successful, and this points to the second requirement for the student. Words such as 'universal', 'essential', 'subjectivity', 'objectivity', have particular meanings in current everyday parlance, but these are not what they originally meant, nor what phenomenologists mean by them. This problem is concatenated on the one hand by geographers' seeming reluctance to adopt philosophical language, and on the other hand, by their persistence in dealing with philosophical issues regardless (a good example here is Johnston, 1983b; 1986). For our present purposes it is important to bear in mind that: (a) it is necessary to use language carefully and exactly when we are trying to avoid the many philosophical pitfalls that have confounded previous attempts to understand the human sciences; (b) this careful use may well have resulted from careful consideration of alternatives, and not from the wholesale adoption of jargon; and (c) the meaning of a term should as far as possible be taken from the text and the tradition to which that text points, and not from a cursory reading of secondary literature or the imposition of other meaning.

The question of method

Before we begin discussing the phenomenological method let us think about 'methods' as we normally understand them. The *Oxford English Dictionary* defines method as a mode of investigation, a procedure for attaining an object, or a special form of procedure or set of rules and practices adopted in any branch of mental activity or in pursuance of a particular goal. More specifically 'method' refers to certain specific procedures in mathematics and the experimental sciences, such as least squares, experimental method or the deductive method. Thus, when turning to a book on qualitative methods one might assume that methods are procedures or rules which, like tools, permit us to construct an account of the way some aspect of the world is. Modern social science often views method in this way, as a series of approaches or techniques, each of which fulfils its function in permitting the researcher to construct another piece of a broader project: an account (or a geography) of intra-urban mobility, an analysis of capital flows in the city, an explanation of settlement patterns in Pennsylvania. Interview and questionnaire schedules, participant observation, archival research, multi-dimensional scaling, correlation and regression techniques; these and others are often seen to be the methods of social science. Thus, when we turn to 'the phenomenological method' we might at first assume it to be of a similar character. Indeed, most of the literature in geography which makes reference to the phenomenological method treats it in this way; it is applied to methods which are descriptive and interpretative, and which are therefore assumed to be qualitative. Moreover, in evaluating claims about phenomenology, geographers have consistently demanded examples of the use of the method as if it were like all these other methods. Calls for doing phenomenology have been calls to put the method into practice in investigating some empirical problem or other.

But this view of method is too narrow for our present purposes: method here will not be a tool or a technique, but will involve a philosophy, an approach to inquiry, and only then specific procedures for the actual conduct of research in a particular science such as geography. Nor will the phenomenological method tell us very much about the kind of techniques we need to use in empirical research, for the very reason that phenomenology does not deal with empirical research as such, but with the essential or invariant structures which found the objectifications of empirical categories. In making such a strong claim, my aim is not to dissuade students and researchers from pursuing phenomenological research. It is to say that, while there may be no straightforward technique to be picked up, the adoption of the method (as we shall come to understand that term henceforth) will be much more productive than any single technique could be. In this sense the 'phenomenological method' is not, nor can it be made into, a method (i.e. a technique) like many others in this book. In large part this is because the phenomenological method, unlike other qualitative methods in this book, does not address empirical issues. Phenomenology indeed tells us how we should go about 'doing' things, but in regional ontologies not in empirical (or positive) science. Thus, calls from geographers for phenomenologists to demonstrate the efficacy of their approach through practical and concrete examples completely miss the point. In this sense the phenomenological method is much closer to what we might call 'ontology of science' than it is to what we call 'empirical research'. Having said this, it is none the less the case that working through the phenomenological method will radically transform both the questions of empirical inquiry and approaches to them.

The phenomenological method

Phenomenology is at once a philosophy and a rigorous science, and thus its scientific character is very different from that of the sciences of nature, life, mind and society (Kockelmans, 1985: 27). Primarily it is a method of philosophy whose aim is to clarify *a priori* and ungrounded assumptions in order to permit phenomena (including things, concepts, experiences) to be shown as they show themselves, and to do so in a way which does not show them in any other way than the way in which they show themselves. Phenomenology thus turns away from the objects themselves and to the way in which the objects are given – to their *objectness*; to their being as phenomena, i.e. objects of experience. With this apparently confusing beginning, phenomenology establishes four important principles often ignored by the social sciences: first, that the objects of science cannot be specified *a priori*; second, that all knowing is intentional; third, that the task of science is the precise and accurate description and account of the phenomena we encounter in the world; and fourth, that the task of phenomenology is methodically to permit this, and to avoid the distorting influence of *a priori* and unclarified assumptions.

Much effort has been expended to apply phenomenological principles to the empirical study of society, but we must be careful with such applications. First and foremost phenomenology is, as Heidegger says, the method of ontology; it seeks to be rigorous and scientific in the sense that it does not want to take its basic concepts for granted. When phenomenologists provocatively call for a return to the things themselves it is a call to arrive at the primary presuppositions, beyond which we cannot go and which do not need to be clarified because they are immediately evident (i.e. apodictic) in direct intuition. Phenomenology is thus an attempt to construct a science of 'ultimate' (not 'unchanging' or 'absolute') grounds: that is, a science based on rationally derived grounds.

Such a study of primary presuppositions is different from the other sciences. It is not concerned with things, which in everyday life (or the natural attitude) are given to us as unquestionably obvious, nor does it take these things as given. Phenomenology is concerned with the way in which objects are constituted; that is, with the conditions or horizon of meaning within which objects have the meaning that they have for us (be we concerned with physical things or non-physical objects such as consciousness, society, place or power). To understand what this means and what implications it holds for our discussion of the phenomenological method, it will be necessary to make a distinction between the natural attitude and the philosophical attitude.

The natural and the philosophical attitudes

The first step in the phenomenological method involves the 'bracketing' of the 'natural attitude': 'that is, suspending the naively held belief that mundane objects exist in themselves in such a way as to be strictly transcendent to our consciousness of them' (Casey, 1977: 74). Husserl makes a clear-cut distinction between the natural and the philosophical attitudes. Much confusion exists as to the nature of this distinction, and the failure to recognize it has greatly influenced the way in which geographers have viewed the phenomenological method and its possible applications in geography.

Kockelmans (1985: 28) has described the natural attitude in the following way:

in the natural attitude one tacitly assumes that we are in a world through which our mind can roam at will and in which we can consider any part we want, without changing the objective nature of what we consider. According to this view, the object-pole of our knowing is an objectively existing, fully explainable world that can be expressed in exact, objective laws. This 'objective' world exists wholly in itself and possesses a rationality that can be fully understood.

Philosophy begins from a different position since it cannot begin as the positive sciences do, naively taking the pre-given world of experience for granted. The philosophical attitude requires that we must return to the original experience in a special way. It is this turn from the natural attitude to the philosophical attitude which is at the root of the phenomenological method, and which, because it is overlooked by geographers, causes so many problems in understanding the phenomenological method. In part, the phenomenological method is this turning to experience not as naively and uncritically given, but as the object of reflection. This is the eidetic reduction (which takes us from the world of facts to the world of ideas), and is what is sometimes called the procedure of 'bracketing': the reduction of the relativities of the cultural world to the invariant or universal structures of the life-world. A second reduction (actually a set of reductions) – the phenomenological reductions – take us from the world of facts to meaning.

In this way the phenomenological method is a problematizing of the everyday, taken-for-granted world. Instead of dealing with the world at the level of facts, phenomenology seeks to deal with the constitution of those facts from and in the pre-scientific life-world. Phenomenology operates at several 'levels'. For its founder (Husserl) it was to be a philosophical method. The need for a philosophical (phenomenological) foundation for empirical science arose because of the way in which empiricism reduced the world to natural and biological phenomena, and the way in which it forgot that its objects were not real objects naively given to immediate perception, but had been constituted through long processes of abstraction and idealization. At this level, phenomenology is the science of regional ontology, which clarifies how the objects of the sciences are constituted; for example, with what space, time, distance and place mean for each domain of the sciences. The regional ontologies thus seek to establish the essential structures of meaning from which each domain of the sciences constitutes its particular view of the world. Such 'essences', it should be noted, are not transhistorical or immutable, but are transformed in the on-going project of scientific inquiry and the changing structure of everyday life. But, it must also be stated that this transformation is itself a bounded one; bounded by the nature of the phenomena taken as objects for each of the sciences. Phenomenology is thus also concerned with the processes by which the sciences transform experiences of the life-world into scientific claims: with the processes of distanciation, thematization, idealization, objectification, abstraction, formalization and possibly quantification, by which science constitutes its objects. Furthermore, since the everyday world is itself not an object of immediate perception but is also constituted, it too has to be investigated as to its constitution. Here phenomenology is both thick description of the structures of signification which constitute the life-world (Geertz, 1973) and an ontological analysis of the constitution of those significations. It is at this level that social scientists have focused most of their attention, and at this level that phenomenology comes closest to ethnography, interpretative sociology, or to the qualitative methods with which this book is concerned. However, this level only makes sense as an inquiry into the constitution of the life-world when situated in the context of the other three levels. Only then is phenomenology a critical enterprise in which life-world descriptions are developed along with the explicit analysis of the constitutive processes adopted by the geographer. Fact (ontic world) and horizon of meaning (ontological world) are thus joint poles of the phenomenological project.

Philosophy, science and everyday worlds are tied together by the investigation of the constitution of objects or objectifications. Because phenomenology seeks to clarify the limits of such objectifications – i.e. to clarify the way in which the world is given to these domains of experience – it is inherently critical.

The issue of phenomena and masked-phenomena

Not all geographers have seen phenomenology in this way. The humanist sees in the individual's striving to make sense of the world the foundation for a phenomenological geography of experience: a world of cognitive maps and developing complexity of representation; a world of social contracts which form a web of social interactions; a system of signs and symbols whose meaning constitutes the lived world of the individual. These and other claims found the humanist's belief in the integrity of individual perception and understanding, and the importance for geography to begin with this subject as the building base for any humane geography (see, for example, Claval, 1983).

Few would argue with the intent behind such claims: the need for science to incorporate the dignity of human beings; the meaningful nature of human action; the symbolic structure of cultural life. This fabric of daily existence fills out a human geography and avoids the bleached bones of many analytical approaches to human behaviour.

But is this position sufficient? Is a phenomenological approach one which permits these phenomena of everyday life to be given central place in the human sciences? Does it embody within it a notion of phenomena which restricts itself to the immediacy of the cultural world? To do so would be to limit itself to treating that world as do those who live in it: surrounded by ambiguity and uncertainty, confused by ideology and distortions, bound by constraints of power and economy. Is the notion of phenomena adopted by phenomenology confined to that which shows itself, and unable to penetrate to that which shows itself as a mask, as a distortion, or as a symptom of some deeper cause?

Since Freud pointed to the unconscious as a crucial element in the explanation of certain behaviour, the issue of masked or hidden phenomena is one with which any phenomenology must deal from the beginning. Its corollary in the social realm is found in Marx's claim about the relationship between bourgeois culture and its economic foundation. In geography its current form is clearest in the relationship between structure and agency, and studies dealing with ideology, power and culture (see Gregory, 1978). In turning to the individual subject, and his or her world of meaning and action, do we approach the phenomena or are we diverted away from critical horizons and issues which would better explain those matters?

While this chapter will not answer these questions in detail, they are raised for two reasons. First, in turning to the phenomenological method, we must ask ourselves what we mean by 'phenomena' and what we may be excluding from our definition. And second, we must give an account of how phenomenology permits masked phenomena and deep structures to enter into its purview. Failure to begin to answer these questions will severely limit the value of any other claims we may make for phenomenology.

The game

Phenomenology claims for itself the role of philosophy of science. What could this mean, and how can it be so? To answer this question, and to clarify the nature of the phenomenologist's interest, let me discuss the issue in terms of the nature of a game.

A game, say a game of soccer, can be 'experienced' in several important ways. First, of course, is the experience of the players in the game. Here immersion in the game is a prerequisite for effective play: only the players who 'give themselves over to the game' can play effectively and well. Here the players immerse themselves in the act of playing, and, much like the conditions of social life, the rules under which they play are present to them only as limits on what constitutes playing and not playing the game. The fully immersed player does not necessarily recognize these rules in the act of playing, but instead may feel that the play of the game is governing his actions. There is a necessary tension between the play of the game carrying the actions of the player and the player controlling the outcomes of parts of the game. Both are necessary for the game to succeed as a game. The player who is unable to concentrate on the game in this way (who is unable to immerse himself in the playing) may find that the attempt to move a spherical object from one end of a field to another, and to shoot it through three pieces of wood, is a less than meaningful activity. Such a player does not submit to the rules and we say he is 'no longer playing the game'.

There are other participants in the game besides the players. The referee in a sense is playing a different game since he is interested in the limits of permissible play; that is, he is interested in the intersection between the game being played and the rules within which it is played. The spectators are also participants in the game, and they like the players must immerse themselves in the game and its rules. To step out of that context is suddenly to find the game to be a rather odd activity.

Several perspectives on the soccer game are independent of participation in it. The investor who has an interest in the success of the club may see the game as a means of financial security or loss. The sociologist who studies the game may see it as an outlet for pent-up aggression, a diversion from unpleasant conditions of work or home, a means of entrenching class interests through the generation of profit and the absorption of surplus on the one hand, and the creation of a large interest group supporting the perpetuation of existing economic relations, on the other hand.

These and other perspectives may be valid claims about the game of soccer. In each the 'object' is 'soccer', but each claim takes that object to mean something different depending upon the framework or horizon within which the claim is situated. In each the object of discourse is constituted differently, and the relations within which it is analysed are also different: for the players these relations are those of each player to all the others and to the rules; for the referee they are the relations of players to the game (that is to a set of rules); for the spectators they are the relations of the players and/or the teams to the game (that is, the rules and the symbolic function that each team plays); for the sociologist the relations are those of the game to broader issues of economy or society.

In each of these the objects so constituted may or may not be constituted accurately in terms of the phenomena themselves, but where they are so constituted each of the claims about the game may be valid claims. We have a set of objects (soccer in each of the different frameworks of analysis) which take their meaning from the horizons within which they are situated.

All social science is of this type. The phenomenologist aims to refocus attention on the rules and the horizons within which each social experience is given to us. The horizon of the players is only one, albeit important, possible horizon.

We have many possible perspectives on society. But are we to accept each of them as equals in the attempt at explanation? This depends to some extent on our purpose. If we want to understand individual and group action then each of the contexts sketched briefly above (and many possible others) describes the elements of such an understanding, and the way actors in each setting understand their actions. To borrow a term from Geertz (1983), we attempt to see 'from the native's point of view' (accepting all the problems that this entails). We have the beginnings of a descriptive ethnography, what Geertz (1973: 27) calls 'thick description' – 'setting down the meaning particular social actions have for the actors whose actions they are.' Are these descriptions sufficient to constitute a phenomenology?

What is missing from each of these descriptions is an analysis of their constitution, both conceptually and historically. When we turn to such a constitutive enterprise we immediately recognize that experience it-self is constituted through its historical formation. As such actions may arise from, and maintain in place, social structures and relationships which are unintended consequences of those actions. Description is thus inadequate where the horizons of meaning have been limited to the intended and examined consequences of 'playing'. These actions may only be intelligible in the context of their origins and unintended consequences. Thus, to refuse to extend ethnographic description to its broader critical base seems to have little justification given science's prior claim to be critical and rational. The logical extension of phenom-enology's claims to describe the phenomena as they show themselves is then that some phenomena show themselves as symptoms of underlying causes, or as phenomena which appear as one thing but really are something else.

Phenomenology must be able to deal with such masked phenomena. It cannot restrict itself merely to the immediate experience and its context of meaning. This second task is for Geertz (1973: 27) 'specification' or 'diagnosis': stating what the knowledge social actors have of their actions demonstrates about the society in which it is found and, beyond that, about social life as such.'

Our double task is to uncover the conceptual structures that inform our subjects' acts, the 'said' of social discourse, and to construct a system of analysis in whose terms what is generic to those structures, what belongs to them because they are what they are, will stand out against the other determinants of human behaviour. (Geertz, 1973: 27)

The phenomenological method and geography

From the above it follows that phenomenology has been greatly mis-understood within geography as to its essential premises and one of its major aims. Phenomenology is not concerned only with naively given experience, neither is it anti-scientific nor a criticism of science. Indeed, one of the major aims of phenomenology is to provide a rational foun-dation for the sciences as well as for life more generally. It would be a mistake to reject phenomenology at this stage because it is inappropriate to spatial analysis, cultural geography, participant observation method-ologies or critical geographies. Because it is about the ontological, and not – unlike these areas of inquiry themselves – about the ontical, it will have much to say about each.

In what follows I shall deal with phenomenology, science and the life-world, and with what phenomenology and a geography of the everyday

244 From Fact-world to Life-world

world must entail. In turning to this everyday world it will be necessary first to discuss several forms of phenomenology, and to show why we shall need a hermeneutic (or interpretative) phenomenology to deal with these issues.

Phenomenology, science and life-world

When Eddington (1929: ix–xvii) raised the question of how we are to understand the fact that the scientist always deals with two tables: the table of atoms and empty space, and the solid table at which he eats or writes, he pointed to an important problem for all the positive (i.e. positing) sciences, be they theoretical or empirical. As scientists pursue their inquiries, the objects of their scientific research become increasingly removed from the same objects in the everyday world. This occurs to such an extent that Eddington is forced to ask whether the two tables have any relationship to each other.

The objectifying tendencies of modern science should neither surprise nor horrify us. Empirical science operates as a positive, that is to say positing, science by setting up (or positing) a framework of meaning within which the world is seen in a particular way; as physical, biological or cultural, for example. In so positing a framework of meaning and its corresponding objects (or objectifications) the community of physicists, biologists, anthropologists, is able to penetrate and explain the abstract relationships between phenomena. These sciences of phenomena are sciences of facts, and to establish their claims they need special languages, methods and procedures. That is, for the most part, what this book on qualitative methods seeks to achieve for aspects of geographic research. The actual procedures of any positive science thus involve methodological procedures for distancing the observer from the observed (distanciation) – and this is equally true, albeit differently so, for participant observation methods and other forms of social analysis. In order to deal with this issue, Geertz (1983: 57) has suggested the use of Heinz Kohut's concepts of 'experience-near' and 'experience-distant' to capture the difference between the actor's frame of reference and the frame of reference established by the scientist. These involve agreed-upon principles and methods, in terms of which the world of everyday experience is constituted as a 'world' of objects for quantum physics, evolutionary biology or descriptive ethnography. These procedures include idealization and thematization, abstraction and objectification, and in certain cases they may include formalization, functionalization and mathematization.

Each procedure entails, to a greater or lesser extent, the distancing of the observer from the observed, or, to be more accurate, each entails the researcher standing back from lived involvement and treating the world as a set of objects (but not necessarily things) of theoretical reflection. Consequently positive science is necessarily forgetful of its origins, or what Whitehead called the 'fallacy of misplaced concreteness', where science forgets that its concepts are abstractions and not concrete objects.

In being forgetful of their origins in this manner the sciences lose touch with (a) their own processes of abstraction and concept formation, i.e. with the way in which they constitute their objects of study; and (b) the origins of their abstractions in the everyday world of experience (the life-world). The project of phenomenology – as a philosophy, a science and a method – is to clarify the way in which objects are constituted in the sciences, the arts and everyday life, *and* to show how these objects relate to the pre-given life-world.

In regard to the mathematical and natural sciences, phenomenology may thus function to provide their rational ground by dealing with the constitution of objects and their relation to the everyday world. In spatial analysis the regional ontology of space, time, place, distance, . . . can thus be clarified. In modern human geography the domains of conflict, power, production, social interaction and sense of place are to be clarified in this manner. In ethnographic geographies the task of phenomenological analysis is the clarification of the structures of signification within which action is meaningful and intelligible. In each of these cases the essential or invariant structures that constitute a particular phenomenon are sought: the essence of the phenomenon.

Defining the eidos

The notion of the eidos or essence of a phenomenon has created much confusion, and a good deal of heated debate. Much of this disagreement is founded on a misunderstanding. The eidos is nothing more than the essential structure that constitutes the being of a particular phenomenon.

We can begin most easily with the geometrical figure. What do we mean when we say that we see a circle? What is it that we see? On the blackboard we see a diagram of a circle, but we know this to be a mere device for aiding our discussion. When I draw a landscape of glacial deposition on the blackboard we do not presume the sketch to be the landscape. Similarly, the sketch of the circle is not what we mean when we refer to a circle. The eidos of a circle is thus necessary for each blackboard sketch to be intelligible as a circle, but the sketches themselves are insufficient to capture the eidos of 'circlehood'. Even given a blackboard full of circles we could not inductively derive the essence of circle, for we might just as easily select the *aspect* of white, of unevenness, of something drawn, of oval shape when viewed from the side. We need some understanding of the eidos of circle – in this case an axiomatic understanding of a geometrical principle – a figure whose sides are all equidistant from its centre. (This, incidentally, explains the problem with those aspects of geography which assume that method is learned by doing independently of clearly specified principles about what constitutes the essential characteristics of the objects under study and the methods of dealing with them. Without such principles the novice has a wide range of possibilities from which to derive the 'essential' characteristics of the enterprise; a factor that very often leads to intense frustration on the part of graduate students as they are apprenticed into an approach, rather than educated about it.)

Such a notion of essence does not invoke any absolute (sometimes called Platonic) essence, although in this example the mathematical is transhistorical in the sense that it is invariant over time and space. Such a geometric figure is by definition invariant only within a particular framework of meaning: that of Euclidean two-dimensional geometry. In the case of social phenomena their essence is not transhistorical, and it is for this reason that we need an interpretative phenomenology.

Phenomenology depends upon this notion of eidos, and it is to be applied to all phenomena if they are to be rationally grounded in a science of objectifications and in a life-world of original experience. Such an eidetic knowledge permits us to distinguish the essential and the accidental in empirical relationships, and thus influences the practice of research in the natural attitude. Above all, such eidetic knowledge raises serious questions about the amount of time and effort that positive social science is spending analysing relationships and testing hypotheses about phenomena which are and can only be related accidentally, not eidetically. To put this another way, meaningful empirical research requires a foundation in ontology, or a preliminary understanding of the essential characteristics of the phenomena with which it deals.

Perhaps we need an example to clarify some of these claims. Social scientists and geographers among them, have suggested that human behaviour in complex urban environments involves spatial search strategies by which route selection occurs and habituated travel paths are established. Such search strategies are often linked to other forms of spatial searching, such as finding an object in a complex array, or to the performance of animals in maze experiments. The links are obvious ones, and have been useful heuristics by which we conceptualize behaviour in space. But is such conceptual linkage phenomenologically valid? If we envisage human behaviour as if it were adapted maze behaviour, or some other stimulus–response relationship, won't we in fact find such a relation? What would we find if we began with several fundamental, but different principles? For example:

1 Human action is intentional, and is thus always to be conceived in terms of its correlate – its object, or in some cases its objective.
2 The intentional structure of experience is not unidimensional or simple. It is layered and complex, composed of multiple intentionalities, where switching between objectives is the norm, not the exception.
3 Human experience is ambiguous in two senses: first, in that the objectives of action may be only partly defined, or they may be satisfied when only partly achieved; second, these objectives are situated in the context of human learning and may thus be transformed in the process of their being consummated.

To begin with principles such as these is not to deny the possibility of operationalizing and formalizing relationships in science. The issue is prior to such formal processes, and indeed the point of the example above is that its thematization and formalization is possible, but would lead to very different conceptual and theoretical accounts of spatial behaviour than those with which we currently work. What would happen, for example, if we added a fourth principle? All human action is social in nature, and social action by its very nature produces and reproduces contexts with intended and unintended consequences. Or a fifth: human action occurs within a context of socially produced meanings, which in turn renews and reproduces those meaning structures.

Phenomenology and the thematization of scientific knowledge

It is a mistake to see phenomenology as in any way a rejection of the rigorous methods of science. As we have seen, phenomenology operates in a different domain from the natural attitude to which the positive sciences are confined. The difference between phenomenology and positive science is hinted at here in the introduction of the qualifier 'positive' science. This is not the philosophical position known as 'positivism', but describes the essential characteristic of modern science: that it is a positing science. (See Pickles (1982) for a brief introduction to this issue.) Modern science posits a framework of meaning within which the world is given as a set of relations which can be thematized and formalized. This positing process occurs as a domain of phenomena is taken as an object for a particular science. The positing of the framework of meaning involves the thematization of the everyday world as a particular world for scientific investigation, and this entails the objectification of that world, i.e. it involves procedures by which the world is taken as the object domain of a particular science. Thematization and objectification constitute the first levels of the abstractive reduction, where the everyday world is reduced and abstracted from. The result is a series of idealizations – the state, the economy, the market, exchange value, profit-maximization – each of which has a correlate in everyday experience, but each of which is transformed into an analytical and formal context. This is the process of formalization, and it results in the problematization of the everyday, taken-for-granted world (see Gregory, 1978).

Degrees of formalization are possible, one such being the formalization which results in establishing relationships which can be expressed as functional relations (functionalization) or in mathematical terms (mathematization).

While phenomenology indeed uncovers these procedures of science, rather than rejects them, it is vital that we recognize the attendant claim that phenomenology always makes: that we must deal with the phenomena as they show themselves to be. It is precisely at this juncture that the debate between quantitative and qualitative approaches to science has arisen. The debate is misspecified if it is seen to be a denial of the validity of quantitative methods. The question is, instead, which levels of formalization are appropriate to the phenomena of human action and behaviour. The choice is not an arbitrary or conventional one, but is conditioned by the phenomena of human behaviour as such. Nor is the decision between the two a fixed solution to the question: one could readily envisage a situation (and time) where social relations were of such a kind that simple or complex mathematics described accurately those relations (as, for example, in the socio-economic system established in Skinner's *Walden II*). Furthermore, we must not forget that the choice of methods, and hence the type of solution to this question, is in part a function of the interests which underpin research, and here we may also readily envisage a situation where quantitative methods served certain interests better than qualitative methods (in geography see Mercer, 1984; Pickles, 1986; more generally see Habermas, 1968). But in both these cases – where social systems take on the character of linear mathematics, or where science is characterized by the interests that underpin it, nothing is said about the fundamental relation of science to the phenomena it studies. It is this about which phenomenology has something to say.

The claim that phenomenology provides a rational foundation and an overcoming of distorted views of phenomena has received much criticism in the literature of the social sciences, and particularly in geography. It is argued that such a project is 'foundational' in nature, by which is meant that it is an attempt to establish solid grounds where we now know none to be possible. In claiming to achieve something like a 'return to things themselves' (that is, a turning back to the consideration of the phenomena as they present themselves – the turn to the philosophical attitude) it is argued that this is an 'essentialist' claim which ignores the social and linguistic construction of reality in favour of something like direct access to phenomena. But both arguments misunderstand the claim to deal with phenomena. Indeed, both arguments show just how far we have gone down the road to irrationalism in science (where the dominance of the fact prevents us from turning to the grounds from which the fact is derived) – a path Husserl warned against taking, and which underpinned his attempt to develop phenomenology in the first place (Husserl, 1910–11). (It is difficult to understand how scientists can deny that the project of science deals with the way the world is known by man, that science seeks to comprehend these phenomena without distortion, and that the truth of a scientific claim is founded upon the actual state of affairs. It is again a characteristic of the loss of understanding that such truisms have to be restated again, and in such a way that today will probably not be universally accepted.)

The misunderstanding rests on the confusion of the term 'phenomena'. Where the arguments of foundationalism and essentialism have been made, 'phenomena' have generally been confused with 'things'. In fact, phenomena refer to the way in which things and objects which are not things are given to us; the way they are constituted. The use of the word 'phenomenon' thus implicates both object and subject, and again places at the centre of our thinking the intentional structure of knowledge and experience.

Understanding 'phenomena' as the correlate of intentionality thus removes the criticisms of essentialism and foundationalism. Knowledge is socially constructed, and it is precisely this phenomenal realm of socially constructed meaning that the phenomenologist seeks to describe. This is not, however, an easy or a straightforward matter. The one thing the phenomenologist cannot do is to accept the naive description of the world. That is, we cannot: (a) assume that appearances give us access to the phenomena, since some phenomena may be masked (social relations under capitalism), distorted (the advertising media in regard to product differentiation and effectiveness), or they may be intended to disseminate; (b) take the world for granted in the way we do in the everyday natural attitude; and (c) describe the world (phenomena) in terms of some other phenomena, to which we ascribe some similarities of appearance.

Science without an explicit phenomenological underpinning frequently makes use of analogy in the construction of its objects in precisely this way. In this view, while analogy may be a useful tool of scientific inquiry, it is a fundamentally distorting one because it is based on the assumption that phenomena can usefully be treated as if they were other phenomena: people can be treated as if they acted like animals; economic agents can be treated as if they operated as independent atoms, and so on.

Such analogical models are common in science and they are productive stimuli to thinking about the world. But they are dangerous because they sacrifice the rigour of phenomenological description for a much easier, and sometimes more readily applicable model: the education of children is like the manufacture of goods; human communication is like the inter-connected flows within a physical system (cybernetics); geographic migration is like the flow of water over a surface with barriers (diffusion); the shipment of goods across land and sea is like the refraction of light through two media (social physics). For the phenom-enologist each of these (possibly 'productive') analogies is distorting because it fails to investigate the phenomenon itself as it shows itself: as educative experiences; communicative action; human interaction and movement; the interaction of social, political and environmental con-texts with an economic system. The importance of qualitative methods (i.e. techniques) in empirical research should be immediately apparent; participant observation, diary keeping, in-depth interviews, etc. permit the researcher to attempt to understand selected domains of experience, behaviour or action which more 'distanced' methods do not.

Investigating the phenomenon as it shows itself is, however, far from straightforward, especially where analogical thinking dominates our encounter with the world. In encountering any new phenomena, or any phenomenon with which we have long been familiar, we give an account of it in terms of the experiences we already have. This claim raises two problems.

First, it suggests that science cannot help but think as people do in their everyday worlds, striving to make sense of the world through the already-known world. But is this claim true of science? At one level it is a truism that cannot be denied – we only have the known world from which to explore the unknown, and we make the unknown known through the language, concepts and categories of the known (at least initially). However, we cannot be satisfied with this claim as it stands. Science claims to be a 'fully transparent', rational and critical enterprise. That is, in principle, all its claims are open to challenge (transparency), claims are made on the basis of accurate evidence and sound argument (rationality), and the intersection of the community of scholars and rational methods permits the commonly assumed, taken-for-granted explanations to be challenged in favour of counter-intuitive accounts of the state of affairs (science is critical). The criticism of the Ptolemaic geocentric theory of the universe by the Copernican heliocentric theory of the solar system was one such massive shift from an immediately perceptible account to a counter-intuitive account. Similarly, when Galileo postulated in a 'thought experiment' the free-fall and the friction-free surfaces, he introduced counter-intuitive accounts of what had previously been intuitively obvious explanations: the property of all substances to achieve their proper place. Or again, when Baran and Sweezy (1966) argue that there is a natural tendency towards crisis (stagnation) under conditions of monopoly capitalism which results from the inability of the economy to absorb the surplus it produces, our naive impression is challenged by what at first glance appears to be counter-intuitive. It is precisely this ability to problematize the taken-for-granted experience which permits science to arrive at new and critical understanding.

Second, however, the claim has a deeper truth to it, and one which Husserl, in attempting to found phenomenology as a pure science of primary presuppositions, may not have fully realized. It is with his student, Martin Heidegger, that the problem is raised and solved. Phenomenology as the return to the things (read 'phenomena') themselves is vital to rational science and philosophy. Such knowledge is, however, always hermeneutical or interpretative, because Dasein (read 'the human being') is always historical, finite and interpretative. The seeming contradiction between these two claims: on the one hand, that phenomenology seeks rationally to ground empirical science, and on the other hand that this is an interpretative project, raises apparent problems of relativity and loss of precision. But they are only apparent, and not real problems. They remain problems only for those who cling to some absolute conception of the truth, or for those who wish to deny all truths in favour of a radical relativism. The point is that we cannot avoid the hermeneutic aspect of knowledge, but that this does not remove the necessity for, nor the possibility of, establishing rational grounds for empirical research. Descriptive phenomenology indeed has a foundational task in that it intersubjectively explains basic assumptions for doing science. In the case of human and social sciences interpretation and critique are necessary where communities or individuals attach meaning to social actions in the historical situation in which they find themselves.

The aim of the phenomenological method

Since concrete, factual propositions belong to the special sciences, the goal as expressed in phenomenology is the . . . foundation and clarification of the essential structures which underlie knowledge and (known or experienced) reality. (Farber, 1943: 572)

In many ways the whole issue of phenomenology has become more complicated than it need be. The most important elements of this method have been in partial use all along, and Husserl's task was partly the clarification and natural extension of generally accepted procedures. Two basic elements are found in all discourse: reflection and essences or universals. The task of phenomenology is to analyse these thoroughly as issues which are prior to all special regions of discourse and the concrete, factual propositions of the special sciences (Farber, 1943: 572). With these remarks we can conclude with a brief summary description and definition of phenomenology.

The aim of the phenomenological method is the rigorous description of the essential structures that constitutes objects in their various modes of givenness. These modes thus include the modes of givenness of scientific objects, but also include the modes of givenness of everyday objects, objects of memory, objects of political discourse, etc. Such a method is not a method concerned with the ontical (that is, the world of things and facts), but with the ontological (that is, the way of being of things, facts, objects, experiences, etc.). Phenomenology thus does not concern itself with the everyday (or natural) attitude, which naively accepts the givenness of the world, but with the philosophical attitude, which asks critically about the intentional structure of experience. This is not, however, a search for transhistorical essences, nor for subjective impressions of the everyday, but it is a search for invariant and universal structures (understood carefully). It is not a retreat into solipsism and consciousness, because from the very beginning the principle of intentionality establishes the intersubjective nature and otherness of all experience, and thus its social construction. Of necessity, then, phenomenology is an interpretative enterprise: it is hermeneutic phenomenology. Moreover in dealing with phenomena, phenomenology must penetrate the differences between phenomena, symptom, distortion and lie. Such an enterprise is a critical one, and is an essential foundation for any science which claims to be rational, and any method which claims to be scientific.

The turn from the natural to the philosophical attitude, bracketing and the reductions, and the description of essences or universals, have been specified. These form the basis of the phenomenological method. But, since phenomenology addresses the ontological, rather than the ontical, the actual practice and achievements of the phenomenological method may be more difficult to specify in the abstract. For one thing, at its best the descriptive phenomenology of essences occurs within the scientific project and alongside all empirical research. In this sense, it cannot be easily abstracted from good scientific practice. For another, like good science, literature and philosophy, abstract principles provide only the framework on which good phenomenology is woven. For the social sciences then, the test is not the production of good phenomenologies, but the production of good, critical scientific research which is grounded explicitly and reflectively in the phenomena, and not based upon unreflective and unexamined presuppositions and assumptions.

Note

I would like to thank Peter Gould and Joseph Kockelmans for their helpful comments on this chapter.

References

Baran, P. A. and Sweezy, P. M. (1966) *Monopoly capital. An essay on the American economic and social order*, Monthly Review, New York.

Casey, E. S. (1977) 'Imagination and the phenomenological method', in F. A. Elliston and P. McCormick (eds), *Husserl: Expositions and appraisals*, University of Notre Dame Press, Notre Dame and London, 70–82.

Claval, P. (1983) *Models of man in geography*, Department of Geography Discussion Paper 79, Syracuse University.

Eddington, A. S. (1929) *The nature of the physical world*, Macmillan, New York.

Entrikin, N. J. (1976) 'Contemporary humanism in geography', *Annals of the Association of American Geographers* 66, 615–32.

Eyles, J. (1985) *Senses of place*, Silverbrook Press, Warrington, Cheshire.

Farber, M. (1943) *The foundation of phenomenology: Edmund Husserl and the quest for a rigorous science of philosophy*, State University of New York Press, Albany.

Geertz, C. (1973) 'Thick description: Toward an interpretive theory of culture', in *The interpretation of cultures. Selected essays*, Basic Books, New York, 3–30.

Geertz, C. (1983) ' "From the Native's Point of View": On the nature of anthropological understanding', in *Local knowledge. Further essays in interpretive anthropology*, Basic Books, New York, 55–70.

Gregory, D. (1978) 'Social change and spatial structures', in T. Carlstein, D. Parkes and N. Thrift (eds), *Making sense of time*, John Wiley, New York, 38–46.

Habermas, J. (1968) *Toward a rational society: Student protest, science and politics*, Beacon Press, Boston.

Heidegger, M. (1927) *Being and time*, Harper and Row, New York.

Husserl, E. (1910–11) 'Philosophy as rigorous science', *Phenomenology and the Crisis of Philosophy*, translated by Q. Lauer, Harper and Row, New York, 71–147.

Husserl, E. (1970) *The crisis of European sciences and transcendental phenomenology*, translated by D. Carr, Northwestern University Press, Evanston, Illinois.

Jackson, P. (1981) 'Phenomenology and social geography', *Area* 13, 299–305.

Johnston, R. J. (1983a) *Geography and geographers. Anglo-American human geography since 1945*, Edward Arnold, London, 2nd edition.

Johnston, R. J. (1983b) *Philosophy and human geography. An introduction to contemporary approaches*, Edward Arnold, London.

Johnston, R. J. (1986) 'Review of *Phenomenology, science and geography*', *Transactions of the Institute of British Geographers* 11, 123–4.

Kisiel, T. J. (1970) 'Phenomenology as the science of science', in J. J. Kockelmans and T. J. Kisiel (eds), *Phenomenology and the natural sciences. Essays and translations*, Northwestern University Press, Evanston, Illinois, 5–44.

Kockelmans, J. J. (1985) *Heidegger and science*, Series in Contemporary Continental Thought, University Press of America.

Mercer, D. (1984) 'Unmasking technocratic geography', in M. Billinge, D. Gregory and R. Martin (eds), *Recollections of a revolution: Geography as spatial science*, St Martin's Press, New York, 153–99.

Pickles, J. (1982) ' "Science" and the funding of human geography', *The Professional Geographer* 34(4), 387–92.

Pickles, J. (1985) *Phenomenology, science and geography: Spatiality and the human sciences*, Cambridge University Press, Cambridge.

Pickles, J. (1986) 'Geographic theory and educating for democracy', *Antipode* 18(2), 136–54.

Relph, E. C. (1981a) *Rational landscapes and humanistic geography*, Croom Helm, London.

Relph, E. C. (1981b) 'Phenomenology', in M. E. Harvey and B. P. Holly (eds), *Themes in geographic thought*, Croom Helm, London, 99–114.

Seamon, D. (1980) 'Concretising phenomenology: a response to Aitchison', *Journal of Geography in Higher Education* 4(2), 89–92.

14

Towards an Interpretative Human Geography

David M. Smith

There can be no ideal goal for human life. Any ideal goal means mechanization, materialism and nullity. There is no pulling open the buds to see what the blossom will be. Leaves must unroll, buds swell and open, and then the blossom. And even after that, when the flower dies and the leaves fall, still we shall not know. There will be more leaves, more buds, more blossom: and again, a blossom is as an unfolding of the creative unknown. Impossible, utterly impossible to preconceive the uncreated blossom. You cannot forestall it from the last blossom. We know the flower of to-day, but the flower of to-morrow is beyond us all. Only in the material-mechanical world can man foresee, foreknow, calculate and establish laws.

D. H. Lawrence, 1936

In the middle of the 1970s these words from Lawrence's essay 'Democracy' seemed to epitomize the uncertainty of human geography, or at least one of its practitioners. This quotation was used to introduce the theoretical part of a text which sought to restructure the field around the theme of human welfare (Smith, 1977). Ambiguity was contrived by juxtaposition with the assertion of August Lösch (1954: 359), that 'Whenever something new is being created, and thus in settlement and spatial planning also, the laws revealed through theory are the sole economic guide to what *should* take place.' The motivation for a welfare approach to human geography was unashamedly human betterment, consistent with Lösch's axiom that the real duty is not to explain our sorry reality, but to improve it. Just as neoclassical economics had provided the conceptual foundations for an earlier generation of human geography in the locational analysis tradition, so welfare economics now permitted the rigorous exploration of the question of what is best, or what should take place in the spatial arrangement of things. The uncertainty arose from recognition that such heady concepts as social well-being and the quality of life, which were central to the welfare perspective, appeared inconsistent with the analytical trappings of economics and its disdain for value judgements. At a deeper level there was an emerging realization that the development of those laws which geographers had been seeking almost as a passport to scientific respectability implied a world vastly different from that of actual human experience.

These uncertainties had already been encountered by nimbler minds and to some extent resolved by espousal either of humanism or of a more active 'radical' stance on social change. They were, however, symptomatic of an era in which great expectations had been aroused by the supposed capacity of the new quantitative and model-building human geography not only to explain reality but also to improve it, facilitated by modern cybernetics and harnessed to the cult of managerial rationality. Urban and regional planning along with development problems were seen as fields in which spatial reorganization could be used to attain specific goals, with almost a mechanical deliberation. Such expectations foundered not only on the limitations of spatial planning revealed in practice, but also on the inability of what passed for geographical theory to make much sense of a world so apparently unyielding to well-intentioned state intervention.

Changing models of humankind

While geography's reconstruction as spatial science had been closely associated with the adoption of numerical and statistical methods, the role of economics had also been significant. Economics had provided the most convincing model of a law-seeking social science, with an enticing battery of supporting graphics and a mathematical rigour the more convincing by its occasional obscurity. It had even become spatial in its regional science offspring. Equally if not more important was that economics provided a convenient model of man(/woman, but necessarily male in this rational world). While *homo economicus* was introduced originally as an ideal type, this perfectly informed and perfectly able being automatically maximizing personal utility or satisfaction through marketplace choices soon became a substitute for something far more complex. He(/she?) was easily understood, and comfortingly infallible in a world of so many fallen angels.

Geographers were by tradition too much empiricist, and engaged in the 'real' world, to be captivated by *homo economicus* for long. However, the variations which we adopted were not much less dauntingly inhuman, even with a few cultural considerations, personal preferences and random variables thrown in as they tried to maximize their place utility. And when a somewhat more imaginative 'behavioural' geography emerged its so-called actors were little more than inanimate participants in some stimulus–response system. Like *homo economicus*, they were good actors in the sense that they learned their lines and put on a predictable performance, but for the most part it was to an implausible script and a plot tedious in its simplicity.

That geography was ready to grapple with a more complex humankind as well as with more subtle processes of causation was signalled by an emerging interest in humanism. But this remained somewhat muted, or relegated to the sidelines of disciplinary restructuring (e.g. Smith, 1977: 370–3). Much more influential was the radical critique built on Marxism. However, the model of humankind provided by the Althusserian reading of Marx which informed geography's early dallying with structuralism turned out to have little depth of character. Indeed, *homo marxicus*, in the form of capital single-mindedly extracting the last drop of surplus value from labour or manipulating state policy to its precisely understood purpose, bore an uncanny resemblance to profit-maximizing *homo economicus*. One cardboard character replaced another.

But, as in conventional economics and the geography built partly upon it, not only was the characterization inadequate, so also was the plot. Explanation came perilously close to determination. The quantitative model-building era was yielding to a no less mechanistic account of the world, in which social superstructure was determined by the economic base or substructure and individual human beings (capitalists as well as workers) appeared captive of macro-structural forces. For the more ardent practitioners of Marxism, simply to evoke 'the law of value' or the 'logic of the accumulation process' was sufficient explanation, with human volition reduced to collective class struggle. It took the penetrating irony of E. P. Thompson to undermine such views (e.g. his brilliant depictions of Althusser's structuralism as machines in Thompson, 1978: 292–4). He pointedly stated, 'if a mode of production is proposed to entail a regular and rational form of sequential development, and a complex (but uniform) internal relational structuration, *independent of the rationality and agency of the human actors who in fact produce and relate*, then, very soon, the questions will be asked: who is the divine will which programmed this automating structure, where is the ulterior "unconscious power"'? (Thompson, 1978: 282).

258   Towards an Interpretative Human Geography

The notion of social structures as not fixed and immutable but the outcome of human action or agency helped to bridge the schism which had hitherto separated Marxism and humanism. The resurgence of humanism actually provided a more persuasive platform for the critique of empiricism and positivism (which are by no means inconsistent with crude Marxist economism), and hence for their partial displacement in human geography by an interpretative approach informed by qualitative methods.

The drama of human life

That this concluding chapter should have taken so many paragraphs to reach the substantive content of the book is no oversight. Our authors have addressed a humankind quite different from the actors to which many readers may have become accustomed in the literature of geography, economics and some other social science. The preceding chapters have in various ways sought to reveal a world of experience, in which the meaning of things and places, and of life itself, is far from self-evident, yet in which commonsense and lay beliefs are as legitimate, as real, as findings of science. It is a world in which human volition is neither determined nor unconstrained, neither predictably responsive to stimuli nor totally lacking in logic or rationality. A world in which people can contradict themselves as well as others, giving different account of their lives in different circumstances – different versions of the truth. This world is a far cry from that of location theory's optimizing entrepreneurs, distance-minimizing consumers, place-utility maximizers and the like, and it is worth a brief reminder of how at least some of us reached it – how our own paths (or understanding of them) changed in the unfolding drama of disciplinary development. We have spared readers the personal biographies which are now being used as explicit accounts of academic experience, having indulged ourselves in that respect elsewhere (Smith, 1984; 1988; Eyles, 1985; 1988), so the above must suffice.

The analogy of drama repeatedly comes to mind, as these sentences are composed. Perhaps it reflects a hitherto unconscious urge to try to step out from and externally observe human activity, consistent with the traditional expectations of the objective and detached scientist. We may watch a play, but we now recognize ourselves as actors in another broader drama. That all the world is a stage and no person an island may be trite but goes to the heart of the interpretative approach, for we are part of and contributors to that which we seek to understand.

The dramaturgical analogy figures prominently in a number of the preceding chapters as a means of understanding. Human life is likened to a drama (sometimes even a game), with a text (or rules), a plot, and roles or parts. Such a perspective helps to illuminate strategies of face-to-face encounters, as Susan Smith explains. Rose stresses that a text may be spoken or written as well as acted out. The interpretation of a written text after the fashion of literary criticism captures the essence of the practice of distillation of meaning which may not be immediately apparent or conveyed by a superficial reading. Burgess and Wood refer to messages and codes, further to underline the indirect, hidden or even deliberately distorted meanings that a text may convey.

A further dimension to this strand of work concerns the role of the media. The press provide a population with access to a plot which may convey a greatly simplified or partial view of social life. As Susan Smith puts it, the script 'is an unfinished checklist of cues providing the public with a basis from which to extemporize', for example with respect to how they deal with crime in relation to race. The performance in which people engage ensures the local reproduction of racial categories set up nationally and internationally; 'such a "production" is acceptable because it works: plot and script offer a pragmatic basis on which to conduct everyday life in any uncertain environment.'

Tomaselli's analysis of Afrikaans-language films demonstrates the role of the media in helping people to make sense of and come to terms with a collective historic experience which has a bearing on their present identity. As he explains, contained within plots, characters and social practices, can be found the suppressed traumas, hopes, fears and preoccupations of Afrikaner culture. At a deeper level he identifies an historical materialistic base in what he describes as capital's ultimate defilement of Afrikaner cultural space. The symbolic transformation of the *uitlander* (outsider) from white English capital to blacks across the border is full of resonant foreboding for white South Africa.

The study by Burgess and Wood of television advertising is more explicitly geographical in its concern with the production of meanings for places. Their text of visual images and spoken script is composed of signs, which they set out to decode. The interpretation of signs depends on 'shared understanding of the codes which structure messages'; their analysis depends on being part of the action, in the sense of being able to grasp the subtleties of use of accent and evocation of characters from both the actual Docklands/East End and TV dramatizations. To them, a new place has been created by advertising: 'Nothing in these commercials signifies geographical or cultural realities.' Yet the image motivates action, as their survey of the response of small businesses revealed. And night after night on TV, *East Enders* becomes real enough to captivate a quarter of Britain's population.

In this confused and confusing world where fantasy becomes a form of reality, it is a sense of place which can give people a location, at least in a tangible environment of bricks (or concrete) and mortar. But there is more to place than built form. Places can become symbolic, of anything from a fading way of life, a lost relationship, a sought-after security or sign of status. People seek to preserve them as they are, as in the Chicago neighbourhood described by Jackson, the Howdendyke of Porteous and the widow's house where she was happy with her husband, and in the affluent Vancouver suburb examined by David Evans. Understanding the meaning of place, what it signifies for people and how the signs are read, are close to some long-standing geographical concerns, even if the route to understanding revealed by some of our contributors is unfamiliar.

Keith provides a particularly vivid illustration of how certain places took on a symbolic significance to black people in Britain. It was in these 'no-go' or 'front-line' places that violent confrontation with the police occurred in the early 1980s, in a struggle for control of crucial territory. The explicit police policy of desymbolizing particular streets reveals a degree of lay understanding greatly at variance with the stimulus – response methods of social control which have come to be expected of police dealing with civil disorder. Keith's reconciliation of the drama-turgical approach with semiotics is a useful reminder that the meaning of action played out on British streets has to be reconstructed with some care rather than read directly from what is visibly manifest.

With the dramaturgical analogy, semiotics (semiology) has emerged as a major theme of this volume. The *Oxford English Dictionary* definition of these terms – a branch of pathology concerned with symptoms – reminds us that signs are but surface manifestations of something deeper. These meanings will be shared by people in a particular locality or otherwise drawn together: devised, articulated, reproduced and possibly changed by discourse, individual conduct and personal inter-action. Symbolic interactionalism 'posits that all objects carry meaning which is socially constructed through group reference' (David Evans). Evans calls on Giddens' notion of structuration to reveal human action and social structure as recursive in a manner which allows for change in the significance of place, in a complex and perhaps contradictory process. He points out that the anti-growth strategy of Vancouver sub-urbanites would ultimately challenge the foundations of the economic system on which the people concerned depended for their employment and affluent lifestyle. The place which they sought to protect, with its symbolic semi-rural exclusivity, somehow existed outside of capitalism and its attendant values: captive of their own imagery, they fail to grasp its intrinsic contradiction.

Central to the interpretative endeavour is hermeneutics, or the theory of the interpretation and clarification of meaning. In its original form hermeneutics was developed to explicate and adjudicate contending theological texts, and was then applied to historical sources more generally. The interpretation of texts involves what Giddens has referred to as a 'double hermeneutic', whereby the analyst attempts to interpret a world which is already interpreted by people living their lives in it. Something of the complexity of modern hermeneutics is explained by Rose in his concluding note on method. It is not simply a matter of finding what lies behind the signs in the text but of looking '*with* the text at what it says to successive generations of interpreters thereby involving the text, the interpreter and the interpretation in an ongoing text-event.' We interpret other texts in a continuing 'self-encounter', while at the same time being concerned with understanding other people's actions.

People's pre-interpretations are important to any explanatory account. They may comprise what are sometimes referred to as 'lay' or 'common-sense' interpretations (even 'theories'). However misguided, or wrong, lay interpretations may appear to be to others or those who may consider themselves experts, what people believe to be true motivates action. In health, for example, lay theories of how the body works and of what it means to be ill influence how people behave in seeking medical care, as Donovan and Cornwell have revealed, even though such beliefs may be discordant with scientific knowledge of anatomy or with how medical practitioners define illness. Health education which disregards lay interpretations runs the risk of failure. Commonsense interpretations of life may be grounded in shrewdly evaluated experience, leading to such conclusions that heavy smokers do not always die of lung cancer and that this complaint can also afflict non-smokers: an intuitive grasp of the distinction between necessary and sufficient conditions. Jackson's assertion in his Chicago study that people 'accurately recognize their own interests and understand the root cause of their problems', however contestible as a generalization, at least reminds us that ordinary people are seldom fools or merely victims of false consciousness – far less playing parts written by others in a drama they cannot comprehend.

Sources, materials, methods and theory

It should be clear by now that an interpretative geography has been informed by sources quite different from those on which the quantitative model-building (empiricist or positivist) paradigm was built. Economics has been displaced by sociology (and in particular interpretative sociology) and anthropology (especially its ethnographic tradition), as major influences on geographical practice. The impact of strands of anthropology is notable, for it could be argued that it is in this discipline that the interplay of case study, method and theory has been most clearly articulated. Philosophy in its strict sense has augmented the customary 'philosophy of geography' discourse. Realist philosophy has been invoked by some (e.g. Smith and Keith) and phenomenology, especially that of Schutz, has been a major influence, for example to Rose and Donovan in this volume.

The final chapter, by Pickles, offers a proclamation of phenomenology as the appropriate philosophy for the qualitative/interpretative endeavour. Pickles underlines the possible confusion of usage in the term method. This book is about method, Eyles announces at the outset, and so it is in the sense both of philosophy (a way of knowing) and practice or technique. In fact, the collective if not entirely consistent sense of philosophy expounded in this volume conforms broadly with phenomenology as Pickles explains it. And from this, specific methods (techniques) of observation and data assembly follow. They are mainly qualitative (as opposed to quantitative) in the case-studies, as might be expected of a philosophy not inclined to accept a world of objects with specific measurable properties. But this is not to say that quantitative methods, even statistics, are no longer useful: they are by no means inconsistent with the interpretative approach, as Eyles and Pickles point out, if it is recognized that some aspects of human experience are capable of sensible measurement, formal tests of association, and so on.

To be somewhat more specific about research material and qualitative methods as techniques, this volume has illustrated a variety of approaches to textual analysis, broadly defined. This can refer to texts in the literal, literary sense, as in the documentary sources examined by Jackson and Porteous, and the newspapers which were part of Smith's material. Of a similar nature are the advertisements looked at by Burgess and Woods, and the films examined by Tomaselli. Informed by semiotics, the techniques employed resemble the critical reading of literature, or even of a painting or piece of sculpture: interpreting in its most obvious colloquial sense. In other work, the material to be interpreted is the spoken word, recorded (by taking notes or use of a tape recorder) for subsequent analysis following what are often long, informal (but not necessarily unstructured) interviews. The chapters by Mel Evans, Donovan and Cornwell rest on this technique. The participant form of observation is a particular means of listening to and observing people in which shared experience should enhance access to research material as well as its interpretation, providing, literally, inside knowledge. Both Evans and Porteous show how participation in local life was an influence on the research process.

Various of our contributors have emphasized and illustrated the demands of qualitative research. An empathetic understanding of the people concerned is important and this may be conveyed as commitment to a cause of theirs, as in Porteous's study of a community being 'erased'. Establishing empathy may come easily living in and being part of a community but is more difficult if there are evident cultural, class or gender barriers. The solution may be unexpected: Donovan found her Jewishness and the shared experience of racism helpful in establishing empathetic relations with blacks. The development of personal skills in communicating (conversation and especially listening), along with verbal improvision, quick thinking and especially knowing when to turn off the tape recorder are essential in informal survey work. So is awareness of self-presentation, including how to dress in a manner which respondents will find acceptable. More generally, Susan Smith stresses the importance of 'an understanding of the active role of the analyst's *self* which is exercised throughout the research process'. Mel Evans suggests that 'the success of participant observation does not primarily depend on the casual adoption of one set of rules against another but upon a profound level of introspection on the part of the researcher.' The supreme challenge is to step back from the inevitable personal involvement, so as to see more than does the mere participant.

Qualitative research raises ethical issues which may not be so starkly revealed in other approaches. Mel Evans's considered use of a hidden tape recorder for covert observation is a case in point. The identity of respondents and even of the location of a study may have to be concealed, as in Cornwell's work, if only to prevent the embarrassment of people finding their frankly expressed views in print in an attributable manner. However, Cornwell did feel impelled to show her work to those who participated in the study. So did Porteous, as part of a research strategy designed to elicit their reaction; this was largely unsuccessful but he also felt he owed it to them, for 'one of the ethical imperatives of qualitative social research is the need to give one's informants the right to comment upon and criticize one's interpretations.'

The rigours of qualitative research are stressed and demonstrated by a number of our writers. Geographers steeped in the practice of numerical measurement and statistical hypothesis testing in the positivist tradition are sometimes tempted to dismiss qualitative work as little more than journalism, which fails to conform to conventional standards of scientific practice, or what Mel Evans terms 'the rigour of an imported logic'. But the rigour of good qualitative research has been convincingly set out by Mitchell (1983) in an exposition of the case-study approach which has influenced a number of contributors, including Susan Smith who claims with ample justification that 'the logical consistency required to validate case analyses is just as scrupulous as the demands of statistical inference and experimental replication.'

The development of theory is also different from, but no less rigorous than, more conventional approaches. Donovan is explicit in the theoretical implications of her eclectic combination of phenomenology, ethnomethodology and ethnography, which provides 'a methodology which is sensitive and flexible, and which embraces the views and opinions of ordinary people in their own terms.' This leads to 'grounded' theory, generated by a grounding in the data collected instead of arising from *a priori* constructs, and refined in the ongoing interaction of data and theory, in what Eyles in the first chapter describes a theory-informed case-studies. But we should not expect too much grand theory, as David Evans suggests in his exploration of structuration as the basis for a case study. At this stage plausible accounts, the validation of which is internal to the discourse of the perspective adopted (to use Eyles' phrase), would itself be quite an achievement. Wider questions of validity involving choice between macro-theories or competing '-isms' (or '-ations') may be more moral than scientific.

The institutional setting

Before concluding, some observations on the institutional setting of the creation of qualitative, interpretative approaches in human geography are in order. Reference was made in the Preface to the fact that seven of the chapters in this book originated in post-graduate research supported by the Economic and Social Research Council or its predecessor the Social Science Research Council. This is not altogether surprising, given the Council's virtual monopoly over the financing of British post-graduate students. There has not, however, been a conscious SSRC/ESRC strategy to encourage qualitative approaches; the studentships in question have usually been allocated on the basis of links with particular topical concerns (e.g. ethnic issues at Oxford and health studies at QMC). Indeed, the qualitative/interpretative approach is hardly consistent with the current established orthodoxy, or what Mel Evans describes as 'the new realism of the ESRC and their obsession with quantitative data and "relevant" research'. This is itself a response to state pressure for more cost-effective research and a better performance defined in terms of PhD completion rates as well as for a more pragmatic problem-solving social science.

As financial support for post-graduate studies and research in Britain becomes more selective by institutions, guided by some bureaucratized conception of research quality or performance, it is worth noting that only a minority of those contributors to this volume who had SSRC/ESRC studentships submitted a PhD thesis within four years, which is the Council's current (1987) criterion of success. All but two have completed, but it took most of them nearer five years than four. This 'performance' is explained to a large extent by the special demands of qualitative research, to which reference has been made above, including the acquisition of special research skills and the necessary self-awareness to use them properly. One contributor (Cornwell) refers to some of the difficulties which she encountered, including a struggle to establish the legitimacy of her approach in a department where alternative perspectives largely prevailed – not least among physical geographers to whom qualitative research bordered on heresy. She was also to some extent a victim of the then SSRC insistence on a more structured research training than in the past, including exposure to a range of research techniques and philosophies which were irrelevant to her project. Learning to be a research worker or scholar is a highly individual experience, involving the supervisory relationship as well as the institutional setting, and cannot helpfully be boxed into a prescribed format. As Cornwell illustrates, part of the process is learning by experience, reflecting on it, and being prepared critically to re-evaluate one's work. As post-graduate research becomes further institutionalized and its practice increasingly codified under pressure to perform by criteria which are not intrinsic to scholarly endeavour, there is a danger of stifling the intellectual innovation which has hitherto been possible under the flexible format of the conventional British PhD experience.

While the focus of this volume has been on geography, and most of its contributors are geographers by self-identity, close relationships with other fields are part of the context in which an interpretative geography has emerged. This refers not only to sources of intellectual influence from other disciplines but also to the setting of some of the work. Cornwell and another post-graduate student who adopted a qualitative approach came to QMC from the medical sociology MSc course at Bedford College and retained a strong sociological affiliation. Another came with a human sciences degree from Oxford. Cornwell and Donovan went on to (non-geographical) academic posts in the health field. Tomaselli went from a geography degree into contemporary cultural studies, which is where his semiotics perspective was developed. The significance of all this to what is sometimes referred to as the production of knowledge is that the interdisciplinary cross-fertilization which has been an important contributing factor in the adoption of qualitative approaches has embodied a fortuitous element arising from the personal forging of specific links into or out from human geography.

Conclusion

Our intention in this volume has not been to proclaim yet another revolution in geography. That a new movement is taking shape is clear, however, and we have sought by demonstration to show some of its character. We believe that the preceding chapters have provided persuasive accounts of ways of interpreting the geographical world which are capable of challenging if not displacing prevailing orthodoxy or at least of providing a convincing alternative. The positivist and empiricist paradigm fixated by mathematical process modelling with a promise of policy relevance, which still tends to dominate geography on both sides of the Atlantic, is already yielding to approaches more sensitive to actual human experience. This volume is a contribution to that development. Our authors have illustrated something of the intellectual excitement and demands of an interpretative approach, and also provided glimpses of the kind of understanding on which a better world might be built.

Having dwelt on method, in both a philosophical and technical sense, it is as well also to recognize that interpretative human geography places the field in a central and integral position in contemporary social inquiry. This is manifest not only in the continuing dissolution of conventional disciplinary boundaries, as human geography increasingly shares the methods and interpretations found fruitful in sociology and anthropology, but also in the explicit incorporation of spatial concepts in other disciplines – from the 'time-space distanciation' of Giddens to the notion of reach in Schutz's phenomenology. What is more, we share with others adopting somewhat different perspectives (e.g. Massey, 1984) an advocacy of the re-emergence of local specificity or uniqueness as intrinsic to human affairs, a development also evident in some contemporary historiography. Local specificity is a challenge requiring different modes of inquiry (Massey and Meegan, 1985), not merely something to be dismissed as aberration in the search for generality.

The new and critical understanding which we seek to promote requires what Pickles has described as the 'ability to problematize the taken for granted'. This is to reveal what would otherwise remain hidden, or 'to uncover the nature of the social world', as Eyles puts it in the first chapter. As we penetrate successfully deeper layers of meaning in 'an unfolding of the creative unknown' (to use Lawrence's phrase from the epigraph to this chapter), we shall come to know more. The flower of tomorrow may be beyond us all, but the more we see the less of a surprise each successive blossom will be – though no less exciting and never totally expected for all that. So it is with the interpretation of human geographical experience.

References

Eyles, J. (1985) *Sense of place*, Silverbrook Press, Warrington.

Eyles, J. (ed.) (1988) *Research in human geography*, Basil Blackwell, Oxford.

Lösch, A. (1954) *The economics of location*, Yale University Press, New Haven, Conn.

Massey, D. (1984) *Spatial divisions of labour*, Macmillan, London.

Massey, D. and Meegan, R. (eds) (1985) *Politics and method*, Methuen, London.

Mitchell, J. C. (1983) 'Case and situation analysis', *Sociological Review* 31, 187–211.

Smith, D. M. (1977) *Human geography: a welfare approach*, Edward Arnold, London.

Smith, D. M. (1984) 'Recollections of a random variable', in Billinge, M. et al. (eds) *Recollection of a revolution: Geography as spatial science*, Macmillan, London, 117–33.

Smith, D. M. (1988) 'A welfare approach to human geography', in Eyles, (1988), *Research in human geography*.

Thompson, E. P. (1978) *The poverty of theory*, Merlin Press, London.

Index

Note: References to authors are confined to substantial treatments of their work; references to places are confined to case studies in this text

accent, 110
access, 206
accounts, private and public (repertoire and dynamic), 227–9
accuracy, 34
action research, 26, 30
advertisements, 94–116
Afrikaners, 136–54, 259
Afro-Caribbeans, 188, 190, 191
agency, 120, 131, 257
analogy, 250
analytical induction, 4
anthropology, 1, 119, 121, 122, 190, 262
apartheid, 152
area-development policies and programmes, 46, 95
Asians, 188, 189, 191
autobiography, 174

Barthes, R., 43–4
behavioural geography, 257
Bethnal Green, 219–31
bilingualism, 60, 168, 170
Birmingham (England), 17–36
blockbusting, 82–5
bracketing, 238, 252
Brixton, 43–7

capitalism, 124, 129, 131, 140, 147–8, 260–1
case analysis/studies, 9, 19, 192, 224, 262, 263

centrality, 103
Chicago, 49–71, 260, 261
Chicago School, 49–50, 51, 67, 70, 118–19
churches, 54–6, 146
Cicouree, A.V., 189–90
cinema, 136–54, 259
class, 4, 110, 111, 119, 136, 137, 142, 143, 145, 149, 170, 188, 205
class struggle, 136
codes, 108
commodification, 94
commonsense, 19, 33, 157, 185, 186, 187, 189, 223, 258, 261
communism, 149, 153
community organisation, 60
community spirit, 205
community studies, 68, 131, 198
consultation, 85–90
contamination, 25–6, 27
content analysis, 126
contradictions, 131–2, 153, 227, 261
conversation, 8, 173–4, 184, 191
Cooke, P., 123–4
covertness, 208, 209–10
creativity, 34–5
crime, 17–36, 40–7, 61–3, 68, 111, 114
cultural conflict, 156
cultural space, 148
culture, 94, 121–2, 165, 181–2, 240, 259
culture of poverty, 221

decoding, 108–114
defensive space, 124, 125, 126
definitions of the situation, 49–71, 77
depth interviews, 76
deviance, 66
dialectics, 174, 203, 211, 212
diary research, 220
Dilthey, W., 172–4
distance, 162, 163
distanciation, 244–5, 266
documentary methods, 49, 71, 76
Docklands, 94–116, 259
double hermeneutic, 77, 121
dramaturgical perspective, 21, 27–32, 46, 258–9
Duncan, J.S., 125

East End (of London), 101, 102–3, 111, 114, 259–60
eclecticism, 193
economics, 255–6, 262
eidos, 245–7
embourgeoisement, 137
empathy, 186, 187, 199, 209, 263
enterprise zone, 97–8, 100, 101, 104, 115
Erlebnis, 172–3
ESRC (Economic and Social Research Council), 123, 216, 264–5
essences, 239, 246, 252
ethical issues, 263
ethnic conflict, 61–7
ethnic politics, 68
ethnic succession, 50, 52, 71
ethnography, 22, 49, 52, 61–6, 68, 69–71, 183, 190–2, 193, 239, 243, 245, 262
ethnomethodology, 183, 188–90, 193, 199
experimental research, 20, 22, 25, 28, 33, 35
experimentalism, 198

face-work, 23–4, 25
fantasy, 115, 260

fatalism, 221
fear, 61–3
felt needs, 222
field relationships, 207–8
field research, 4, 5
film, see cinema
folk definitions, 77; see also lay beliefs
formalization, 247–8
front lines, 42–3, 46, 260
French (in Quebec), 156, 168–71

Gadamer, H.G., 173–4
games, 21, 22–7, 241–3
gangs, 63–4, 66, 67
Gans, H.J., 9
gatekeepers, 23, 206
Geertz, C., 3–4, 28, 242–4
gender, 188
gentrification, 59–60, 65
Giddens, A., 118, 120–3, 126–9, 132–3
Glaser, B.G. and Strauss, A.C., 186–7
Goffman, E., 23–4, 28–9, 42, 46
graffiti, 63–4, 69
Gregson, N., 122–3
grounded theory, 186–7, 264

Hackney, 43–7
health, 180–93, 219–31, 261
hermeneutics, 10, 20, 77, 119, 172–5, 190, 261; double, 77, 121, 261
homo economicus, 256–7
homo marxicus, 257
Howdendyke, 76–92, 260
humanism, 119, 120, 202, 240, 256, 257, 258
humanistic geography, 2
humour, 111
Husserl, E., 157–8, 183, 184

iconic signs, 108, 110
ideal types, 12–13, 185, 186, 256
ideology, 29, 121, 123, 124, 137, 152–3, 202–3, 205, 206, 211–16, 222, 240

images, 18–36, 95, 101–2, 114, 154, 259
imperialism, 153
indexical signs, 108, 110
industrial change, 77–90
insider, 76–7
insider knowledge, 2
insider accounts, 8, 11–12, 13
institutional setting, 264–5
interaction, 23, 118–33, 161, 184, 189
interviews, 7–8, 9, 39, 49, 76, 98, 126, 186, 189, 190–1, 203, 223–8, 262; depth, 9; ethnographic, 8; informal, 8–7; multiple, 227–8; non-directive, 8; semi-structured, 98, 126, 186, 190–1; unstructured, 186, 190–1

key informants, 49, 191
knowledge, stocks of, 159–60, 162, 164, 167, 185, 186, 188

landmarks, 110
landscape, 120, 124–5, 130, 132
language, 10–11, 108, 154, 156, 168, 171, 189, 234–5; see also bilingualism
lay beliefs/ideas/theories, 181, 187, 210, 219–31, 258, 260, 261; see also folk definitions
Ley, D., 118–19
linguistic metaphor, 40
linguistic symbolism, 43–7
local knowledge, 66, 68
locale, 95
localism, 123, 124, 125, 126
locality, 205
location decisions, 101
location theory, 94, 258
logo, 104–5
London, 41–7, 94–116, 180–93, 219–31
London Docklands Development Corporation (LDDC), 97, 99, 100, 102–4, 110, 115

Malinowski, B., 5
Marsh, C., 6–7
Marxism, 119, 136, 202, 212, 257–8
material, research, 262–3
media, mass, 29, 84, 116; cinema (film), 136–54, 259; newspapers, 103, 126; press, 30; radio, 103; television, 94, 102, 103, 111, 115–16, 259
medical sociology, 221–2
memory, 165; popular, 136–54
method, 1, 235–8, 262
metonymy, 45, 47
moral order, 52, 65, 67, 70, 118
moral panic, 29
multiple research strategy, 4–5, 13
myth, 41, 104, 137

natural attitude, 158, 161, 238, 252
natural sciences, 198
naturalism, 198–9, 201
negotiation, 22, 187–8
networks, 226
newspapers, 103, 126
no-go areas, 39–47, 260
nostalgia, 139, 141
Nottingham health profile, 5
Notting Hill, 43–7
nouveaux riches, 129–30, 140

objects, 239, 242, 244, 250, 252
Oxford University, 264–6

participant observation, 6–7, 8–9, 27, 30, 33, 39, 126, 186, 189, 190, 197–216, 224, 263
peers, 18, 21, 35
perception, 180, 240
perception geography, 6, 18–19
performance, 265
phenomena, 249–50
phenomenology, 10, 156, 157, 183–90, 193, 199, 233–53, 262
philosophical attitude, 238, 249, 252
philosophy, 235, 237, 238, 241, 245, 262

place advertising, 95–116
place, sense of, 39, 42, 95, 154, 260
planning, 75–92
police, 39–47, 260
politics, 30, 57–61
Polish-Americans, 49–71
pollution, 83
popular memory, 136–54
positivism, 183, 184, 186, 198, 201, 202, 203, 233, 244, 247–8
post-graduate studies, 264–6
power, 123, 184, 188, 240
pragmatism, 118–19
press, 30
productive forces, 136
proletarianization, 137
prototypical knowledge, 229–30
Puerto Ricans (in Chicago), 62–4

quality of life, 256
quantitative analysis/methods, 5, 248, 262
Quebec, 156–7, 164–75
Queen Mary College, 264–6
questioning and listening, 208–9
questionnaires, 7, 116, 183, 198, 203, 224

race, 17–36, 39–47, 180–93
racism, 194
radio, 103
rationalizations, 45
reach, 156–75, 266
realism, 133
recipes, 159, 181, 185, 189
reciprocity of perspectives, 158–9
recording data, 209–10; see also tape recording
recruitment, 225–6
recurrent practices, 121–2
referent systems, 108
reflexivity, 200–1, 211, 214–15
regional antelogy, 234, 236, 239
relevance, 19, 216, 264–5
repeatability, 201

representativeness, 192
reputation, 24–5
research design, 204–6
riots, 43
risk, 101
role expectation, 212–14
Rorty, R., 177
ruling ideas, 137
rumour, 30, 63, 65
routinization, 212–14

sampling, 192, 198; theoretical and snowball, 191
Schutz, A. 157–64, 166, 172–3, 184
search, 100
second-order constructs, 186
semiology (semiotics), 10, 43–7, 95–116, 136, 260–1, 262
sense of place, 39, 42, 95, 154, 260
service activities, 100
sex, 142, 149, 151
signs, 41–7, 108–16, 145, 240, 259–60; iconic, 108, 110; indexical, 108, 110; symbolic, 108, 110; see also symbols
small businesses, 95–116
social administration, 222, 223
social disorganisation, 50, 52, 61, 65, 66, 69, 70, 71, 151
social pathologies, 50
social relationships, 160–1, 228
sociology, 1, 20, 118–19, 121, 122, 262; medical, 221–2
sources, 261–2
South Africa, 136–54, 259
spatial imagination, 136
spatial mythology, 154
speech, 110
statistical inference, 192
story-boards, 98, 101–2, 111, 116
structuralism, 10, 119, 202, 257
structural functionalism, 183, 184
structuration, 20, 118–33, 257, 260
suburbs, 123–32
survey research, 6–7
surveys, 5, 6, 192, 198, 203

symbolic interactionalism, 26, 42, 119, 120, 190, 260

symbolic locations, 41–7

symbols, 125, 142, 150, 166, 215, 240, 260; *see also* signs

syntagm, 45, 47

tape-recording, 189, 191, 209–10, 224

technique, 236

television, 94, 102, 103, 111, 115–16, 259

texts, 10–11, 21, 33–5, 110, 136, 137, 172–5, 229, 259–63

thematization, 247–51

theory, 4–5, 264; grounded, 186–7, 264

thick description, 3, 239, 242

Thomas, W.I., 49–50, 70

topocide, 75–92

triangulation, 13

typologies, 12–13

urban ethniography, 69

urban renewal, 58–9

urbanization, 143, 144, 146

validation, 11–13, 19, 191, 192, 193, 201

Vancouver, 125–32, 260

verification, 187, 201, 203

Verstehen, 157, 186, 199–200, 216

welfare approach, 255–6

Young, A., 229–30

Znaniecki, F., 49–50